New Market Mavericks

WILEY TRADING SERIES

NEW MARKET MAVERICKS

Geoff Cutmore

JOHN WILEY & SONS, LTD

Other Wiley Editorial Offices

John Wiley & Sons Inc., 111 River Street, Hoboken, NJ 07030, USA

Jossey-Bass, 989 Market Street, San Francisco, CA 94103-1741, USA

Wiley-VCH Verlag GmbH, Boschstr. 12, D-69469 Weinheim, Germany

John Wiley & Sons Australia Ltd, 33 Park Road, Milton, Queensland 4064, Australia

John Wiley & Sons (Asia) Pte Ltd, 2 Clementi Loop #02-01, Jin Xing Distripark, Singapore 129809

John Wiley & Sons Canada Ltd, 22 Worcester Road, Etobicoke, Ontario, Canada M9W 1L1

Wiley also publishes its books in a variety of electronic formats. Some content that appears in print may
not be available in electronic books.

Library of Congress Cataloging-in-Publication Data

Cutmore, Geoff.
  New market mavericks / Geoff Cutmore.
    p. cm. — (Wiley trading series)
  Includes index.
  ISBN 0-470-87046-X (cloth : alk. paper)
    1. Investments—Case studies. 2. Investment analysis—Case studies.
I. Title. II. Series.
HG4521 C978 2004
332.6—dc22   2004007931

British Library Cataloguing in Publication Data
A catalogue record for this book is available from the British Library

ISBN 0-470-87046-X

Typeset in 10/12 Times by TechBooks, New Delhi, India
Printed and bound in Great Britain by Antony Rowe Ltd, Chippenham, Wiltshire
This book is printed on acid-free paper responsibly manufactured from sustainable forestry
in which at least two trees are planted for each one used for paper production.

For Marian, Georgie and my Mother

Contents

Preface

This is a book about eight individuals and their unique approaches to investing. I hope it also adds to the debate about whether we are at a profound turning point for financial markets. In writing this book my intention is twofold: to introduce the novice and experienced investor to a variety of investing approaches, and to offer some alternative perspectives on the markets. Some of the investing styles are unorthodox but in a book about Mavericks they could hardly be anything else. If this book helps just one investor make a better decision then it will have been worth the writing.

In my mind the question that stands above all others is whether Western equity markets are in a secular bear market. Is a shift in market dynamics taking place that requires investors to think again about such strategies as 'buy-and-hold' that worked through the long bull years?

The lessons from previous bear markets are informative, if not prescriptive. The great Wall Street crash of 1929 created long-term financial misery and the market took 25 years to recover its pre-crash level. A more recent example is the decade-long fall in Japanese share prices. The Nikkei share index may have re-visited 11 000, but that compares with highs of almost 40 000 points in 1989. In both cases initial sharp falls in equity prices were followed by market rallies that encouraged investors to re-commit to equities only to be caught in a further down-leg. Clearly these are two of the twentieth-century's worst bear markets, but can they help us to answer the question: Will the rest of this decade be marked by a similar challenge for Western bourses?

In February 2003 I read an academic case made by London Business School Professors, Elroy Dimson, Paul Marsh and Mike Staunton. They theorised that, by the end of 2018, there is only a 50% chance that the FTSE 100 will recapture its end of 1999 high. Take a moment to digest this theory. As they see it, there is a 50% chance that the UK benchmark index will take more than 15 years to rise a little over 3500 points. As it transpired, they were writing these words – part of their Global Investment Returns Yearbook – a month or so before the FTSE bounced strongly off its 2003 bear market low.

Will they be right? Ask me that question again in 2018. Their prediction, nevertheless, encouraged me to think about the issues that weigh, and will continue to weigh, on investors over the next decade. This is a brief list of what I consider to be the main issues:

- *From Enron to Parmalat – an alphabet of scandal.* The experiences of Enron, WorldCom, Parmalat in Europe and the excess in the technology bubble proved again and again that companies are not the guardians of shareholder equity, nor are executives always likely to act in the best interests of the owners of the companies.

- *Your money safe in their hands?* As sure-win investing philosophies like buy-and-hold and Relative Return were destroying investors' wealth, the financial industry was unwittingly doing its part to discourage people from buying shares. The fund management timing scandal, and the fines paid to settle claims over misleading stock tips, have done little for the industry's reputation.

- *The war on terror.* Geopolitical risk is hardly a new phenomenon for investors, but the attack on the World Trade Centre in 2001 has clearly changed the dynamics permanently. Terrorism post-Gulf War 2 will be an ongoing issue for investors.

- *The demographic time bomb.* Much has been written about falling Western populations. It will start to matter over the next few years as the baby-boomers retire, stop working and stop saving. If you're under 50, you should start to look forward to paying two pensions – yours and your parents'.

- *Pension funds.* Where does that pension money go? Whether correct or not, savers are sceptical about the worth of committing money to private pension schemes. The experience of a million policy holders at Equitable Life in the UK has damaged the image of organised schemes. At the same time, their performance record in the bear market has raised questions about their investment acumen.

- *Credit and debt.* The concerns about America's government and trade deficits are already well documented. The underlying condition of the US consumer is a further worry. According to the Federal Reserve, consumer debt topped 2 trillion dollars for the first time ever in November 2003, having doubled in less than 10 years. If you add in mortgage debt, the American public owes nearly 9 trillion dollars. With personal bankruptcies hitting a record high in 2003, one has to ask this question: If the American consumer is supporting world economic growth, who's going to support the American consumer?

- *China and India: a force for deflation.* Western economies are already witnessing low inflation from overcapacity and moderate wage growth, and the effect of production moving to the East is only adding to the cap on prices. Production moving to China and India will continue to push prices lower, which will inhibit Western companies from raising prices, reigning in profits.

Can the investing gods teach us anything about the outlook for financial markets? Already a number of wise heads in the investment world have publicly sworn-off investing in stocks in the current climate. At the tail end of 2003 I interviewed Jim Rogers on CNBC Europe. The legendary 'global investor' insisted that there was little for him in Western share prices. He preferred to do his hunting among commodities and Asian equity markets. Rogers still believes that Western stock markets are due a sharper correction in prices.

Sir John Templeton, who founded the Templeton Growth Fund and Templeton World Fund, was reported in 2003 as being worried about the US economy and stock market. The decline in the value of the dollar is at the heart of his concerns. Logic suggests the US currency's weakness will hasten rising interest rates as foreign holders of dollars decide they no longer wish to fund the budget or current account trade deficits. This, in turn, will send a shock wave through the economy. Over-borrowed consumers will be under pressure to service their debts, and Corporate America will be unable to pass on price rises because of the increased competition from Chinese and Indian imports.

Are we then at a profound transition point for Western markets? Is a steady low-return-environment marked by weak equity and bond market performances the best that can be hoped for? In this world, anaemic inflation holds back growth and makes the repayment of consumer and corporate debts a slow, grinding process. The stimulus from low interest rates and giving cash back to consumers through tax cuts has run its course. The implication is a decade of financial dreariness.

Or, have the bears missed the point? The inherent dynamism of the Western capitalist model will allow it to outgrow its problems. The emerging economies of China and India will certainly be a force for disinflation on Western economies (a slower rate of inflation growth), but their hunger for financial and intellectual capital will be sated by the mature Western markets. The West supplies capital, expertise and the global companies that know how to operate across international frontiers. Subscribers to this view talk about a re-run of the first wave of globalisation from 1870 to 1910. It was during that period that North America graduated to the international economic club. This theory has the third wave of globalisation, creating a deflationary boom for the world.

The answers to these questions will shape the behaviour of financial markets over the next decade. Recognising the trends, and investing to advantage, will separate the investor from the speculator. What follows is an examination of different investment styles, and some thoughtful reflection on the future for markets. I have called these individuals 'New Market Mavericks' because their methods represent a departure from the approach of the bulk of the traditional long-only investment industry.

Investing is a discretionary business. The individuals, their personalities and their techniques are all part of the story. Consequently, I have spent time painting in backgrounds where I think they are relevant to the process. I appreciate that some may feel this to be an arbitrary list, but I found it interesting that – across a range of styles and techniques, during the 2000–03 bear market – they all recognised the need for capital protection as much as the desire for capital appreciation, and acted accordingly.

Beyond this they also share a number of other important similarities:

1.   *The Market Mavericks in this book are all directly financially bound to their investment process.* This makes them significantly different from the bulk of the investment industry. The mainstay of the asset management business is still traditional long (buy only) funds. In these operations the manager taking the investment decision is paid a salary, may rarely sees the client face to face and has only a tangential bearing on the company's survival.

        The hedge fund managers here are shareholders in their own companies and have their own money in their funds. This rule also applies to Peter Toogood who operates in the fund of funds arena, and Richard Cunningham who runs a managed accounts investment business. In the case of those who trade individually on their own behalf, such as market historian David Schwartz or technical analyst Chris Locke, they do not invest other people's money but are active traders on their own behalf.

2.   *They have been prepared to put their record up for public discussion.* The investment industry is full of smart people, but only a few are willing to stand up and be counted. I know from a decade of hunting for money managers who were willing to talk on television, that for every one prepared to go public with their thoughts there are at least a dozen who do not have the stomach to submit their ideas to public debate. If the last four years have taught investors anything it should be that they now demand clarity and accountability from those who manage their money, punishing the bad by removing their mandate and supporting the good through difficult days.

3.   *This book is as much about personalities as it is about investment techniques and methods.* Investors who whole-heartedly embrace one investment process rarely find that it is immediately successful and can often spend years roaming from one technique to the next in the hope of finding one that works for them. This approach can be costly and is rarely satisfying. If there is one key message from this book, it is that properly assessing your own attitude to risk and reward, and recognising your ability to understand the type of coming market environment, is as important as mastering an investment technique.

The Mavericks in this book use many different styles of investing, and have found methodologies that suit their own personalities and backgrounds. That ought to put the lie to the idea that there is one approach that is clearly the 'best'. In the area of discretionary money management I would urge any investors prepared to hand over their hard-earned cash to do as much homework on a manager's personality and background as they would do on their investment process and historic returns. Be prepared to ask questions, and walk away if you do not get the answers or access you desire.

AND FINALLY...

Let me put the reader's mind at rest: I have no conflict of interest in writing about these Mavericks. In the interests of objectivity, I have no money invested with any of the money managers in this book. I have chosen Mavericks whose investment approach I find refreshing, but their inclusion should in no way be interpreted as my validation of their methods or a solicitation to use their products.

It should also be made clear that any errors or mistakes in relaying their investment approach are my responsibility alone.

Geoff Cutmore
August 2004

Acknowledgements

I would like to thank the eight Mavericks for allowing me to put their thoughts on the record. While they all have different approaches to the markets they share the same passion to call the future correctly. I am grateful for the time they have given and the patience with which they have dealt with my questions. For that I sincerely thank them, and I hope that I have properly and accurately reflected their investment process and forecasts.

There are several other people who have helped in the production of this book. I wish to put on record my appreciation of the positive feedback from Bob Parker at Credit Suisse Asset Management. I also want to thank Don Spain, formerly a colleague at CNBC, for checking the first draft.

Part I
THE HEDGE FUND MANAGERS

1
Hugh Hendry: The Antithesis of the Past

'The returns from 1982–1999 I suspect will never be seen again. The great money was a function of a very specific period in history.'

Hugh Hendry buys 'train wrecks' – i.e. stocks that have probably lost 80% of their value in companies that have gone to the brink of closure. He is drawn to small businesses that have stared bankruptcy in the face and survived. In fund manager parlance they are called 'special situation deep value' stocks and he cannot get his hands on enough of them. At the start of 2004 he held 560 positions in his $116 million hedge fund Eclectica; 520 of those were holdings in individual stocks and the rest formed a collection of derivative and commodity trades.

Hendry calls it the Centipede approach to investing. Like the Centipede's legs he has a lot of stocks in his portfolio, and if a few companies fail along the way it is hardly going to slow the fund's performance. In 2003 the approach worked extremely well as his hedge fund notched up a 50% gain. He achieved that in a market environment where he was reluctant to buy stocks and was using derivatives and other fixed income trades to offset the risk of an equity market decline. Hendry's refrain throughout 2003 was how uncomfortable he felt buying into the momentum that propelled many Western equity markets to their best closes in four years.

That reluctance to chase money going into technology and 'poor valuation' stocks dampened the performance of the long-only Continental European fund he also manages. The fund made 3% compared to the Dow Jones Stoxx 50 European Blue Chip Index which returned 10.5%. But investors who have stayed fully invested with Hendry should forgive the hiccup as his Continental European Fund is one of only three

European unit trusts that have made money for investors in every year since 1998. Some modest underperformance in one year is a small price for a fund manager who is very conscious of capital preservation, and works to an absolute return rather than a relative return benchmark.

Hendry's five-year record puts him among a small group that fought the worst bear market for equities since the Wall Street crash and came out on top. He did that with the limitations that a long-only fund imposes. He was not able to short the market or individual stocks, and where he was unable to identify companies that were likely to rise in value, he took his money out of the market rather than remain invested. Hendry manages a half a billion dollars across three funds. During the last bear market he had no compunction in moving more than half of the Continental European fund into cash and bonds when he could not find companies to invest in. Hendry says that that is just a common-sense way to protect the cash under management. 'The clients pay me to invest their money, but they also expect me not to lose it for them when markets go down.'

VALUE INVESTOR

Hendry is at heart a value investor. He would rather buy a dollar's worth of value at 50 cents than pay a dollar in the hope that it will double to two dollars. He buys hundreds of stocks to build insurance into his fund. The strategy assumes that some may fail and some may be unremarkable, but enough will generate sufficiently good returns to outweigh the laggards. Inherent in this approach is a bias away from big Blue Chip companies towards the small and mid-cap segment of markets. To work successfully he needs the businesses to have a relatively low profile with other investors, but not so low that the companies are always overlooked. Hendry wants to buy them well before their perceived value is reflected in their share price. To find companies that fit the profile Hendry is supported by a team of researchers at his hedge fund company Odey Asset Management. They screen thousands of businesses around the world for deep value characteristics.

Hendry combines this basic value technique with a top-down assessment of both the macro-economic trends and the underlying state of financial markets. This is the starting point for any investment, in any asset class. Before he goes fishing for stocks in any sector, he creates a mental model for why that sector should be favoured. He wants to know whether the primary market trend is bullish or bearish. Is the economic environment good for earnings growth? Is it inflationary or deflationary? Are interest rates rising or falling? Does that suit- a defensive or an aggressive portfolio? These are all items on Hendry's investment checklist.

MAKING THE TRADE

When it comes to pulling the trigger and buying a stock Hendry has married fundamental work on value with a technical overlay. The fundamentals determine the price he is willing to pay for the business, while the chart work determines his timing in and out of the stock. Hendry is searching for stocks that are already breaking out of a trading range. He wants to buy companies in which the share price over at least three months has outperformed its recent trading record.

The break-out confirms that investors are reassessing the company's prospects. The rising share price indicates that other investors are beginning to notice better profitability, or an improvement in the industry that will benefit the business. He looks for that signal to show that investors are chasing the price up, and that, 'smart people are increasingly willing to pay a little bit more and that in turn is attracting other market participants'. The ideal target stock is already making new multi-year highs, showing that the break-out is a valid technical indicator of a new long-term trend.

From barely using a chart in the first eight years of his financial career, Hendry will no longer make an investment in any asset until he sees a pattern that suggests a break-out in the price. It may take several months of watching the chart for higher highs and higher lows before he commits money to the company, but he says he is happy to wait. Because he will only buy stocks that are already rising Hendry often misses out on initial gains. He is, however, willing to make that sacrifice if it means that he eliminates the risks of chasing a false break-out. He would rather buy a stock that has been rising for several weeks than risk being too early and wrongly calling the break-out.

Hendry enters the trade with a rough idea of what he thinks the stock is worth, but pays closer attention to the patterns on the charts for sell signals. He is analysing the market's emotional view towards the stock, as a break in the new trend could indicate a turn in sentiment towards the company. He is content to sit in a stock for many months, even years, if the new trend remains intact. Always conscious of protecting his portfolio from positions that fail, he runs stop–loss positions (stops) tight to the stock price to limit the downside if the new trend breaks. If the uptrend is breached he sells the stock, even if the share price falls for just one day. He would rather sell than risk holding a losing position. It's a rule, he says, that removes any subjectivity from the selling decision.

But what if the fundamental idea is a good one? Won't he regret not having held on to the position? A typical trader's frustration comes from selling in weakness just before the stock turns higher. But Hendry says he is delighted to buy back companies at more expensive prices because it has confirmed that the uptrend is still relevant. 'If you do buy things that are going down, where do you sell? Where do you recognise that your timing was off – if the price falls another 5, 6 or 7%? What happens time and time again is the stock falls more like 30%, 40% or 50% because it has a profit warning. The market is so smart it picks it up so quickly, it sees the warning coming. So hopefully if we buy in an uptrend we avoid the profit warnings.'

Hendry stresses the importance of 'listening' to the market. The inherent risk in the fundamental approach is believing in the rightness of the reasons for buying a stock when the rest of the market doesn't care. You may be a genius that has discovered a great company that no one else knows about, but if no one else knows about it the stock price will not go up. Hendry faced this in 2003 when he was still bearish on the bigger trend for Western equities but knew that he had to buy into the momentum as the markets rose. Fighting the tape is not his style. When Western equity markets bounced in March 2003 he ran down his cash positions and by the middle of the year his European fund was once again fully invested.

Hendry says too many investors get over-analytical and ignore the message from the market. They buy companies because they like the business model but disregard the fact that the share price is falling. He calls it the Taliban version of stock selection, where investors become fundamentalists. They get excited by the company story and lose sight of the future. This is where Hendry parts company with investors wedded to fundamentals alone. He argues that if the stock is going down even for a single day, at best the market is saying that the future looks uncertain. Investors not disciplined enough to sell are ignoring the market wisdom. They are also failing to examine the flaws in their investment process if they are prepared to sit and watch their holdings fall in value.

To recap, Hendry's reasons for buying a stock can be broken down into five basic points:

1.   Relative out-performance over a three-month period.
2.   A clearly charted uptrend.
3. .   A solid profit margin.
4.   Valuation – Hendry uses Enterprise Value to Sales. This reflects the firm's economic value and is a measure of what the company would cost to buy relative to the sales it generates.
5.   The interplay between points 1–4 should confirm the company's quality.

STOCKS THAT FIT THE PROFILE

Devro is a good example of Hendry's technique. He bought stock in the Scotland-based sausage-skin maker in January 2003. It fulfilled his search for deep value, and had a chart pattern that was telegraphing a change in sentiment towards the company. Devro's share price halved in 2002 after a negative trading statement about full-year profits. The London listed group also announced a charge from restructuring its loss-making cellulose casings business. The message on earnings told the market to sell more of the stock.

A five-year chart (Figure 1.1) reveals the extent of the company's woes. The price pattern shows a business that has stoically faced a difficult past. Hendry saw a company that had been beaten up and survived. Surely, he reasoned, if it could survive its past, with better management and some luck the likelihood is that the future would be brighter. The stock came to Hendry's attention in late 2002 when the tell-tale signs of a reassessment in Devro's fortunes was indicated in the rise in the share price. Investors had begun to notice the turnaround in the company's profits and were beginning to pick up shares.

Hendry paid 44 pence a share for his Devro holding. He says, given the company's track record, that price represented the problems the company had faced but none

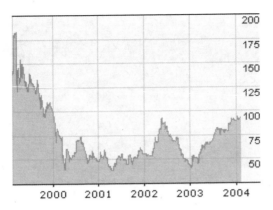

Figure 1.1 Devro: 5-year chart.
Source: Reuters, reproduced with permission

of the potential. At the end of 2003 Devro was trading at around £1 a share, giving Hendry back one and half times his money.

In 2002 he talked a lot about Atria, a Finnish meat-packing company. In media interviews he colourfully described the firm as a reindeer slaughterhouse. The company listed on the Helsinki stock exchange was turning over $600 million a year but had a market value of just $100 million. The valuation reflected investor fears of being caught up in a catalogue of bad news flow for Atria. The company had been adversely affected by the discovery of a case of BSE in Finland in December 2001. The threat of 'mad cow disease' worried investors who headed for the exits. To compound the problems, pressure from EU competition was squeezing prices, forcing Atria to focus on fighting off rivals in its local market where the firm enjoyed a dominant market share.

But, in a bear market for equities investors had missed the dividend story at Atria. The focus in the markets had shifted from capital appreciation to income, and here was a company generating a dividend yield of 3.8%. Again, this is a company that fitted Hendry's profile. Atria had suffered a difficult history, but not so bad that it didn't have a future (Figure 1.2).

Hendry bought the stock in mid-2001 for 4.5 euros. He was still holding a position in the company as it finished 2003 priced at 9 euros. Since buying into the company the earnings news has improved. Atria's statement for the nine months up to September 2003 showed an 11% rise in turnover, while operating profit for the period was up more than 13%. By 2003 the company's recovery was confirmed.

Hendry has made good money in Devro and Atria but he says there have been plenty of mistakes. The benefit of his 'Centipede legs' approach is that he can afford to suffer the failures without damaging the bulk of the fund. The loss of a few positions is the price of doing business. The mistakes do not stay in the portfolio too long, which is another element of Hendry's risk control. A consequence of his discipline of selling

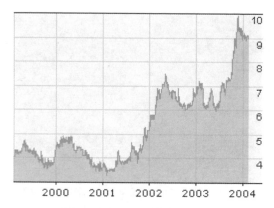

Figure 1.2   Atria: 5-year chart.
Source: Reuters, reproduced with permission

if the price breaks its up trend is that he trades aggressively. He is happy to pay the dealing charges if it means avoiding exposure to a stock that goes into freefall.

This is vital to the day-to-day management of his portfolio. He carries a small financial pager at all times, which alerts him if his positions are stopped out. During periods of high volatility the pager chirps away signalling that his stop–loss safety net has been struck in position after position. Any time spent with Hendry during market hours is punctuated with apologies for the interruption and hasty calls made to brokers. The level of active trading he does is much higher than would normally be found with long-only fund managers. Hendry says the hedge fund model is much more geared to avoiding losses and he probably spends as much time on not losing money as he does on making it.

BASICALLY BEARISH

Hendry believes the primary trend for markets is still negative. The market recovery of 2003 is but a prelude to the reassertion of the bear; it is a temporary cyclical recovery in a secular bear market. At the core of his concerns is the dramatic expansion of credit since the early 1990s and in his view the US economy has been mismanaged.

His Continental European Fund and the Eclectica Hedge Fund are constructed with this perspective in mind. This first shows itself in his asset allocation process – Hendry was a buyer of stocks through the 2003 rally because he is a pragmatic money manager. But he tried to 'stay close to the exits', ready to liquidate his positions quickly if the market fell sharply. He had to balance his enthusiasm for smaller capitalised stocks with the liquidity constraints of less frequently traded companies. He participated in the rally, but continued to buy insurance on the downside by hedging his fund with derivatives contracts on the S&P 500 that would pay out if the markets dropped.

Even his most 'positive' outlook, if it unfolds, will be extremely negative for the bulk of investors. In his scenario for markets over the next 10–20 years the best that can be hoped for is a stagnant US stock market that trades sideways. The Dow may make 12,000, says Hendry, but the bad news is that it will still be at that level in 20 years' time. This 'positive' version of the world depends on America successfully reflating its economy. The US Central Bank, The Federal Reserve, and the American government keep recession at bay by holding interest rates low and giving money back to consumers with tax cuts. By continuing to add easy money to the economy, Federal Reserve Governor, Alan Greenspan encourages consumption and prevents a rise in savings rates that would weaken domestic demand.

The problem with this scenario, says Hendry, is that Greenspan is mortgaging tomorrow to prevent economic weakness today. 'Debt in the US economy is already in excess of 360% of GDP. Greenspan cannot allow interest rates to rise too quickly because of the damage they would wreak on rate-sensitive property and equity markets.' If Greenspan manages to hold rates at low levels to head off a collapse in asset prices, the burden of the debt overhang will be borne by the dollar.

THE TALE OF JOHN LAW

Hendry says students of financial history have witnessed this phenomenon before. The US today is taking big risks with the dollar. The politicians are desperate to remain in power and are prepared to debase the currency by printing more. It is a larger more sophisticated version of the scandal that rocked the French establishment 300 years ago. In 1716, Scotsman John Law, knowledgeable about banking and credit, started the first government-approved bank which replaced coins with paper notes. Hendry thinks the similarities are compelling.

> 'The striking thing is how much this smells of Paris in 1720–24. The politicians got carried away and saw they could be popular by issuing more money. The money gave the illusion of growth and prosperity, but all that was being added to the economy were promises. The markets have been going up for the wrong reasons, it's a phantom, a function of money, just like the Mississippi Trading Company it's a bubble.'

The Mississippi Trading Company was another Law creation. The company was formed to take up trading rights with Louisiana when the previous monopoly on the route was surrendered. Law created the bank and the company with the highest intentions. Stock in the newly formed company was sold to the public. For many years the projects succeeded and he made a smart decision to have all his notes payable on sight and in the coinage that was appropriate for the time they were issued. Law's notes commanded a premium, while the debt notes run up by Louis XIV sold at more than a 20% discount to their face value. All seemed well until Law's paper money was issued in huge amounts in excess of the bank's underlying funds. The paper money stoked speculation in Mississippi Trading Company shares and the whole project collapsed as the public finally lost confidence in the value of the currency.

Hendry says the effects of credit expansion in eighteenth century, and on modern-day Western financial markets, are strikingly similar. In France stock in the Mississippi Trading Company went from 500 Livre a share to 12 500 Livre, a 24-fold rise in three years. Hendry says the parallels are in the property and stock markets in the US and the unrestrained credit expansion is now driving up commodity and emerging markets stock prices. That begs the question: Will the consequences be the same? The bust in France was as dramatic as the speculative frenzy that pushed up asset prices. When the public lost faith in the currency as its purchasing power collapsed, John Law was driven out of Paris, blamed for a system that might have worked had it not been so badly abused.

In the excellent classic text on the history of speculation written by Charles Mackay, *Extraordinary Popular Delusions and the Madness of Crowds,* Law is depicted as a victim of the greed of politicians and speculators.

> 'He was thoroughly acquainted with the philosophy and true principles of credit. He understood the monetary question better than any man of his day; and if his system fell with a crash so tremendous, it was not so much his fault as that of the people amongst whom he had erected it. He did not calculate upon the avaricious frenzy of a whole nation . . . '

For Law, Hendry suggests substituting the name Alan Greenspan, the Head of the Federal Reserve. Both, he says, started with good intentions but were unable to control the outcome of the actions they were encouraged to take by politicians.

Hendry says the roots of the current credit problem can be found in the replacement of the gold standard with the dollar standard in 1971. This has allowed the US government to use and abuse its position as guardian of the world's reserve currency for its own purposes. He believes that change altered for good the long-term relationship between credit and money, with governments able to subsidise their fiscal profligacy by devaluing the currency. Current debt obligations are now out of line with the ability of the US economy to repay them.

The catalyst for the imminent collapse in asset prices has evolved from the point in the late 1990s where Greenspan cut interest rates in reaction to the triple threats to the international financial system from the Asian currency crisis, the collapse of the LTCM hedge fund and the debt default in Russia. The effect of that easy money was to stoke the NASDAQ bubble, pushing the tech index from 3500 to 5000 in the 12 months leading up to March 2000. Hendry says the US is now so desperate to prevent an economic slowdown that it is encouraging reckless credit expansion. 'Greenspan is getting more and more compromised, he's doing everything he can to stop people saving. So what he has done is take a bull market in equities and pushed it into the housing market, he knows money will chase any assets that will go up in price.'

Hendry's greatest worry is the reassertion of a 1930s style depression. If his positive version of the coming decade has the US market trading sideways, his negative version looks like depression. The party stops when people decide to rebuild their savings and tackle their debt, and when enough people collectively stop spending, the economy goes into recession. Even though asset valuations fall to levels that start to look attractive again, no one is willing to buy because they are debt heavy and savings light. Psychologically the experience of wealth destruction gives them a depression type mindset.

In Hendry's doomsday scenario for the world, US equity markets shed 80% of their value. Asset prices fall because the Federal Reserve is unable to stop interest rates rising. Several pressures come to bear at the same time, pushing rates higher. The Fed is trying to stimulate growth to stave off a recession, but if the US economy continues to show strong quarter-on-quarter growth, past experience suggests that corporate borrowing and mortgage rates will have to rise as capital is rationed. The other pressure comes from the US government's need to finance the deficits. The US is forced to raise rates to support the US dollar because its declining value threatens to dissuade foreigners from financing the spending habits of the US government or consumer.

Will foreigners be happy to continue the purchase of US government bonds? At the time of writing the amount of US debt owed to foreigners was about 60% of GDP, or $6.5 trillion. Asian central banks represent a good chunk of the holders of existing and new US Treasury bonds. The symbiotic nature of the trade has Asian Central banks financing US purchasing of Asian goods. Buying US Treasury debt underwrites continued US borrowing and spending. But, the dollar's decline reduces the value of those Treasury bills, begging the question: Will the US have to raise short-term rates to stabilise the dollar and persuade foreigners to continue funding trade and government deficits?

Clearly Asian banks defending their currencies have an interest in buying dollars to halt the rise in the value of their own currencies. This protects domestic exporters, but the Bank of Japan's experience of spending trillions of Yen in the forex markets has merely slowed the pace of the dollar's decline. The sustainability of this arrangement will determine the bigger monetary forces on Western equity markets. Any rise in interest rates to firm up the dollar threatens to cause the US economy to stall. Given the world's dependence on the US as the main driver of growth, the implications for European equities are also bleak. Hendry sees severe asset price adjustments ahead for Europe too.

BUY JAPAN

Japan, like the US, says Hendry, has embraced inflationary economic policies. Interest rates have been kept at zero, the Bank of Japan has intervened in the currency markets to weaken the Yen, and the government has spent money on public works programmes. Japan's economic recovery may be fragile, but he feels that there are compelling reasons to buy Japanese stocks. The country has already witnessed a decade of collapsing asset prices and the domestic economy still has thousands of companies that look like 'special situation deep value' opportunities.

It's the valuation story that convinced Hendry's company, Odey Asset Management, to launch a long-only Japanese equity fund in November 2003. Looking at the valuations available in the domestic economy, Hendry describes himself as the proverbial kid in a candy store; he believes the risks that Japan is promising only a short-term recovery are mitigated by the prices he is paying for companies. He says that any company still alive after the decade through which the Japanese economy has struggled, has demonstrated the robustness of their business model. The valuations are seductive; in Japan he can buy companies on 3% of sales – like Kanaden, an electronics component manufacturer he owns, which has a billion dollars in revenue but is valued by the market at only $30 million.

> 'There are two tranches in Japan; there is big boring Japan which has the same stocks you could buy in the US and Europe, and then there are these bankrupt domestic businesses, these electrical wholesalers, manufacturers and construction companies. They are remarkably cheap; they're trading at 3, 4 or even 5 standard deviations away from where they should be, with a price at maybe 6 or 7 times earnings.'

The history of the Japanese economy charts a country that came out of the Second World War destroyed and destitute, and spent the rest of the century evolving into a world-beater. But, says Hendry, a reading of the Japanese stock market reveals that it was only in 2003 that the market touched its 50-year moving average. The moving average is the average of so many days share price movements. Technical analysts take its movements as a signal that the price is likely to rise or fall. Looking at a simplistic model of dollar cost averaging into the market since 1950, Hendry says that the best the investor could hope for is break-even. A 50-year buy-and-hold strategy would have done no better than come out with even money.

How does Hendry feel about the headline index when Japan has already witnessed a number of false starts since the Nikkei hovered at 39 000 in the late 1980s? He thinks that the best money will be made in the short to medium term by staying out of the big blue chip stocks. The Nikkei has been a disappointment to investors who have been too early in calling the turn. The market may have climbed from the 20-year low of 7607.88 it hit in late April 2003, but the seven years prior to 2003 have seen the Nikkei end the year in positive territory only once, and that was 1999. Hendry thinks that there are meaningful comparisons between the Dow and the Japanese market, and has been studying the 1929 crash for answers.

He feels that Japan could be where the US market was in 1933. That year was the best ever for buying American equities - the Dow saw a 70% move. The rise sucked investors back into the market who then made no money in the nine years from 1933 to 1942 when the index basically traded sideways. The money was made outside the index among the smaller companies operating in the domestic economy.

Hendry says that this is the way to play Japan – look for the deepest value and buy fast-growing smaller companies. Tread carefully around the bigger exporting businesses that operate on the same terms as blue chips in Europe and the US. Following the Dow analogy, ultimately the US market didn't truly break-out until 1952 where, from 1952 to 1966, the Dow went from 300 to 1200 – a 400% gain. If Hendry's hunch is right, Japan has already seen its bear market bottom, but the Nikkei may settle down to a listless decade of sideways trade. It may take 10 years or so for the Nikkei to make a strong break-out of that range, and only then will investors in the index see 4–5 times their money made from Japanese blue chips.

Extending the 1929 analogy, Hendry says he is trying to replicate the investment strategy of economist, John Maynard Keynes. As well as giving his name to an economic theory, Keynes invested heavily in beaten-up US companies in the early 1930s and amassed a fortune for Kings College, Cambridge. Hendry insists that now is a historic opportunity to find the same returns in the domestic economy in Japan. He is buying heavily into Japanese property which has been trading at rock bottom valuations. Among his real estate holdings in Japan are the Japan Real Estate Investment Trust and Nippon Building Fund.

> 'We're buying Japanese real estate trusts because the pricing is all wrong. In 1989 the Emperor's garden had the same value as all of the real estate in California, clearly that was absurd. But we have seen an 89% fall in the price of Japanese property, and the trusts are valuing it as though it will be worthless in 20 years' time. That is also absurd. With a gross yield of eight and a half percent investors, are demanding a high nominal yield to offset the expected capital loss. We think these are attractive numbers.'

HOLD GOLD

Beyond the opportunities in Japan, Hendry thinks that the other dominant theme for investing over the next decade will be in gold and other commodities. 'We are on the cusp of one of the greatest commodity booms of the past 200 years. When this bull market is over gold, oil and mining stocks will look like they were at deep value at current prices.'

Hendry sees a bright outlook for commodities, whichever of his economic visions come true. If there is a long-term reflation of the global economy, leading to a pick-up in sustained growth, then that would drive prices, and monetary inflation will lift the value of commodities as it bids up prices generally across the economy. Mining stocks should also specifically benefit from growth in the emerging economies of China and India, which are hungry for raw materials.

In Hendry's nightmare depression economic scenario, the growth drivers for owning commodities become less important than owning a tangible resource itself. If the Western world goes into recession, commodities will see a less steep fall off in value.

Deflation will be damaging for all stocks, but commodity producers already short on capacity will perform less badly. He likes the fact the commodity markets are emerging from 20 years in the wilderness, where analysts cut back their coverage and producers closed down plants because they were uneconomic to operate. There will therefore be a lag before mines and farmers are able to raise supply. The short-term impact will be a rise in prices to ration demand, and the downside should be capped.

He was adding to positions in mining stocks throughout 2003. Minara for instance met his requirements for deep value and his macro view on commodities. Minara used to be called Anaconda Nickel and operated a technology for bleaching out nickel. Ultimately it was less effective than predicted, but exploration efforts for nickel had been wound down because the technology was expected to satisfy existing demand. As a result of the disappointment with the technology, Minara's share price fell from A$15 to 70 cents. Hendry bought the stock in August 2003 for 73 cents and has made four times his money (Figure 1.3).

Gold has the benefit of being a commodity and having an investment function. As a store of value, gold has traditionally done well in periods of inflation, its last major peak was seen 20 years ago as Western governments battled a period of energy-fuelled stagflation. In a deflationary world gold still represents a non-paper store of value and investors will choose to hold it over monetary assets that are declining in worth.

Hendry also sees good long-term technical reasons to hold gold; the precious metal has broken its 25-year downtrend. In both 2002 and 2003, in dollar terms, gold put in annual 20% gains, and until that rising pattern is broken he will stay with gold stocks.

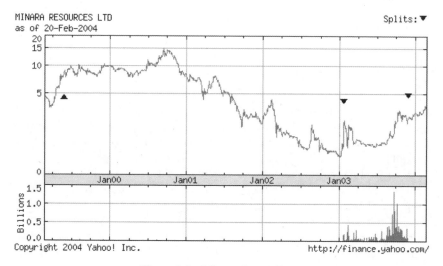

Figure 1.3 Minara: 5-year chart.
Source: Yahoo! Reproduced with permission of Yahoo! Inc. © 2004 by Yahoo! Inc. YAHOO! and the YAHOO! logo are trademarks of Yahoo! Inc.

He believes that it is not inconceivable to see bullion back above $800 an ounce. Through 2003 Hendry held his bigger long equity positions in gold mining stocks, Newmont Mining, Placer Dome and Ashanti Goldfields. The holdings reflect his ongoing concern about the dollar (where gold has traded inversely to the dollar) and his view that gold will continue to be a beneficiary of the current economic environment.

BUY THE ANTITHESIS OF THE PAST

Both Gold and Japan are examples of Hendry's entreaty to investors to buy the antithesis of the past. It is a philosophy he follows in both asset allocation and stock selection. Devro, Atria and Minara had all had ugly pasts, but brighter looking futures. He says investors get stuck on the stocks that just made them money, or regret missing the sectors that have just risen most strongly.

He calls it the Greyfriars Bobby effect. In the story the Skye terrier became famous in Edinburgh when his master, John Grey, died in 1858 and was buried in Greyfriars churchyard. For 14 years after Grey's death the small terrier refused to stray from the churchyard. Hendry says stocks fall to attractive valuations often because investors have given up on them, and they fall off the investment radar screen. He believes investors should focus on trying to spot these companies rather than riding on the back of last year's heroes.

> 'Too many investors act like Greyfriars Bobby. Like the little Terrier they keep going back and sitting on the graves of yesterday's ideas. They go back four or five years and they say we made loads of money in the semiconductor stocks, and when they feel emboldened again as they did in 2003 to take on risk, they go back into technology and semiconductors. They should really be looking back to 1971, or even 1723 for ideas.'

In the market rebound in 2003, investors returned to sectors that had rewarded them prior to the bear market. Hendry acknowledges the gains made, but insists that any understanding of the economics of the business reveals that the best returns have already been seen. 'Semiconductors was a hot area, and hot areas attract money and capital, they attract very bright people who ultimately end up working against each other which in the end negates the uniqueness of the sector. Finally, too much capital creates too much competition, the entrepreneurs and investors no longer get rewarded and the cycle peaks.'

If that experience is still too recent for investors to get a clear sense of perspective, Hendry suggests that investors do some reading up on the oil stocks in the late 1970s. Fears of an energy crisis and inflation drove valuations of oil companies to record highs. Even though the prices peaked, well into the mid-80s investment banks were still running huge investor conferences focused on oil stocks. They were arguing that a company like Slumberger was the equivalent of a high-growth IT company. By that time, however, the big money had already been made in the sector.

Buying the antithesis of the past makes good economic sense. Over the four-year business cycle it is akin to recognising that one cycle has finished and, for one company or sector, a new cycle is just beginning. In stock price terms that cycle might extend out much longer. Hendry believes that for technology stocks the turn in the cycle has come. Another sector that he suspects may have reached its peak are the big pharmaceutical companies that have thrived on selling drugs on generous profit margins. He expects them to face more pressure as societies around the world refuse to accept the high prices for drugs. He says the tide is already turning on drug company profits. Investors looking at the medical sector should focus more on the generic drug makers that offer better promise.

BONDS STILL LOOK INTERESTING

Current market orthodoxy suggests that the bond market rally of the last 20 years is over, and that, over time, as the interest rate cycle turns and rates start to go up in Western economies, bonds will be sold. Investors chasing returns are not going to buy an asset that appears set to decline in value, and government bond prices fall as interest rates rise. Should investors therefore be shunning US Treasuries now that the opportunity for capital appreciation has passed?

Maybe investors should not be too hasty in selling their bonds. Hendry considers that investors can comfortably continue to own treasuries because they will do well in both his best and worst case scenario for the US economy. If the US authorities are able to hold interest rates down there are two major forces that have an interest in buying bonds:

1. *Fannie Mae and Freddie Mac.* These are privately held companies that are chartered by Congress to provide money to mortgage lending companies. These government-sponsored enterprises are victims of the Federal Reserves desire to keep 10-year bond yields as close to 3% as possible. At that level the domestic consumer opts instead of saving to continue refinancing their mortgage and spending the windfall. But each refinancing at a lower rate of interest takes the higher interest rate payment away from Fannie Mae or Freddie Mac. To hedge against the lost income that both organisations expected over 10 years plus, they in turn buy US government bonds.

2. *Asian Central Banks.* These are primarily the Bank of Japan and the Bank of China. They are active in the currency markets selling their own currencies and buying the dollar. Both are keen to defend export-led growth by trying to weaken their currencies, and so are supporting US government bond prices.

These two powerful institutions will continue buying Treasuries while the status quo remains in place. The US Federal Reserve is implicitly supporting and encouraging that action in order to hold yields down, and keep interest rates low. If the Fed succeeds, bond prices will go up, or at worst will remain steady.

If the status quo changes and the US authorities lose control of the dollar, the outcome will still be supportive for treasuries. The impact would push bond yields up and stall growth. The US economy might catch a serious bout of deflation, but Hendry notes that bonds are one of few asset classes that do well in a deflationary environment. As far as he is concerned, it is the only time in history that he could construct an argument where bonds win in both scenarios. He calls it a "bizarre Alice in Wonderland environment" that has sustained oil prices above $30 a barrel, pushed gold over $400 an ounce and primed a new bubble in equity prices.

MISERABLE SCOTTISH TROUBLE-MAKER

Hendry has described himself as a 'miserable Scottish trouble-maker'. But it's a self-depreciating title that is some way from the truth. He likes to be controversial but that comes from a passion for the job, and is more a function of intellectual curiosity than a desire to simply be difficult. In fact Hendry is very likeable in person and has none of the snobbery or affectation that can infect the attitudes of high-earning fund managers. More likely to be found in an open-neck shirt and cords than a business suit and wing-tips, in conversation he is softly spoken, almost shy. There is something of the country minister about his manner. But raise the markets or his own industry and he speaks with the energy of a Presbyterian firebrand, his Glasgow accent pithy with invective for his chosen target. More likely than not, his fire is levelled at the investment industry, or the author of a recently published article on the economy.

He is antagonistic towards the Fund Management business and scathing about its performance during the 2000–2003 bear market. His great bugbear is that so many fund managers in the long-only side of the industry did not cut losses to preserve capital. He complains that the fund management community is incentivised to line its own pockets and bemoans the way it collects money, not on the basis of returns, but on the strength of marketing budgets. Hendry hasn't enamoured himself to his peers by calling the industry complacent and overpaid, but then he isn't the type to step away from a public row.

When he shifted half of his Continental European portfolio into cash in 2002 he stirred-up the ire of the Investment Management Association. The UK industry body fired off a letter warning that he was flouting IMA principles by not being at least 80% invested in stocks. The guidelines are designed to establish a uniform set of rules for investors to understand how fund managers run their funds, and to allow equal comparison of performance. They are not binding or legally enforceable but ignoring them may deter some investors from looking at the fund.

Hendry took the debate public and railed against the apparent absurdity of a set of guidelines which he felt would have made it tough to deliver positive returns for his investors. Ultimately, after several months of running skirmishes in the media, Hendry and the IMA made their peace and the Scot was fully invested back in the market before the row could escalate. Hendry scored a moral victory; he managed to achieve a positive return in 2002 when nearly all rival European Funds lost money.

STARTING OUT

Despite his occasional shots at the industry Hendry is grateful for his two big breaks; the job offer from Ballie Gifford that brought him into fund management, and the chance meeting with Crispin Odey that took him into the business of running a Hedge Fund. Without the intervention of a Senior Partner at Ballie Gifford, the Edinburgh-based Asset Management Company, Hendry might still now be a Chartered Accountant for the accountancy firm KPMG.

He had persuaded the accountants to give him £2000 as a down-payment on his career, and to provide a little comfort in the final year of his accountancy degree in Glasgow. It was 1989, and £2000 and job at KPMG looked good to a working-class son of a truck driver. But the accountants wouldn't get their man. Hendry, armed with the fuzziest notion of what fund managers do, secured himself an interview with Ballie Gifford.

Hendry recalls the job interview. He was very taken with the idea of investing in Hungary at the time. The Berlin Wall had just fallen and, at the time, the country was just rewriting the constitution to enshrine a free market economy with protection for businesses in both the state and private sector. Western asset management companies were taking a keen interest in developments in Eastern Europe and Hendry's arguments appeared to please the interviewer. The Partner at KPMG was less happy to hear that he would be getting his £2000 back. His parting shot was to castigate the young graduate with the censorious comment, 'Young man you will always regret this decision'.

He spent the next eight years at Ballie Gifford getting an education in fund management. Professionally it was a crash course in the world's major equity markets. Socially, there was a culture shock for the young working-class graduate.

> 'They usually got fund managers straight from Oxford or Cambridge so it seemed strange they wanted me, but I must have struck a cord. There was this austere Presbyterian atmosphere and they couldn't understand my accent. They were all very blue-blooded, up from London, so it took a little while for me to get used to; confidence has to be high in this business.'

With hindsight, his biggest criticism with the investment process that he learned through those eight years was the absence of charts. Technical analysis (TA) wasn't considered worth bothering with. Hendry says chart analysis was viewed with some disdain; he was encouraged to dismiss technical analysis and the notion that historical prices can convey any information about future prices. He now views charts as an essential insight into the emotional behaviour of investors, and, as we have already seen, he uses them to time-buying decisions. Before he used TA, Hendry says his trading record was poor, and the blending of charts into his company analysis convinced him that he had been missing the essential emotional content in the share price. Incidentally, he believes that too many fund managers performed badly in the 2000–03 bear market because years of positive gains had made them blind to the message in the price patterns.

> 'They did well investing in a bull market, but in a bull market the emotional content is less, good ideas get rewarded and bad ideas get rewarded, in fact everything gets rewarded in a bull market because everything goes up. So they all came from a frame of reference weighted in the fundamental end of market analysis.'

His time at Ballie Gifford also gave Hendry an appreciation that markets can go down as well as up. He worked on a series of markets that were just hitting pivotal events. Ballie Gifford's method was to put its trainee fund managers through tours of duty as an analyst: one year covering Japanese equities, one year on UK equities and a final year working on US equities. After that the trainee fund managers took up longer positions with separate market teams.

Starting on the Japanese market in September 1990, Hendry spent the year watching the Nikkei index fall from 28 000 to 21 000. The year he covered the UK culminated in the exchange rate crisis which pushed interest rates to 15% and forced the country to abandon the Exchange Rate Mechanism. He started covering US equities in 1994, the worst year for some time for American stocks, when Dow bell weather General Electric ended the year lower than it had started, the only year in 20 up to that point that GE had fallen. The Dow dropped 16% in 7 months and worried investors because it broke below an important support level. Hendry says the period has groomed him well for the coming years of falling prices, and has left a 'deep vein of cynicism' about how markets wait to catch investors as they feel at their most comfortable.

His reincarnation as a hedge fund manager at Odey Asset Management came courtesy of a brief stint with the asset management arm of Swiss investment bank Credit Suisse. His career at Ballie Gifford ended while he was covering the UK smaller-cap market in 1998. He was clashing with managers and neither side could see much future in the relationship continuing. Hendry took a job in the asset management unit of Credit Suisse but his tenure lasted just a few months. The Swiss group had money invested with Crispin Odey's hedge fund and because a colleague was absent, Hendry was asked to attend an investment review meeting with Odey. The two hit it off, resulting in the job offer that brought him into the hedge fund world. Hendry describes the meeting as a revelation.

> 'You feel fantastic, there is this great mind (Odey) who asks you to join his business, but of course when you get there your confidence collapses. There was this quite weird experience of 6 months when I had to learn to embrace the charts. There was Crispin firing off in all these different directions and he was using charts. I had never used charts before and now I had to recognise there was this very bright person successfully using technical analysis.'

Before Hendry joined the company, Crispin Odey was left in no doubt that the young Scot was coming with a reputation. Apparently when seeking a reference from Hendry's previous employer Ballie Gifford, Odey was informed that he should think carefully before hiring a potential trouble maker. Odey patently ignored the advice and Hendry is now a senior manager in the company. What about the trouble-making? There is plenty of shouting in their Mayfair offices, and he says there are many times he disagrees with Odey but the creative tension in the process is good for thrashing out new ideas.

Hendry says his commitment to the job leaves little time for friends. Not for him the social carousal of dinner parties and bars that might typify the life of the average 34 year old. His staff might like a distraction or two to take his mind off the job. He insists that they all work at a temperature of 56 degrees, which is actually quite chilly. He read somewhere that an old hand in the fund management business had done the same and it had done wonders for staff productivity. Hendry says it focuses the mind and 'keeps sharp pencils pointed at the spines'. When they ask if the temperature can be turned up, they are told that if they are cold they are not working hard enough!

PUTTING THE CLIENT BEFORE MANAGEMENT

Many fund managers who invest using fundamental techniques visit companies. They consider the trip to see management an important part of learning what is beyond the accounts. Hendry doesn't. The system may have been a part of his training at Ballie Gifford, but he has dropped the practice finding that it inhibits the objectivity of his investment process. 'Many CEOs by definition are charismatic people, the risk is when you talk to them that you begin to fall under their spell and fall in love with the company. What I am trying to perfect instead is an emotional intelligence.'

Hendry says retaining objectivity is hard in the face of prejudice everywhere about companies, currencies or economies. His advice to investors is to try to keep some distance and focus on your own research.

He may not have much interest in meeting the management of the companies he buys, but it's a different matter with his own investors. He makes a point of meeting the clients face to face to explain Odey's investment process. This is not a practice throughout the industry where some institutions prefer their managers to focus on stock selection while the asset gatherers and the marketing and sales staff worry about the clients. Hendry says pointedly that all managers who pursue 'relative performance' benchmarks ought to meet the person whose money they are losing. 'It is harder to justify when an investor has just given you the fruits of his life's work to steer through the shark infested waters of the financial markets.'

As Hendry sees it, people give their money to a fund manager because that person will protect it and possibly make some on top. 'Even though they can't understand why he is so well paid they think the generous compensation he earns will ensure he sells their holdings when the markets go down.' If the market is going up they assume that he will stay in the market and try to make them some money. Hendry says that in 2000 most people who invested in equities discovered that their well-paid fund managers didn't do either of those things very well.

Hendry says that investors must seek out managers who offer absolute returns over relative returns. They must also recognise that the period under which relative returns flourished was a function of a very specific time in history that will not be repeated for some years, if at all. 'During the period 1982–1999, for example, the UK stock market generated 15% compound returns, which meant that investors could double their money every five years by just being invested in the index.'

The certainty of year-on-year index gains, Hendry complains, moulded an industry more interested in collecting money than managing it better for higher returns. He says, 'too many clever minds are involved in a dysfunctional overpaid industry that is incentivised to maintain the status quo rather than strive for excellence'.

When I point out that Hedge Funds, including his own, traditionally take a 20% performance fee from their clients, which doesn't seem ungenerous, Hendry immediately agrees. 'Yep, we're greedy, but that money comes from profit. If we are doing our job properly the clients are getting rich and so are we.'

DEALING WITH RISK

By bitter experience the Odey group places a great onus on managing risk. Hendry's technique of buying out of fashion sectors and stocks already contains an element of risk control through price. But the Odey group as a whole has been forced to implement a stricter system of cash management. This is a systematic measurement of money at risk in the markets and is designed, like most similar models, to prevent the company going bust from a few bad investments. The risk controls were all tightened up after Crispin Odey took big bets in the debt market.

The lesson bears repeating here and has a direct impact on everything Odey Asset Management now does. In 1994, when the company was in its infancy (before Hendry's arrival), Odey took a large bet on UK government War Loan. War Loan is the most leveraged fixed income debt issued by the British government, and Crispin had charted a 17-year break-out.

Odey was gambling that disinflation, a slowdown in rising prices (inflation), would continue to assert itself in the 1990s, driving down interest rates. As rates fell the expectation was that bond prices would rise as investors tried to lock in higher rates paid by the bonds. The bond holders would enjoy tremendous capital appreciation in the assets they owned. The price broke out to a 13-year high which appeared to confirm Crispin Odey's hunch, so he bought generously to the tune of hundreds of millions of dollars, eventually buying up 40% of the issuance.

It was the right trade, at the right price. But, says Hendry, when the market knows that you own such a large position, you are a target unless your pockets are very deep. There is an intellectual conviction that drives Hendry's investment process, and that owes much to the guidance of Crispin Odey. At the time Odey was sure the War bond was the right investment and, rewarded by the market with rising prices, loaded up heavily on the basis of a single trade.

At that point the market delivered an unwelcome surprise. The price checked back to its break-out level, leaving him stretched and needing to sell some of his holding. But, as he now owned 40% of the issuance he was at the mercy of the market makers who knew he needed to sell. Odey had no choice but to lighten his position to mitigate the risk of a more serious loss. The price did start to move back in Crispin Odey's favour, but by then it was too late. His hedge fund had lost 43% of its value. By the end of 1994 those losses, and the withdrawals from spooked clients, saw assets under management fall from a billion dollars to just $40 million.

Hendry says that the experience has had a profound effect on the company's risk control. A hedge fund company either goes out of business when something of that magnitude happens or it changes its business practices. The company has now changed the way it operates to allow it to accommodate mistakes and survive. Inevitably that means taking on smaller bets. On a company-wide level, because of the concern about the current environment for financial markets, there is a focus on liquidating to cash at the sign of any serious sell-off.

Strategically, because of Hendry's view on the bubble-like conditions that markets are still exhibiting, his aim is to take a lot of negative bets on European and American stocks while running faster long positions in Japan. He also hedges his portfolio by buying derivatives in the S&P 500. A significant part of his strategy through 2003 was to buy S&P 500 index Puts for his hedge fund. These are options contracts that give him the right to buy the index back at a lower price if it falls. The contracts are a basic insurance policy against downside risk, and while they do cost money to arrange, they earn their keep in declining markets. At any one time in 2003 the contracts may have cost him 3–4% of the fund's net asset value.

SPOTTING THE BREAKDOWN

Does Hendry have a view on the timing of a fresh bear leg down? If, as he fears, there is a broader bear market at work, the tricky part is timing the next break. There are precedents from the bear markets of 1929 and 1989 for a fourth year of positive trade, but Hendry says that even that was ultimately only a brief reprieve from the bears. He likes to quote the example from 1929 when investors got drawn back in, after the market bottomed on the 13 November of that year on 10 times earnings and a 5% dividend yield.

> 'All the bears who had made money, reinvested their cash and the market rallied by 50% from November to the following June. Thereafter, everyone lost 80% of their money, and it didn't matter that the market was on ten times earnings or that the market was statistically cheap because the US got depression.'

Hendry suspects that the next major down leg will come quickly with little warning. Although he uses charts to identify price trends he feels that this time they may be poor harbingers of weakness. Contrarian investors argue that when a theme or style of investing becomes ubiquitous it is time to take the opposite position. Hendry's fear is that investors now wedded to technical analysis will fail to see the market correction coming. He suggests that they might do better by using a little common sense to recognise when a company or market is overvalued or undervalued. He is dismissive of more complicated forms of technical analysis, like Elliott Wave theory, which is meant to give time signals. He says it is too prescriptive and too complicated.

The prospect of being locked into losing positions haunts Hendry. His fear is of another 1987 type crash, where the first day sees the market lose 15%, the second day another 15% and by day 3 the portfolio is down a third. So what do investors do to minimise their risk? They leave the market before the correction comes. Hendry says that emotionally it is very hard to walk away from a great party, but capital preservation demands just that. His partner and founder of the company, Crispin Odey, was lightening holdings in 1999 and shifting to a defensive profile, while others where rushing to participate in the technology bubble. Odey's fund put in a little over 6%, its worst year ever, while others were making high double-digit returns. Ultimately, while he may have been a little early, Odey would continue to make positive returns for clients through the bear market where the other funds gave back their gains. According to Hendry, all investors can learn from that. It is the lack of losses, and not always the gains, that singles out a good investor.

THE GAP IN THE CURTAIN

Hendry, to borrow a phrase 'feels the hand of history' upon his shoulder. He is fond of using literary or movie references to demystify the investment process, and a current favourite metaphor is John Buchan's 1932 novel, *The Gap in the Curtain*. In Buchan's story a group of characters come together for a weekend country house party. They are trained by a German Professor to read the front page of the London *Times* newspaper as it will appear on a specific date one year in the future. But each character comes away with only a small snapshot of the front page. Each character then acts on that scrap of information only to find that life does not turn out quite how each expected.

Hendry says that investors now are getting a scrap of the future. It is in the economic data, in the market noise and in the stock charts. These are like pieces of a jigsaw puzzle, but it is an incomplete picture. 'Life has these capricious turns, so the hardest part is patience. The charts only represent about one-third of the journey to the pot of gold.' In 2003, where markets were down 50% from their peak in 2000, a rally was due. That rally served a function of making bearish investors bullish as they became emboldened to take on margin and more aggressive bets. But, he counsels, remember the 'Gap in the Curtain', the danger is that in their haste to participate and recover earlier losses investors lose sight of the medium and longer-term picture. By not understanding the bigger negative themes investors will again commit expensive mistakes. Hendry, his pager bleeping to signal that another position has been stopped out, says cheerily that he'll be waiting close to the exits when the markets finally recognise the dangers from the credit bubble.

> 'I feel incredibly honoured to be associated with the stock market right now, to be out there trying to navigate a course through this period. Its not that we're in uncharted waters, but this is going to be one of the big ones. People will look back and wonder how fund managers reacted, they will wonder why the hell they got it all wrong, why they were buying stocks when they should have been selling them.'

2
Michael Browne: European Value Stocks

'For the bears I have one message, you do not have a monopoly on wisdom. But, any investor looking to make money in Europe over the next decade has to understand a combination of structural problems will make the equity investor's life difficult.'

Want to know where the global markets are going? Dust off the history books and turn the clock back 130 years. Michael Browne thinks investors could do themselves a favour by taking another look at the pattern of growth when Queen Victoria sat on the British throne. Then the challenge for companies was adapting to the new competition from the United States. Today the emergence of China and India is presenting the same threats and opportunities.

In the nineteenth century the opening up of the US to business was marked by falling transportation costs as trains and faster ships reduced the time it took to get new products to market. Today technology and its adoption in the emerging world is having the same effect on prices. Both the cost of capital and the improved efficiency of capital markets are directing money to the economies that can use it most productively: namely, the emerging markets where the profit potential is greatest. The future says Browne, for the next few years at least, will see emerging economies grow quickly, while growth in the mature Western economies stabilises and the world witnesses a deflationary boom.

For equity investors, that could generate some turbulence in financial markets over the next decade, but, says Browne, there will still be plenty of opportunity to make money from stocks. Ironically, since he manages a Hedge Fund at Sofaer Capital that only invests in European shares he says the better gains will probably come from the US where he expects an annualised return of between 7 and 12% over the next few years.

DON'T BELIEVE THE DOOMSAYERS

Browne is confident about the US economy's underlying strength, and is dismissive of the voices predicting a significant breakdown in financial markets. As long as capital projects in Asia are generating double-digit returns and the products are supplied into the US market, there will not be a problem. The falling costs of production in Asia will help to suppress the threat of inflation that could push interest rates higher, avoiding, "the kind of debt meltdown and consumer blackout that some people are forecasting." says Browne, "European economists have basically called the US economy wrong for as long as I have covered the markets, they just don't understand the sheer dynamism of the US. They always underestimate it and expect a crash. Why? Because that's what you get in Europe, you always get trouble."

At the start of 2004 Browne's outlook for global growth forecasts an improving tone in most parts of the world except Europe, where he believes the bigger economies will struggle. He supports the view that low interest rates and a weaker currency will underpin US growth, leading to a pick-up in capital expenditure, inventory rebuild and an increase in employment. Those economists who predicted a jobless recovery will, Browne says, be proved comprehensively wrong. Companies that have been running at very low capacity utilisation rates will see a surge in profitability which will justify higher stock market valuations.

In Browne's forecast, China's growth moderates from the mid-teens pencilled in by some economists, while Japan, still a beneficiary of US consumer spending, gets an extra boost from the yen's fall against the euro. If his world view holds, the economies of the US and Asia remain strong, Latin America benefits, and Europe becomes the weak link. Europe's domestic markets suffer fragile growth and European exporters struggle in overseas markets because of a stronger single currency. 'I can see how the Europeans may not like this, but they don't realise how sweet a spot the rest of the world is in.'

The bears are haunted by the thought that consumer and corporate debt levels in the US may bring a halt to spending. Browne is sanguine, he believes that the key is ability to pay and not the headline credit number. It is a relative story, and as long as interest rates remain low and growth and employment improve, lines of credit will remain good. If the borrowers are able to service their debt they won't be worried, and neither should anyone else. If debt servicing isn't a problem, corporate and consumer spending may slow but won't drop sharply enough to cause a recession.

Investors who are pessimistic, Browne says, are missing the importance of monetary stimulus, and are worrying instead about underlying demand. In his opinion the US economy is well constructed and responsive to the challenges. The bears are not seeing how much shorter the economic cycles have become compared to five or six years ago. Companies are switching between cost-cutting and growth strategies faster than they have ever done before. 'There will be slower, steadier growth. There will also be blips, excesses in demand and supply, but our ability to control those blips will be better than it was five or six years ago.'

Entering 2004, Browne says that there is still overcapacity in Western economies. Interest rates, however, will remain low for some time with little threat of inflation, which is a positive combination as long as the easy money is recycled and used profitably to acquire productive assets. As a student of economic history (it was his degree), Browne has studied five hundred years of economic activity and points to just two real threats to his upbeat assessment:

1. If the money isn't recycled, there may be a blockage in the international financial system.
2. If the US decides it is no longer open for business, then, for political reasons, it may adopt a protectionist agenda.

Does a pick-up in inflation concern him, with a consequent tightening of interest rates? Browne says that if inflation were to go back to the 5–6% level the US has seen before, there would be some pain as borrowing is choked off, but people forget that the US Federal Reserve would react very quickly to balance the risks to the economy. 'Because of the shortness of the economic cycles, 3 years rather than the typical 7–8 years, the outcome could be a series of volatile mini-cycles less damaging than a full-blown cyclical downturn.' Browne points to the year 2000 when the US experienced what he describes as a conceptual recession. 'Talk to people on the streets and they'll say, what recession? It wasn't a real recession on the ground as in the early '90s when everybody knew somebody who had lost their job.'

Won't the borrowing catch up with consumers? Browne again stresses the importance of interest coverage rather than the level of debt, and as long as the interest coverage remains good, inflation remains moderate and people keep their jobs it won't be an issue. 'It's a very different economic position we have at this point in time – the monetarists and central bankers will claim this is a triumph for monetarist policy, this is exactly what monetary policy is designed to do . . . '

What about capital spending levels, don't they need to rise to support equity prices? Shouldn't companies be investing in new plant and machinery to meet sustained demand? Browne says, give it time. In the current low interest rate environment company managers feel more confident about spending money, and that feeds directly into corporate decision-making. Browne says the 15 years he spent examining when and why companies invest in their own growth suggests that the current timing is good. He believes that the earnings flow is built on solid foundations. Low interest rates support demand, which encourages companies to raise production. Companies have used the period of benign interest rates to improve their balance sheets by restructuring their debts. The combination of cost-cutting through 2000–03 and stronger balance sheets has improved their operational gearing. This will continue to be seen in the earnings that will support stock prices.

But what happens when the Federal Reserve starts to raise interest rates? Browne considers that the Fed will obviously have to put up rates eventually to slow the economy and head off inflation because its job is to manage growth and control inflation levels. But he has faith in the Fed's ability to time the size of the rate increases. Current credit levels only make the interest rate tool more effective. 'Because the level of indebtedness is so high the interest cover will deteriorate faster – if the Fed reads it right the market should feel more confident, not less confident.' That will demonstrate to the market that the monetarists are in control. Browne is looking for a decent economic cycle in 2005, and the Fed he stresses will provide guidance. Moves ultimately to take interest rates higher will show that America's central bank believes growth to be sufficiently sturdy to withstand the rate move.

THINK 1870s, NOT 1970s

There is a resonance, then, with the turn of the nineteenth century. Browne insists, it's about cheap money, prolonged growth and the occasional financial crisis (probably corporate). Mostly, however, for financial markets it was a good time to be invested in bonds and a fine time to be invested in equities.

> 'You have got to ask yourself, are we in a 1950–70 type period when we continue to create supply bottlenecks and ultimately lived through a period of high inflation, or is this 1870–1910 where we were creating new economies that were opening up, and giving you cheaper production. Which kind of world do we seem closer to at the moment!'

The economic bears continue to growl about government deficits, easy money-fuelled spending and rising corporate and consumer debt reminiscent of the early 1970s. But, says Browne, where is the inflation? Instead it is rather more like 1870–1910 when great new economies were starting to suck in cash and commodities and were in turn lowering global production costs.

What is the risk to Western markets? There is some industrial decay in established economies as production moves to the new country to exploit lower costs, but that labour is recycled. The speed with which that happens depends on structural flexibility. Much has been said about the current trend for outsourcing services like software development and call centres to Asia. Browne points out it has its precedent in the British textile industry's relocation to India. The British economy adapted by shifting those jobs into coal mining.

Browne is convinced that the way to capitalise on this story, globally, is to pursue a twin track investment strategy. Recognise the risk and return potential and invest according to your appetite for growth.

'You get steady low-risk returns in the US, nothing spectacular but you can trust the government and the regulatory regime. Then you look to Asia and other emerging markets to put some fire in the portfolio; it is higher risk but these markets have the potential for better returns.'

What long-term returns might an investor in the US markets expect if Browne is right? Under this scenario, he anticipates that the S&P 500 will be at around 2000 in 10 years' time. He suggests the caveat that long-range forecasts should be treated with a measure of caution. He believes the market peak may be reached earlier, in about four to five years. Then as demographic forces weaken the equity story, baby-boomers will start a process of equity withdrawal to finance their retirements.

1870–1910 REVISITED

If the US's emergence as an economic force at the turn of the nineteenth century hastened the peak and passing of the British Empire, does China's growth in the East represent the same threat to the US? Possibly, is Browne's answer, but it is too difficult to make much sense of the question at present. We may be seeing the high point for America's economic and political power, but we won't recognise it for another 20 years. The focus should, instead, be on China's growth which Browne believes will have as great an impact on the twenty-first century as America's had on the twentieth century. Browne suggests that investors need to be careful not to see that as a one-way bet,

'You will get bubbles occurring in economies that are on a long-term growth path; China, though, will continue to take in more than it produces. It may shock some people that the reality on a three-year view is that demand, especially in basic industries, will continue to outstrip production.'

What about other emerging markets. Does Russia interest him? Russia's financial boom is a function of the oil price, 'everybody who has been to Moscow tells me it's the most amazing city, but it ought to be if oil stays at $30 a barrel'. He says there are more interesting places to look for opportunities in Eastern Europe and points daring investors in the direction of the Ukraine as the place to build a factory.

EUROPE'S WEAK DECADE

The next 10 years promise to be a testing time for European companies. Browne believes that anyone buying European stocks on a long-term view needs to understand how the economies of Europe will be challenged by the reduction in the numbers of productive workers over the decade. Structurally, Europe is less well prepared than the US to adapt to the ageing workforce. 'For the real story from 2003 to 2013 you have to go to demographics. It is critical to understanding this period. First of all Europe becomes completely grey, then there are fewer people working than there are claiming pension benefits.'

The pension funding crisis in Europe is well understood by governments but is only just starting to mean something to the public at large. States are dependent on a falling number of workers paying higher taxes to support a larger number of pensioners. Any shortfall has to be met from increased government borrowing which will be a drag on the private sector economy. The outlook is depressing. Declining working populations and increased demands from retiring pensioners and higher health costs add up to governments struggling to limit spending deficits. 'I am just not sure how the French think they are going to get their debt to GDP ratio sub 3% in the next 3–4 years.'

There is no way to square the circle says Browne, EU states like Germany and France which face the largest retirement funding gaps are starting to look at the options, but few are politically palatable. The likelihood is a combination of longer working years before retirement and/or a much lower level of state benefit provision. The alternative is higher taxes, which electorates tend not to vote for. In economic terms reductions in the value of pensions and increased transfer of wealth from private to public hands will only suppress domestic demand. That is not good for the profits of listed companies geared to the domestic economy.

The demographic time-bomb also comes with a sting in the tail for equity markets, says Browne – that is, the slowness of generational wealth transfers. The baby-boomers are not releasing their wealth to the next generation. The wealth was built up as a result, says Browne, of one of the sweet spots in history, anyone coming into the labour market between 1968 and 1982 saw their debts continually eroded by inflation. Consequently, the period saw a huge creation of value in the property market as prices rose. The high rate of inflation helped to pay off mortgages. Wages were indexed to inflation, and pensions were planned at rates of return that look positively generous by today's standards. In essence those pension rights were unsustainably large in relation to worker productivity over that period of time. Browne says what we now see around Europe, but particularly with the prevalence of property ownership in the UK, is a coagulation of wealth in the 50+ population.

For the post baby-boomers or anyone under 40 the financial burden is rising. They will have to pay real interest rates for property in a low inflation environment and pick up the bill for two pensions, their own and their parents. Browne says that European consumption is low in economic terms and will probably remain low as these demographic trends take hold.

Browne thinks the great natural story that European equities witnessed in 1994–95 is gone. Instead, a younger generation with less available surplus cash will run a more conservative portfolio with perhaps only 20–30% of their wealth in stocks. Europe becomes a net exporter of cash. Low interest rates, high free-cash flows and a lot of private equity takes companies out of the public domain. The risk-averse baby-boomers have fixed liabilities in retirement and have this coagulation of stored wealth, but if they have already cut their equity holdings they are unlikely to return to stocks. 'They've got fixed liabilities these people, they are very risk adverse because of their age, and they've got this great bulk of wealth.'

Incidentally, he believes that in the US, 30–40 year olds will still choose to run equities to about half their portfolios. The baby-boomer overhang is not as big a problem in the US where the population is not declining, and new immigrants have added to the working population.

How does the 'stuck' wealth get recycled back into the economy? Browne thinks the experience of Japan is useful, but not encouraging.

> 'You could argue that European governments are doing a grand job running huge deficits and that that is one way of turning the cash into demand. Taking money back through tax would be a logical way of trying to recycle cash through the system. But as the Japanese have found you cannot politically go after the older generation because they are not going to vote for a government that wants to raise taxes.'

THE GERMAN BANKING PUZZLE

Within Europe, Browne believes there is one story that has sufficient magnitude to once again stir up interest in owning equity. That is for a substantial chunk of the publicly owned German banking system to find its way onto the markets. A substantial programme of privatisation or liberalisation in the German banking system would bring new money into the market. If it were to mirror the process that occurred in Britain or, to a lesser extent, in France it could bring thousands of small private investors into stock ownership. 'This is the last major piece of equity that is out there and not quoted today. The issue will appear beautifully within the 10-year time-frame.'

The German public banks do a significant percentage of the banking that occurs in the country. These are the Landesbanken (regional land banks) and the Sparkassen (savings banks) – public banks that are part of the social fabric of the country. Along with the credit cooperatives (Kreditgenossenschaften) these institutions, of which there are around 2000, are integral to the German economy. They service 90 million retail and commercial customers and, because of their public status, enjoy a triple 'A' credit rating. This allows them to lend money at lower rates than the country's listed banks. They are the prime lenders to the small and medium-sized companies that represent 80% of Germany's GDP.

There are laws that govern whether these banks can be bought or sold, and because the German banking system is rooted in the idea of social responsibility any attempt to privatise them could be deeply unpopular with the general public. That doesn't mean it can't happen, says Browne; Germans who don't believe that the process will unfold over the next 10 years are missing the bigger picture, many of the States and City's that own them will be inclined to sell to meet their own financial obligations.

'I have friends in Germany who tell me these banks will never demutualise but look at other examples in Britain, and in France with Credit Agricole, no one would have thought they would come to the market.'

TRADING THEMES

Browne's investment process is classic fundamental bottom-up stock selection. He works hard on basic measures of performance like free cash flow generation to come to an understanding of what he thinks a company is worth. He wants, through research, to identify stocks that are not being correctly valued and then assign them a target price, buying and holding them until that price is achieved. He is happy to hold the stock for a year or so if the price is rising. In fact core positions in his fund may be held for two years with positions actively traded. He spends a lot of the research time working on themes, like the German banking story, or new legislation where the impact on stock prices has yet to be recognised by the market. He uses stop-losses on both long and short holdings to minimise losses, which raises the level of trading the fund does to protect assets.

No hedge fund manager can exist in a fundamental bubble, and Browne's asset allocation approach within the fund is based on a top-down model of the world. He has very clear ideas about the direction in which the world economy is travelling and those ideas shape his current positive outlook on the equity markets. In Browne's model Europe has some issues to face that will weaken interest in equities, but he says there are sufficient new catalysts to enable an astute asset manager to uncover undervalued stocks.

The $360 million long/short fund is diversified across industries, market caps and countries and there is a bias against over-weighting in one industry or market. Browne has managed the fund since the beginning of 2001, after operating a hedge fund at Chase for three years. In the bear market of 2000–03 the fund made money in every year. Measured against the Dow Jones Stoxx index of European companies it was up 11% in euros in 2001 against the Stoxx 50's minus 18.7%. In 2002 it returned 6% against minus 35% for the Stoxx 50. In 2003 the fund made 2.2% against the Stoxx 50's 10.5%.

As with most hedge funds the investment philosophy is absolute return, with the standard 20% performance fee; Browne's in trouble if the fund losses money. The focus on absolute return means that funds like Browne's sacrifice performance for a lower risk profile. The benefits of that are evident in a bear market where they still make money, but during a bull market they can lag the index. His fund typically runs between 50 to 60 positions, with each averaging about 1.4% of the total portfolio. The fund closed to new investors in the middle of 2003 having reached its target size.

TRADING LONG

A strong idea that worked for Browne between the years 2000 and 2003 involved figuring out which companies would lead out of the bear market. He assumed that investors who had lost money to technology stocks would seek out companies that looked different. He reasoned that risk-averse investors would return to valuation first-principles, wanting to own firms already generating cash with strong balance sheets. There ought to be some companies he could buy and squirrel away for the market recovery. Maybe even technology businesses that had been sold indiscriminately because of their association with an unloved sector.

Browne began screening for companies with a good business model, plenty of growth potential and plenty of money already on the balance sheet. An out-of-favour technology company was exactly what was thrown up by the screening process. Wanadoo (Figure 2.1) is a French Internet Service Provider that is the gateway to the internet for millions of computer users across Europe. It appeared to be making a lot of money and yet had suffered in the bear market. The growth potential was apparent, the company was rolling out a broadband service and had over 8 million users of its internet connection. Browne decided he should pay the company a visit to confirm that the business model looked as good on the inside as it appeared from the outside.

What he saw was a business that fulfilled his valuation requirements. It came with the added benefit of a much improved valuation proposition, having been a casualty of the tech fall-out. That put the current stock price well below what he thought the company was worth: 'It was unloved not because of how it operates but just because it was an ISP.' Browne bought at 6.5 euros and has seen his holding double in value.

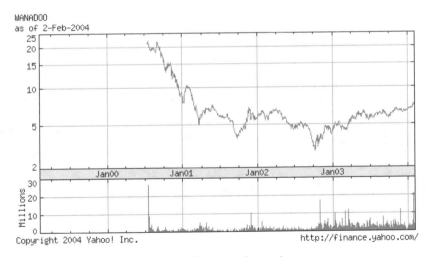

Figure 2.1   Wanadoo: 5-year chart.
Source: Yahoo! Reproduced with permission of Yahoo! Inc. © 2004 by Yahoo! Inc. YAHOO! and the YAHOO! logo are trademarks of Yahoo! Inc.

Good investment ideas are too precious to be squandered. Browne realised that if Wanadoo fitted the profile there might be other European ISPs that were also generating good cash flow. He also bought shares in T-Online, Germany's largest ISP and a unit of the country's telecom giant, Deutsche Telekom. Both companies were starting to capitalise on a new business opportunity he thought would be extremely lucrative. While carrying out research work on the telecom sector he had noticed rising levels of broadband use among home computer users. An army of armchair internet browsers fed up with slow connection speeds were prepared to pay extra for faster downloads. The ISPs were in the prime position of already serving those customers. They could therefore offer a premium broadband service at a premium price with few start-up costs. This was all good news for company profit margins, and Browne's stock positions.

Another company that has made Browne's long book is Anglo Irish Bank (Figure 2.2). The Dublin headquartered company is listed on both the Irish and London stock exchanges; it's a niche business bank more interested in lending to other companies than chasing the retail consumer market.

Small companies can struggle with financing. They are too small to tap the equity market, they are often misunderstood by the high street retail banks, and private equity money often demands an ownership stake. Browne had an idea at the start of 2003 that he should examine the players lending money to small companies. Banks that understood small companies and their desire to borrow in a low interest rate environment ought to be thriving. Browne says that Anglo Irish just leapt out of the screen: 'it had a 30% return on equity, an established management team and the lending book looked to be of good quality.'

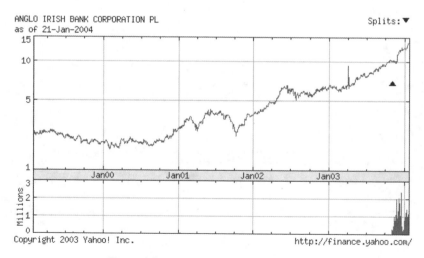

Figure 2.2   Anglo Irish Bank: 5-year chart.
Source: Yahoo! Reproduced with permission of Yahoo! Inc. © 2004 by Yahoo! Inc. YAHOO! and the YAHOO! logo are trademarks of Yahoo! Inc.

The early research work looked promising. Browne next sought out information on any future plans the bank might have for raising cash. There are few things that frustrate a fund manager more than buying a company's stock only to see their holding diluted by further shares being put into the market. There was nothing to indicate that Anglo Irish intended to raise cash by issuing more shares to existing shareholders. In fact Browne's research highlighted the management team's desire to develop the business organically. Browne bought the company's stock at the start of 2003 and has watched the price double. 'This was the right company with the right balance sheet in the right segment of the market at the right time.'

TRADING SHORT

A consistent theme for Browne's shorts is companies that are exhibiting signs of balance sheet distress which the broader market has not yet picked up. The Swiss–Swedish engineering company ABB (Figure 2.3) has been a very good short play for the hedge fund. In the middle of 2000 Browne was looking at what he figured was a 15% premium to the market in the ABB share price. On the surface the company's balance sheet looked reasonable; cash had been flowing in from the sale of power-generating businesses and the market, says Browne, had difficulty seeing beyond the money. On his calculation of what the company was earning, the share price looked as though it ought to be 10-15% below the market. He decided to start shorting the stock. Browne initially sold the stock at 26 euros and sat in the short position for several years.

The timing was fortuitous for him if not for ABB. He had decided to short the stock just as the company was pitched into the kind of litigation that would keep any

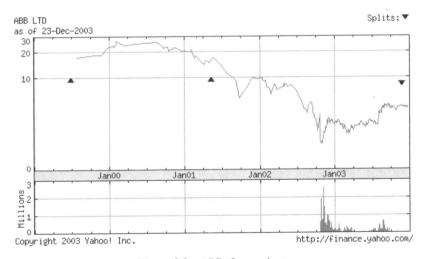

Figure 2.3   ABB: 5-year chart.
Source: Yahoo! Reproduced with permission of Yahoo! Inc. © 2004 by Yahoo! Inc. YAHOO! and the YAHOO! logo are trademarks of Yahoo! Inc.

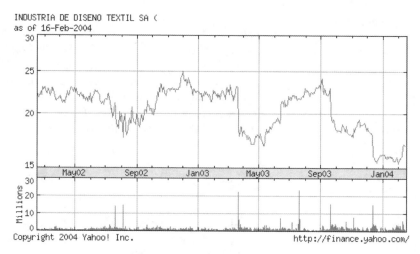

INDUSTRIA DE DISENO TEXTIL SA (
as of 16-Feb-2004

Copyright 2004 Yahoo! Inc.   http://finance.yahoo.com/

Figure 2.4   Inditex: 5-year chart.
Source: Yahoo! Reproduced with permission of Yahoo! Inc. © 2004 by Yahoo! Inc. YAHOO!
and the YAHOO! logo are trademarks of Yahoo! Inc.

CEO awake at night. ABB was sued by over 100 000 individuals claiming exposure
to asbestos from boilers produced by a unit of the company. ABB's share price went
into free-fall as the litigation risk threatened to push the company close to bankruptcy.
After shorting at 26 euros, he closed the short when the price hit 4.50 euros.

At the time of writing, Browne was still actively shorting the Spanish retailer
Inditex: 'It is the only retailer that still produces its own products. Vertical integration
is wrong for retailers.' Browne's beef with Inditex (Figure 2.4) is the group's insistence
on producing its goods in Spain when there are lower cost centres of production for
clothing, such as China or India. At the time of the company's IPO in May 2001
analysts hailed the vertical model praising the idea of 'just in time' delivery of new
fashions to the stores every two or three weeks. Browne says that the idea is no longer
new and the company's rivals can achieve the same turnaround by using lower cost
manufacturers. Through the last six months of 2003 the Inditex share price fell from
24 euros to a little over its IPO price of 14.70 euros.

FINDING STOCKS

As a European long–short manager, Browne says his potential universe of stocks is
realistically somewhere between 350 and 400 companies. He is most active in the large
and mid-cap space, seeing better visibility in businesses of that size. When Browne
gets an idea for a theme that might lead to a change in valuation for one or several
companies, he runs a screen to discover the firms most likely to be affected. The
research process evaluates corporate strategy, strength of business franchise, current
market value, industry fortunes and barriers to entry. The screening process aims to

reduce the number to about 20 stocks, a top 10 and bottom 10 on which more detailed work can be done.

Typically with core and non-core holdings Browne is hoping to find companies that have similar characteristics:

- High-quality management
- Businesses that enjoy competitive advantages
- Companies that generate free cash flow
- Companies that consistently earn a high return on equity, typically more than 20%.

The screen will usually run the numbers for stocks on price/book value, price/earnings and price sales. The rationale is that companies at the low end of their valuation range suggest less downside risk than those at the high end of their valuation range.

Satisfied with his list of 20 stocks, he goes on to isolate 3–4 companies from either group for further research. He wants to focus on the companies that may have the greatest reaction on the upside and downside. Browne tries to imagine running the company himself and says that helps him to better understand its future prospects. Does the company have the right product? What is the business risk? How high are barriers to entry? Is the management good? What balance sheet risks are they carrying? Are they targeting the right strategic goals? And so the list of questions continues until he feels he is getting close to a valuation and can predict where the stock price could be in 3–6 months.

When Browne is comfortable with the valuation he has placed on the business and has a clear price target he will enter the trade. He looks at the stock charts for confirmation of trends and assistance in timing entry points, but that is the extent of their usefulness. He places stop-loss positions on all trades.

Browne isn't interested in trading a short-term punt unless he is stopped out of the position. The goal is to uncover real value rather than trying to play a trading opportunity. If he decides to take a position in a stock it could remain in the fund for many months, even years. At the beginning of 2004 he was starting to extend the holding period for his long positions. His assessment of reduced economic risk, and a reduction in market shocks encouraged him to take a medium-term view.

If he is right, the better environment for corporate decision will embolden company managers to think more aggressively about pushing through expansionary business plans. As managers become less risk-adverse, Browne thinks they will expand business either through capital expenditure and increased merger and acquisitions activity. As he sees it, the major problem issues of 2003 – the Iraq war, SARS and economic uncertainty – have diminished in importance for the markets. This has removed constraints on management's willingness to push through change.

THE COMPANY VISIT

The company visit is an important part of Browne's stock selection process. He also keeps in close contact with companies in which he has holdings. Some fund managers view company visits as a distraction, and prefer to buy a stock on its price record, its earnings history and the valuation metrics already in the public domain. As company executives become slicker at presenting their business there is also an argument that little new can be learned from several hours spent walking the factory floor. Browne strongly disagrees. He currently visits about 200 companies a year, and says it is still the best way of getting confirmation of his ideas.

He meets with senior managers to discuss their strategy and the company's future prospects. The management is also under scrutiny. He says it is important to see how the management is communicating with the investment industry. In Browne's stock selection process good management gets a high weighting. The experience has been that good management traditionally produces higher returns on capital than bad management, regardless of the industry.

A typical week of company meetings is presented in Table 2.1.

Do companies mind talking to a hedge fund that might short their stock? Browne says that most of them realise there is a possibility that he could close out a short position if the company visit throws up better than anticipated news. In fact, he says it happens frequently enough to more than justify the modest effort and expense involved. The bigger companies around Europe understand that the hedge fund genie is already out of the box and the shorting of stock is just one more aspect of being a publicly listed business.

He did just that with short positions he was running in German financial stocks at the beginning of 2003. Browne had taken a view that one or two German banks would see their share price hit by the restructuring programmes they had in place. It was only after visiting the institutions and learning that the restructuring was more far-reaching than he had anticipated that the shorts were quickly covered and long positions taken instead. The programmes he decided were likely to be well received by the market as they suggested a real commitment to growing profits.

Sometimes the company visits produce unexpected and welcome results. Browne recalls a trip to see a German company that made locks for cars. The meeting appeared

Table 2.1 Appointments for week beginning 18 April 2004

Monday in London:	Acerinox
	DFS
Tuesday in Paris:	Atos
	Peugeot
	Thales
Wednesday in Dublin:	Speak at the EuroHedge Conference
	Fly to Dublin
	Meeting with Aer Lingus
Thursday in Dublin:	Speak at European Investors Relations conference
	Meetings with IAWS Group and Irish Life and
	Permanent
Friday:	Weekly fund review
	Strategy Lunch

to be making little progress: 'the German executive was explaining how the car locks work in fine detail. I looked at my watch and wondered if this is what I had to look forward to for the next hour and a quarter.' Fortunately, the executive suggested a tour of the factory and Browne leapt at the chance to avoid the car lock lecture.

Walking around the plant Browne noticed that orders for the production of the locks were pasted up on notices, specifying the company they were intended for and the delivery size. From the numbers, Browne could see the car company's internal vehicle production plans. After that it was a simple task to match up reported sales with the production numbers to measure production to sales. "The visits were purgatory, but a trip to the factory floor was always necessary to see how many locks they were producing for the different car manufacturers."

DON'T STYLE DRIFT

The year 2003 to be proved to be a tough environment for fund managers rooted in a fundamental valuation approach to stocks. From the 12 March market low money flowed back into the equity markets but the stocks that had the fastest rise were not those that stood out on valuation terms. Browne started 2003 concerned about valuations, particularly in the tech and telecoms plays that took the greatest hit during the bear market. But the sheer weight of money going into the market lifted these companies despite little change in their underlying business models. Running a hedge fund allowed Browne to use derivatives to secure some positions, but the year tested all managers wedded to a bottom-up approach: 'It was a hard year for us, we were bouncing around up a few percent to flat all the time because it was a difficult year to differentiate through analysis.'

Browne says, three years ago the macro-managers couldn't make money, but since the end of the bear market they bought into sectors that still exhibited the worst earnings news and the sectors went up. That wasn't about good company analysis, he argues but about opportunistic trading, or, to describe it more technically, about managers who can trade volatility.

> 'I look at the market and think there are so many good companies with stack loads of free cash flow that I want to buy, but you know what, I don't like the tone to the market. I like the stocks, but I don't like the tone to the market.
>
> 'What do I do? I run a neutral book. I build it up, I buy all the stuff I don't want, then I use futures to cover it because that is the right structure for this particular market. The bulls say we may go up another 400–500 points before we get to the top. Fine, let's get the froth out of the system and then set about building regular steady normal market growth.'

Browne is philosophical about the competition. He says the managers who achieved 20% plus last year generally will have performed less well in 2002, or previous years where the market suited his style. He is comfortable knowing his fund covered the cost of capital and he has not lost any of his clients' money.

I suggested that he could think about changing his style to adapt to the market. Browne shook his head, warning that trying to be master of all markets is the quickest way to lose a fortune. It is critical not to abandon what has worked in good years just because it is less successful in others. He has used his own methods of assessing bottom-up value since 1986 and has beaten the index and his peer group over that period. Browne says he isn't good at trading volatility, it is not his skill set, and his clients know that is not the type of manager they have running their money.

But what if the clients want better returns in all years? If the clients don't like his investment style they can take their money to another fund. Browne says they all understand what his approach is and see the benefit that comes from rigorous stock selection rather than chasing the market.

> 'Understand what your added-value is and don't style drift. If you think my kind of market (valuation driven) is never going to come back then I should be pensioned off, but I know the market will come back to me.'

Browne says that investors have to decide whether they agree with the fundamental approach and then stick with it. If they agree that a company's assets are worth the cash flows they produce, and have an expectation of greater or lesser cash flows through analysis, then over time that analysis ought to predict the value of a company.

RECOGNISING THE MARKET

Browne says no one should put money into stocks until they understand the broader market tone. Is it a market of buyers or sellers? A simple measure is to watch how a stock reacts to news-flow which is both company specific and relevant to the market. If a share price reacts badly to bad news he will be cautious about investing early. It is a signal that there are still potential sellers waiting for a better price. If it doesn't rise on good news, he views that as a valuation statement telling you that the stock is already fully valued and the company will have to produce significantly better news before the stock can start rising again. 'I think we are in a period where most of the good news is already discounted in the price, so you don't see much reaction to the figures.'

Browne says it is a simplistic but effective tool. It works equally well in the context of how whole markets react to economic news. Another important measure is the market's sense of the future. He thinks investors must understand the length of the current market horizon, or how far ahead prices are already discounting the future He thinks investor horizons, like corporate horizons, are slowly lengthening after a period where fragile market confidence reduced the outlook to a business quarter or three months.

For managers trying to build a value-based portfolio, short market horizons add more risk to stock selection. Long-term valuation models inevitably lose their effectiveness where the market is fickle about news flow. Browne says that it requires strong conviction in your stock-picking ability to ride the volatility. Ultimately investors should remember that they may have picked the right company from studying its future cash flows, but until the rest of the market starts to see it in the same way the share price won't move.

A WORD ON CHARTS

Browne's investment process may be rooted firmly in traditional valuation methods, but there is some room for charts. He uses technical analysis for confirmation of trends. He is sceptical about the value of technical analysis as a predictive tool. The charts are not very good at forecasting the direction in which prices are about to go and only reaffirm the current direction, or trend. For this reason Browne gives the charts more attention when market volatility is high, but finds them less helpful when markets are drifting.

> 'Charts only work when a strong trend is in place; you need to have a clear trend line. I'm talking mainly about European markets here. When you don't have a clear direction it is basically telling you that buyers and sellers are matched.'

Browne's other problem with charts is the favour they currently enjoy. Inherent in that view is the likelihood that if many investors are using similar techniques they will quickly cancel out its advantages: 'When everybody starts doing the same thing it stops working.' He says market participants become wedded to chart analysis through the market extremes of the technology bubble and the bust that followed; but now, as market conditions have changed, the charts have become less helpful.

BEAR-MARKET LESSONS

The experience of the last bear-market will change the nature of the next boom for markets. Browne says the technology bubble was the result of a phenomenon that had its parallel in the business boom at the end of the last century. 'What we had was something we haven't seen for 100 years. We financed venture capital through listed equity.' The money for the technology bubble came from companies listing themselves on equity markets rather than using the more traditional routes of debt sales, bank borrowing or mezzanine finance. He argues that it shouldn't have been through equity, but the environment of easy money through relaxed monetary policy and the peak in the investment industry made that possible.

The consequence of that has been to scare off, for good, potential equity investors. Too many shareholders were left exposed in the market sell-off. Ultimately the bad taste left by the destruction of wealth will make investors reticent about supporting new technology via share issuance. Any new boom will be supported by debt, says Browne, because when the time comes to raise new capital the collective memory will make equity investors reluctant financiers. 'Nobody is going to give anybody 400 million dollars for putting up an internet site and seeing how many eyeballs they can get to it.'

Lenders will also be more rational, and that means refusing capital to a business with no clear revenue model. The next boom, when it comes, will be in businesses with cash-flow, and that will make it a different type of boom to that witnessed in the late 1990s. Again this confirms for him the idea that what we are witnessing is the return of a 'normal' business cycle, as opposed to anything more sinister.

Browne says that if the bear market has been good for anything, it's in making fund management companies pay more attention to their clients, and forcing them to acknowledge that absolute return must become the dominant investment goal. Having worked in an environment where money was managed on a relative performance basis, Browne says that there is a totally different mindset among managers when they are only trying to beat their benchmark index. Managing money for absolute returns drives a process that is not content to sit in the safety of the herd. Ruefully, however, Browne observes that a six-month bull market is enough to push the absolute return issue off the agenda; the collective memory is short and when markets go up investors tend to care less about process than they do about participation.

BACKGROUND

Barely a couple of blocks away from Buckingham Palace, Browne and his team at Sofaer monitor the European markets and generate ideas for their next investments. He is tall, and of medium build. He could be described as traditionally good looking with a neat side parting and square jaw. His energy for life is infectious, and he is naturally enthusiastic about most projects. He is passionate about the job.

The office is a grand Regency town house with a white stucco frontage that sits on a broad sweeping terrace of similar properties. The rooms are spacious and have high ceilings with plaster moulded cornices. The modern desks, computers and televisions look incongruous in rooms that would once have been the living area of a wealthy nineteenth century family.

The working conditions are more comfortable than the Barclays bank counter in Balham south London where Browne started his career in the financial industry. He joined the graduate trainee programme at Barclays after earning a degree in Economic History at Durham University in the UK. The bank believed that new graduates should get a taste of the shop floor and put the young recruits on the front line. That meant removing sleepy drunks from the doorway to open the bank each morning. Browne calls the experience horrendous. When a table was smashed up in front of him he decided he was losing interest in retail banking. A short spell on debt collecting duty in Brixton, another London neighbourhood with a tough reputation, only confirmed that he wasn't cut out for the retail side of the business.

Rather than let him leave the bank, Browne was encouraged to apply to the investment management unit. It was at BZW that Browne started his career as a fund manager and that is where he stayed for nine years running traditional long only European equity mutual funds. He was tempted away to Chase in 1994 to set up their institutional asset management business in London. It was at Chase that Browne had a taste of trading both long and short, essentially acting as a hedge fund manager. The company seeded a fund with $5 million of its own money. Browne ran the fund with a team that included Steve Frost, who would eventually leave Chase with Browne in 2000. The pair moved to Sofaer to manage the groups long/short European equity fund. He is now a partner in the business and locked into the company's financial future.

THE JOY OF SHORTING

Did he find it difficult to mentally adjust from buying stocks to also being able to sell them short? The learning curve was steep at Chase, but the two years spent running the bank's own money gave Browne a sheltered environment to make early mistakes. It also gave him the opportunity to put into practice some of the ideas thrown up by company visits. One of the frustrations of being a long-only manager was finding poorly managed companies through research but not having the ability to properly exploit them by shorting the stock. He says it was depressing visiting 5–6 companies in a day and coming away thinking that at least one had the wrong business model for their product or maybe the wrong senior management or cost structure. 'It was frustrating, it was 2–3 hours each day wasted. You couldn't profit from the information and that was frustrating because you could see the opportunity.'

Finding the shorting opportunities wasn't difficult; understanding and intellectually embracing the risk-reward of putting on a short trade took a little more time. As Browne reminds me: unlike buying a stock where the profit upside is infinity but the maximum loss is limited to 100% of your investment, shorting a stock limits your maximum profit to 100% but the potential loss is infinity. In other words, if you buy a stock the maximum loss is what you paid. If you short a stock there is no maximum loss, the loss is as high as the stock rises. Protecting against that infinitesimal loss, says Browne, means trading more often and more aggressively than a long-only manager.

RECOGNISE WEAKNESSES

Does he ever become emotionally attached to the companies? Browne says it is a risk he always has to fight against – particularly when he likes the management, or their approach to the business. One of the benefits of working closely with a team is that another manager may have a different view. He says that an alarm goes off in his head when a colleague gives equally valid reasons not to buy or retain a stock. The other obvious clue that the analysis is wrong is that the stock price is not doing what you want. Then it's time to re-examine what went wrong.

Browne says his 10-year working relationship with Steve Frost, another manager at Sofaer, is invaluable for bouncing ideas around and filling gaps in his own analysis. He describes their roles as being similar to an attacker and defender in a football team – both elements are equally vital to the success of the venture. He admits that he is not good at analysing some companies, and these are better left to Frost. The oil industry in particular has proved a frustration in the past, defeating his attempts to get the valuation right. He recommends investing with others as a way of stress testing ideas. His advice for people new to the field is: accept that there are some things you will never do well and move on, the time will be better used elsewhere.

RISK MANAGEMENT

Browne calls this process of recognising weaknesses 'attribution analysis'. It is about trying to understand where an individual fund manager can add value to stock selection. Browne and his colleagues expend considerable energy protecting their portfolio from losses. The primary aim is to do that through stock selection, and then twice a week he carries out a review of each holding stock by stock on chart technicals and fundamentals. There are fixed rules to the process:

1.   *Stop-loss – driven by chart technicals.* A 10% capital loss on holdings will trigger a reduction in the size of holding. That is a strict rule; however, a trading stop-loss might be tighter than this on either a long or short position. It depends, Browne says, on the current information, and how that information changes will determine whether the stop-loss is widened or narrowed in relation to the market price.

2.   *Price targets – fundamentally driven.* Price targets are set on all holdings. If the target is achieved Browne will usually reduce the holding.

Browne says the rigours of stop-loss and price target management can raise the fund's turnover in volatile markets but that's better than having to explain why losing positions were not cut.

He and his colleagues produce spreadsheets with their own assumptions recorded, noting their expectations for the next 12–24 months. It is a blueprint that is constantly re-checked to compare expectations with reality. This enables them to quickly know if news is disappointing or positive. If a stock is not outperforming the relevant benchmark, this is sufficient reason to re-evaluate the investment thesis.

ADVICE

Browne says that the key to investing is keeping your radar on the world that hasn't happened yet. Following that simple but effective principle could stop a few people losing money, chasing today's company news. Being a fund manager is about forecasting the future, and understanding how much of the future is already in a share price. Pay attention to today's news but pay more attention to what will happen in a year's time.

> 'Company earnings may have come out today but that is history, the stock may be overpriced or underpriced relative to the numbers today but that will be corrected very quickly. The important question is where this stock will be in 6 months', 12 months' or 18 months' time.'

What writers can give insights into today's markets? If his market outlook is right, investors could do themselves a favour by dipping into the histories of companies that were successful in the Victorian era. He suggests reading works on the Baring family and the Cazenoves. Browne also thinks that investors should take another look at the work of John Maynard Keynes, an economist who was also a very successful investor and understood the need to spend for gowth. 'He is a man for our times. He understood the importance of demand. He is definitely one to dust off and read again.'

3
David Murrin:
Trading the Roadmap

'The genie is out of the bottle, the ongoing fight against proliferation will be a long-term process and will throw up other trading ideas.'

David Murrin's investment process is built on a model of a world that is locked in a battle to control the disbursement of nuclear technology. Potential clients at Murrin's hedge fund company Emergent Asset Management get a lesson on global power politics before they hand their cash. Murrin is keen for all who put money into his funds to understand how they are going to profit from the West's desire to halt nuclear proliferation. The key, he says, is in finding emerging markets where that policy drives a change in sentiment and the valuation is an incentive to invest.

Geopolitical risk normally scares investors away from financial markets as they seek safety in cash. That is no problem for hedge funds like Murrin's which can buy or sell the market. How then does the fight against nuclear-proliferation create opportunities? Murrin says the war on terrorism and the US goal of gaining influence in the Middle East should be viewed in the context of the broader battle against the spread of nuclear technology.

For instance, in 2003, Murrin made money from the row over US military bases in Turkey. In March of that year, ahead of the start of the invasion of Iraq, the Turkish Parliament voted against having 62 000 extra American troops stationed in the country. The bases would have helped to provide air support to operations in the region. The Americans were offering a $30 billion aid package in return for access, but the Turkish government resisted the money. The reaction on the Istanbul Stock Exchange (ISE) knocked 10% off the market. Murrin reasoned that once US forces had secured a base

in Iraq they no longer had to depend on Turkey. The disagreement over the bases
looked likely to end the large lending packages Washington had delivered to support
the Turkish economy.

The loss of aid was a negative for the Turks, but Murrin figured it might force the
government to tackle deeper economic problems. Without that aid, but a desire to
meet fiscal rules for convergence with the European Union, the government would
have to take action to stimulate the economy. His hunch paid off. Under a new reform
programme the government set targets to bring inflation under 20%, and for economic
growth of 5% for the year. In September of 2003 official interest rates were cut aggressively, with the central bank lopping three percentage points off short-term rates.

Murrin was already in the market. In July 2003 he bought the Turkish stock market
index when it stood at 10 500 points and rode the market to his exit at 17 000 points in
mid-December 2003. He says that he feels better about a trade if he is early and alone.
After the row with the US and a struggling economy there was general disinterest in
the country from other investors. That allowed him to buy at a price he felt undervalued
the market's potential. Murrin always validates his trades with technical price analysis
and, in the case of Turkey, his model suggested a low volatility entry point with plenty
of risk already built into the price. Figure 3.1 shows how he traded the ISE with a
stop-loss marker tight to the purchase price to limit any potential downside.

Murrin says success in event-driven trades is about understanding both the state
of the market and its linkage to the catalyst for changing the price. In this case the
market condition in Turkey was fragile and the threatened removal of US aid hurt
the currency and the equity market. The art comes in thinking beyond the short term.
Murrin anticipated the Turkish reaction to implement reforms, and recognised that
the valuation made the market too cheap to ignore.

The Iraq invasion generated several trading ideas. Murrin also bought more direct
exposure to Iraq in the form of the rights to $6 million of defaulted loans to the

Figure 3.1   Trading with a stop-loss marker.

country's old regime. When his funds picked up the debt in early 2003 the paper was trading at around 16 cents on the dollar and had doubled from 8 cents in September 2002. Murrin reasoned that the inflow of US cash into the country should help to bolster Iraq's economic foundations. Ultimately it was a calculated gamble on the Saddam Hussein era debt being repaid close to face value. At the time of writing Murrin was still waiting for the pay off. He described the debt's performance so far as disappointing; the price had barely changed from where he bought it and he was still a holder.

How does Iraq fit into the nuclear proliferation story? Murrin feels that analysts who view the US invasion of Iraq as driven by a desire to secure oil supplies from the Middle East are missing the bigger picture. The powers that toppled Saddam Hussein's regime justified their action by pressing the cause for finding Weapons of Mass Destruction. But, he argues, the strategic purpose was much wider. Securing territory in the Middle East by force sent a message to any state in the region that was in the process of developing nuclear technology.

> 'The US wanted to let Iran know it would take action over proliferation. With US forces in Iraq, Iran now had this western gorilla just over the border. Would Libya have been willing to do a deal on nuclear inspections with British Prime Minister Tony Blair if there had been no invasion of Iraq? Libya had centrifuges; these are a vital piece of equipment for refining Uranium.'

Murrin believes the World Trade Centre attacks in 2001 forced Washington and London to face the reality of a world where terrorists have the resources and intent to commit atrocities. The greatest fear in both governments is that the terrorists are supplied with nuclear technology. Preventing that from happening means cutting off the most likely source. These are mainly the governments of countries that have a record of aiding anti-Western terrorist cells. He says that Western efforts since September 2001 have focused on preventing proliferation from 'hostile' governments by imposing diplomatic or military pressure on countries labelled 'rogue states'. It is a story, he says, that will rumble on through the rest of the decade, and Murrin thinks it is a difficult policy to sell directly to democratic electorates. Nonetheless it is a campaign already underway with democracies forced to respond to the threat even if they don't come out and say so explicitly.

> 'The democracies have to be pro-active without declaring it to their electorates, which is why in Britain we had an intense debate about whether we should be in Iraq. The leaders have understood the change in the paradigm but the populace has not.'

What other opportunities does Murrin see in the nuclear issue? South Korea is another market where Murrin has sought to benefit from the proliferation trade. On 10 January 2003 the North Koreans announced they would withdraw from the nuclear non-proliferation treaty. The South Korean equity market, the KOSPI, lost 8% over the next month. This time he was banking on heightened tension with North Korea dampening interest in the market. Nervous investors were already worried about a fresh campaign in Iraq, and the local accounting scandal at SK group. The KOSPI struggled through the first quarter of 2003. Murrin couldn't see anything that would change the negative sentiment and he entered trades shorting the market.

This trade was less successful, as the KOSPI benefited from the push of liquidity into global markets in the second half of the year. Murrin closed out the shorts as foreign investors poured money in the Korean market. By the end of the year foreigners owned more than 40% of the market cap, the first time that has ever happened. Despite the retreat from his short position Murrin will watch Korea for further opportunities. He believes tensions with Pyongyang will rumble on, creating opportunities to short share prices in Seoul.

Murrin says that this is a feature of the proliferation trade. The markets become sensitive at different times and investment tactics depend on reading the ebb and flow of the story. There will be periods when confidence and money push the issue out of investors' minds. But a spate of negative news flow combined with weak market sentiment will put the potential trades back on his radar screen. 'The genie is out of the bottle, the ongoing fight against proliferation will be a long-term process and will throw up other trading ideas.'

At a broader level, the nuclear story is an important theme for opportunities in emerging markets because the issue frames the way the West reacts to the emerging world. Although he doesn't see too many direct trading stories in Pakistan the country remains a particular area of concern for him because the nuclear technology is aligned with an Islamic country. Murrin believes that that will keep Pakistan close to the heart of the issue for Western governments and it will remain the potential flashpoint with the greatest risk of nuclear conflagration.

THE ROADMAP

The proliferation theme is part of a larger model of the world Murrin and his team have created called the Roadmap. The Roadmap is modelled on the price of financial assets, and an understanding of economic and historical cycles. It is an educated guess at how financial markets and the world will change during this decade. It is a fluid model and is continually updated as the forecasts are compared with the unfolding reality. Assumptions are amended and modified where the two conflict. Murrin's Roadmap is designed to have predictive value until the year 2009 and is built on several core ideas:

*   1929–2000 represents one growth cycle. The dates mark the two worst bear markets in history and periods of distress in corporate America – particularly the insurance industry. A repeat of the pattern suggests a decade where equity prices fall from January 2004 levels.
*   The correction is played out in shorter time-frame moves. These are smaller versions of the longer time-frame trend. The technical term for these is

fractals – imagine a pattern which, when subdivided, reveals identical smaller patterns. For instance, think of looking at a stock chart from some distance. The price line is downward sloping. As you move closer to the chart the line is still downward sloping but you start to notice the line zig-zags on its way down. Even closer and the bigger move becomes blurred, but you notice within the shorter time-frames that the same downward zig-zag pattern is repeated. These are fractals and Murrin considers them to be vital trading patterns.

- January 2000 to March 2003 was the first bear cycle. Until the end of 2005 the US markets will stay in a large trading range. From 2005 to 2009 expect a powerful deflationary market in US and European stocks.
- Japan's 1989–March 2003 corrective cycle is complete. A new bull cycle is underway. The recovery will benefit the Asian basin.
- Some Emerging markets will enjoy a primary bull trend in this environment.

Murrin's aim is to exploit these themes going both long and short equities, the flexibility of running a hedge fund means he can also trade using derivatives, bonds, gold, commodities and currencies.

Emergent, as the name implies, specialises in uncovering opportunities in the emerging markets. In Asia, where he is generally bullish on the outlook for markets he has taken on several trades in Thailand. A currency position in the second half of 2003 capitalised on the perceived economic strength of Thailand and the problems in South Korea. He opened a position long the Thai baht and short the Korean won in August. The baht was the strongest regional currency; the Korean won was the weakest with low domestic demand from the overhang of the threat from North Korea. Again Murrin looked for confirmation in the price pattern and entered the trade at 28.2 won to the baht, with a tight stop-loss at 28 (Figure 3.2).

Figure 3.2   Trading the won against the baht with a stop-loss marker.

Murrin enters positions with a specified price target. By November 2003 he closed out the baht/won trade having reached the price target.

MAKING TRADES

Murrin's company, Emergent, offers three themed funds called: Ballistic, Cosmopolitan and Alternative. Their respective focus is on Emerging equity markets, developed G10 equity and fixed income markets, and Emerging debt and currencies. Two other products, Global Macro and Diversified, are blended versions of the main three themed funds. All of the products target a 20% annual return, and carry a 20% performance fee.

These are relatively early days for Murrin's hedge funds but returns already look promising and have been achieved in both bull and bear market conditions. The Alternative fund was ranked number 1 in its class by S&P Micropal in 2001. It has beaten its internal 20% target for four of the six years it has been running. In performance terms Ballistic has been the star, producing annualised returns of 30% since its inception in January 2001. In 2002, a bear year for Western equity markets, the fund made 50% and was ranked number 1 in its class by S&P Micropal. The fund benefited from long holdings in Russian and Chinese oil companies and South African gold. Murrin shorted financial stocks in Latin America and technology in Taiwan and South Korea.

Cosmopolitan was launched in March 2003 and, despite gaining 34% in nine months of pre-launch trading, struggled to find its feet in the rally and ended the full year with a modest 3% rise. The fund was up 22% from March to September 2003 but lost ground in the last three months of the year as Murrin shorted G10 equities and bonds. He was expecting the bombings in Turkey on 21 November 2003 to dampen European equity market performance towards the year end but, in the event the sell-off proved to be short lived. A correct call on the dollar mitigated some of the losses. 'We looked for a turn in equities and were negative on treasuries. Both strategies proving incorrect. The G7 gave a good launch to a $ bear move which we shorted.'

The trading process for all Emergent funds starts with the idea. That is generated by a combination of market awareness and price analysis. The awareness comes from a view on how economic and geopolitical events will affect financial markets and commodity prices. The price analysis comes from Murrin's technical work using Elliott Wave theory to detect price trends. Once the idea develops momentum, more work is done to confirm its validity. It is cross-checked with the Roadmap, and assessed historically over long and medium time-frames.

The investment process for identifying and placing trades can be broken down into three-stages. Murrin uses Figure 3.3 to describe the process to clients.

Murrin's approach to any asset is to seek out Elliott Wave price patterns and, as accurately as possible, identify the correct wave count. As a discipline, Elliott Wave has a loyal following among some technical analysts. For readers unfamiliar with

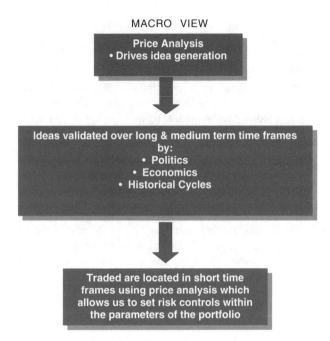

Figure 3.3 Trade idea generation.

the theory, in the 1920s Ralph Elliott studied decades of US market price charts and concluded there were patterns that repeated. He identified sets of eight waves – five trend waves and three subsequent corrective waves. Remember the fractals? This is an important point for trading; the Elliott Wave pattern is repeated within junior patterns.

Murrin stresses that the pattern reflects the state of mind in the market. Each rising wave is a reflection of buyers in control until the risk in the price is greater than the momentum to take it higher. The discomfort for buyers' increases as the price rises, until some buyers become sellers. When the sellers outnumber the buyers the price drops, forming the down wave. Murrin's own research sums up the emotional element.

> 'For the purposes of market analysis, we may conclude that the market has a collective consciousness that processes information and then responds predominantly on an emotional basis, reflecting fear and greed. For the individual this equates to the fear of losing money, employment and self-respect, and the greed associated with a higher standard of living, freedom of action and increased self-esteem.'

After a series of rises (higher highs), buyers become more cautious. The Elliott Wave pattern shows the subsequent falling price as a 3-wave corrective cycle. Murrin says that corrective patterns are vital for identifying trading opportunities on the short side of the market, but are harder to get right because the pattern loses some resolution.

'The psychology becomes more mixed as investors lose conviction after a correctional move. The degree of fear and greed falls and so the quality of the pattern falls and the certainty of the pattern becomes lower.'

Recognising the strength of the pattern and identifying its relative magnitude are the tools Murrin uses to confirm an investment idea. In over two decades of using the same methods he says he has never seen a period when at least somewhere in the world the analysis couldn't be applied. It then comes down to the experience of the manager in deciding when the signals are strong enough in a particular asset or market to warrant a trade.

Murrin has defined two directional trading methods that capitalise on the price development patterns:

- Contra entry point – where the initiation of the trade is contra to the prevailing trend, which, if correctly located, is also at the end of the trend. From this entry point the duration of the trade can be varied across all time-frames.
- Trend trading – where the initiation of the trade only occurs a considerable time after the new trend has commenced. To take advantage of such trades the duration of the trade has to match the duration of the trend. This style tends to be that of longer time-frame traders.

Murrin combines the trading technique with a close attention to risk control. He runs stop-loss positions close to entry points to protect the downside. If a trade works and the trend is still intact he may have several attempts at exploiting the same theme. If the analysis is wrong he takes the loss quickly and re-examines the strategy.

An old Chicago pit trader once made a great impression on Murrin by relating a story about how, over 40 years in the pit, the traders alongside him came and went. Their styles were fixed and as the markets changed they weren't able to adjust and went out of business. Murrin has tried to integrate the lesson into his trading, and that means recognising when the ideas aren't working. 'You need to build an adaptive system for changing with the market environment.'

This chart of the Dow Jones Index (Figure 3.4) encapsulates all of these elements at work. In June of 2002 Murrin was bullish on equities and expecting a rally before a significant bear move towards the end of August. He made two attempts to buy the Dow for the rally but was stopped out on both occasions at critical levels.

Murrin then reversed his view on the market. He says the WorldCom default coupled with some financial market instability in Brazil over the possible election of the leader of the left-wing Workers Party, Luiz Inacio 'Lula' da Silva, as President had accelerated the time-frame for the bear market. From late July into mid-August Murrin initiated three new profitable bear trades. The chart shows:

1.   risk control when the ideas are wrong;
2.   bull to bear changes in strategy;
3.   several bites at the same trade where the idea can be exploited.

Figure 3.4   The Dow Jones Index.

RUSSIA

The Russian debt crisis in 1998 almost sank Murrin's business. Emergent's funds have been open to all investors since 2001, but the company has invested in Emerging markets since its inception in 1996. At that time any investment fund worth the name was active in Russia in the mid-1990s. In the post-Soviet experiment of shock capitalism Russia was pumped full of foreign cash that inflated the price of financial assets. When the party stopped, the foreign investors were trapped by an overnight devaluation and a government debt default. Murrin's funds suffered an option default that would end up costing a quarter of the portfolio. 'It was a defining moment in the business. We could have closed but we decided to stay with it and we slowly recovered. That is where we learnt that even though we were directional traders once in a thousand years credit is a diabolical situation.'

The experience brought a dramatic change in Murrin's attitude to risk. Having once nearly lost the business on a concentrated trade, there are now strict limits on how much is ventured and how much can be safely lost. In the emerging equity fund, Ballistic, a very strong idea might see at most 25% of the portfolio spread over 7–8 stocks. Elsewhere, on a single trade Murrin says the maximum bet might be 0.5% of Net Asset Value. He prefers not to think of diversification as protection, but instead chooses to concentrate on good ideas. Where he doesn't see opportunities there is no requirement to stay invested, which is the main advantage of being a hedge fund. 'The biggest discipline is not to be overactive and waste money before something really good comes up. We think that through understanding long-term pictures, transcended into short-term movements, we can choose timing.'

Murrin was actively trading in Asian markets before the region's currency crises in 1997. He considers that, unlike Russia, the Asian problems were easier to identify. He liquidated all positions in Asia before the crisis took hold. The chart patterns were showing that the Asian bull had run its course; he had seen signs of completion of the market rally. The forecast allowed him to sidestep a business offer that probably would have finished the company.

'Before the crisis a Korean bank came and offered to invest $200 million with us, but we would have gone from $17 million to $217 million and then back to nothing. They couldn't understand why we refused. We said there are problems coming and you are going to be in trouble.'

THE MINDSET OF MARKETS

Murrin's commitment to charts and price patterns evolved from an event that left a profound impression on his life 20 years ago. He is a physicist by training and his approach to markets reflects a scientific mind searching for rational explanation in all things. Watch, learn, observe and make your own decisions is Murrin's credo. If it is possible to see what happens, why it happens, what effect it creates, and whether the outcome perpetuates the cause – that's halfway towards predicting the future. Where a stock chart is in its simplest form a reflection of investor behaviour, understanding the motivation and cause of that behaviour ought to have some predictive value.

This is the guiding principle in Murrin's investment process. Improbable as it may sound, it was a frightening showdown with natives in the jungles of Papua New Guinea that set him on this course. He graduated from university as a physicist specialising in geophysics. In his first job after university he joined an oil exploration company. His first task in the field saw him transported thousands of miles to the Papuan jungles, where within hours he was set to work managing a crew of 60 Papuans cutting a swathe through the undergrowth. After a cold and wet first night, Murrin awoke to a terrific rain beating on the tent canvas, and was presented with his first problem of how to motivate the disconsolate native workforce.

With a lack of diplomacy Murrin explains away as the arrogance of youth, he told the reluctant workers he understood they didn't want to work in the wet conditions, but in his country even women and babies worked in the rain. The translated slur upset the son of the local chief and the anger spread quickly through the assembled Papuans. As the workers' anger escalated they became more hostile towards Murrin until fearing for his life he retreated to his tent. As calmly as he could he began writing out a letter to his mother explaining why her son had died at the hands of enraged Papuans.

Slowly their anger dissipated and some hours later they were once again behaving in a friendly fashion to the young English geophysicist. In Murrin's mind the experience was an early primer on understanding financial market psychology. The lessons were essentially two-fold: firstly, crowds run on emotion and that the group will at times behave together, either desiring or rejecting the object of their attention; secondly, those who are able to exercise personal self-control can ignore or move in opposition to the crowd if their will is strong enough. This is an approach to markets that any contrarian investor would understand.

Murrin later put the jungle experience into the context of financial markets on the trading floor at JP Morgan. Joining up the dots as a 23-year-old new boy at the American investment bank's operations in London, Murrin watched the way the best traders made money. It didn't appear to correlate with academic qualifications or even fundamental knowledge; instead the best traders understood the emotional state of the market. Within the first 10 days on the trading floor at JP Morgan Murrin had determined that the correct approach to markets was directional trading, basically taking on long or short positions by analysing the price and predicting its movement.

'So there it was, investment is an emotional process and the emotion is linked to price. From that it was clear, price is the only quantifiable variable and it is tied to emotions that create eclectic behaviour patterns.'

Early on, Murrin posed himself the question whether price patterns are fundamental in nature or self-fulfilling. Intuitively he felt there were two elements, an underlying fundamental shape and a feedback loop where investors have some awareness of the pattern and, in their behaviour, force the pattern to sub-evolve into a slightly different shape. Emerging markets provided a promising testing ground because the relatively lower number of market participants and the smaller size of the markets would give the fundamental pattern clearer definition.

'It proved to me once and for all that there is a basic embedded pattern, but that as you go up the financial food chain towards bonds where there are more and more people involved in trading them and there is more awareness of the patterns, the patterns inevitably become more complicated.'

JP Morgan gave Murrin his first job in the financial industry. His career as a geophysicist was memorable but brief. After some months being helicoptered from one inhospitable landscape to the next to take mineral samples, he quit. Instead he decided to seek out an industry that was both better compensated and recognised advancement on the basis of ability. It was at JP Morgan where he discovered charts and directional trading and finally found his way onto the Prop desk in the treasury. This is the operation where the bank does some trading on the markets for its own account, and is in nature very similar to the operations of a hedge fund. Prop traders move between asset classes; they can use leverage and are able to short the market. The Prop traders are considered to be the trading superstars in the institution and are entrusted with the firm's own cash.

Later Murrin was plucked from his trading tasks to work as a strategic adviser to the Head of Trading. He says there weren't many people in the bank in London at the time who shared his view of the world. The position put him at the top table when bank strategy was discussed. Murrin stayed at JP Morgan for seven years, he left in 1993 at the age of 30 to start his own trading consultancy, Apollo.

He continued to provide directional trading advice to JP Morgan and any other investment bank willing to pay. The consultancy business still exists alongside Emergent and the work it does ties-in directly with the original research on price patterns Murrin generates for the hedge funds. Emergent was founded in 1996 and is currently based in Surrey in the UK.

LOCATION, LOCATION, LOCATION

Murrin's office comes directly from a scene in a James Bond movie. After some time on quiet country roads a turn-off down a barely made track ends in a tarmac turning area. There are two houses, both many hundreds of years old, built on the side of a valley giving unspoilt views across the lush Surrey countryside. Murrin and his family live in the main house; the other is Emergent's headquarters. Beyond an unusually high number of cars for two residential properties there is little to give away the location of the team inside electronically monitoring the world's financial markets for trading opportunities.

Pop the latch and step through the old-fashioned wooden door and the countryside gives way to a snug L-shaped room humming with computing power. There are several large flat screen televisions fixed to the walls. The televisions are permanently tuned into 24-hour business and news channels. Desks are covered with computer monitors and trading research. The screens show fund positions and a range of bond and stock prices. The small team of managers that work alongside Murrin are constantly making calls and checking prices. There is the atmosphere of tidy efficiency, of people getting on with the business of trying to stay one step ahead of the competition.

Apart from being conveniently situated a 10-second walk from his own front door, Murrin makes a virtue of his managers' distance from the City of London. The old joke about hedge funds described them in the early days as akin to two guys in a log cabin in Montana. This is as close to the European equivalent as it is possible to find. Murrin says the out-of-town location keeps costs down, and limits the influence of peer and other environmental pressures on his team's market analysis.

LEFT-EYE DOMINANT

Murrin is tall, of slim build and, when working, is most likely to be found in a pullover or turtle neck top. In conversation there are traces of the scientist; the approach is direct and the answer considered. His manner is intense, and he relates his investment process with deep conviction.

He describes his early teens in an English state school as tough and not much fun. Murrin grappled with slight dyslexia, which wasn't recognised at the time. With a strong internal desire to learn and take head-on life's challenges, Murrin stuck with the school when a private alternative was offered. He says he later only took a physics degree because it seemed a difficult subject to master. Sport proved a useful diversion, and when he began to excel, other areas of school life settled into a more comfortable routine.

Much later in life Murrin identified himself as left-eye dominant, a characteristic that appears to be more common to left-handed people (although the evidence seems inconclusive). This is now widely recognised as being related to creativity and a non-linear outlook on the world. The hard wiring of the brain brings the right hemisphere to prominence. Murrin contends that left-eye dominant people take a different approach to problem-solving from the majority of the population. It is thought that around 70% of the population is right-eye dominant.

In trading terms he thinks left-eye dominant people make better wave counters. They are superior at pattern recognition because they have strong visual perception skills. Right-eye dominant traders should show a more linear thought process that is better suited to systematic trend trading. A simple test for eye dominance is to hold at arm's length a piece of A4 paper with a small hole in the centre. Look through the hole and focus with both eyes open on an object in the distance. Close the right eye. If the object is no longer visible through the hole you are right-eye dominant.

Murrin has extended his work on eye dominance into other areas of brain activity. He is intrigued by the idea of honing the mind, like an athlete's body, to a peak of performance. The research continues in that field: 'I'm looking at this a lot, if you can train your body, why not your mind.'

THE DESIRE TO SUCCEED

I asked him whether his trading system could be taught to any investor. It is based on clear rules and uses a traditional Elliott Wave charting process. Murrin agreed that the mechanical side could probably be passed on but he insists its success, or indeed the success of any trading system, lies with the individual rather than the system.

'Think about it,' says Murrin, 'by far the most important part of any trading process is the trader. If the trader is not open-minded, unstressed and self-aware the best trading programme on the planet is not going to make them a success.' Self-awareness comes up continually during our interviews. Murrin describes it as the ability to stand back a little from yourself to observe and understand why you are making certain decisions and how you, in turn, are being affected by events and the decisions made. When I suggested the sporting analogy of being in the 'zone', Murrin agreed that it must feel as though all senses are geared to the one goal of beating the market. He has a deep interest in martial arts and Eastern religions as routes to a greater awareness. He is fascinated with spirituality, and the idea that it can bring clarity of thought and process. He is a great believer in rhythms and cycles in all things, and that extends to his managers' feel for the markets on any given day. 'You have a rhythm, the universe has a rhythm; when the two of you are synchronised that is when the opportunity will appear. So you can't try to force it, but recognise the rhythm instead.'

Murrin sees no division between working life and private life – in fact he thinks making such a distinction is a barrier to success. Investors who view the process of buying assets as work will probably not succeed. He believes in the philosophy that the working life and the non-working life should be extensions of each another. 'You see self-sabotage in the fund management business all the time. What it comes down to is the conflict between what people say they want, and what they really want inside.'

Murrin says he can tell which managers are going to make money from their mental attitude. The starting point is to open the mind of any prejudices before coming to the market. He says managers are successful when they are not trying to project their own desires and needs into the trade. Murrin's method over two decades boils down into three components:

1.   Build a risk management structure or system that is designed for the person using it, implicit in this is the understanding that the risk system will be different for each person according to their personality.
2.   Take a model of the world that you think is successful and adaptable. Any model will contain many assumptions about future and current events. Where it is predictive, assign values of probability to those outcomes. It should be a model that is applicable in both bear and bull market environments. It should also work across different time-frames – in essence it should be linear.
3.   Finally, understand that the first two principles will only continue to work if you recognise that your abilities are the key to their success. The third principle then requires a constant questioning of your own capabilities to act and react appropriately to circumstance.

WHEN IT GETS HARD – STOP

Murrin says when it is no longer easy to make money stop trading. It is an unwritten rule in the Emergent office. When it starts to get difficult to find ideas that generate good profits it is probably a good time to take a break from trading. Murrin describes it as being out of phase with the market, and sometimes no amount of cool detachment or self-awareness makes it any easier. Recognising it when it happens could be one of the best investment decisions any trader makes. 'You go through periods when it is just like pulling your own teeth without anaesthetic, then it is just a question of managing your risk.'

Murrin says it is usually 'easy' when all elements of the trade come together:

•   There is a long-term pattern – which manifests itself in a shorter time-frame. There is very strong clarity in the price pattern.

- That corresponds to corroboration of political, economic and all other price related variables.
- You are alone in the trade – are you seeing it differently from other people. The risk reward is well covered in the price, and there is time to run the trade several times if the idea is confirmed.

BUY AND HOLD THE DECADE?

If I were to buy a portfolio in 2004 based on the Roadmap and then hold it for the decade, what should that portfolio contain? After making it clear that no one should ever just buy and hold because it's a recipe for losing money, Murrin was willing to play along with the scenario as an intellectual exercise.

'Coming to the end of 2004 and then into 2005 there may be a lift for US equities, this would coincide with the Presidential elections. But I would reduce positions in equities in Europe and the US coming to the end of 2005. If you need to be long equities stay in Asian markets there will also be the benefit of currency appreciation. If that down cycle for European and US equities is correct, buying bonds in '04 and '05 might be the right decision.'

Murrin thinks investors need to make diversification a high priority through the decade and must not limit their trading or investing to a single asset class. That also applies to the geographical breakdown of holdings. He stresses that there will be emerging markets, and developed and emerging markets, that trade in opposing directions. 'The last 10 years has seen a cementing together of asset classes – equities and bonds in developed markets became highly correlated. That relationship will breakdown.'

He says that sharp-eyed investors will be able to find pricing anomalies and make money. There is a simple example from Emergent's holdings in 2000 where the group bought Colombian government debt. It carried the same internationally recognised debt rating as the government paper issued by Argentina but was cheaper. It ought to have traded at the about the same price as it carried the same likelihood of default. At some point that gap would be noticed and start to close, giving Murrin's team a profit.

WHAT CURRENCY?

Murrin's current preference in the foreign exchange markets is for Asian currencies because he cannot see the justification for the appreciation in the euro. The dollars decline will be tempered in his view by problems in Europe, because 'Europe is structurally much weaker than the United States'. He says people who took their money out of the dollar and put it in the euro were just responding to a desire to get out of the dollar. When they sit down and examine the situation they will realise the last currency they want to be in is the euro.

Murrin does see the dollar regaining some strength around the end of 2004 but the move will be temporary. His confidence in the Japanese recovery means that the yen will remain favoured among the major currencies. He believes that the start of a new bull cycle will support the yen, pushing it to 80 to the dollar by the end of 2004.

GOLD

Murrin actively traded the rise in gold in 2002, but he thinks the precious metal has further room to appreciate. He started buying at $316 in December 2002 and sold at $355 as the volatility increased. He intends to trade in and out of gold believing it will reach $800 by the end of the cycle. The $800 level is modelled in the Roadmap. He dismisses those who still don't view gold as a significant store of value. Murrin says there will be a time when investors will want to have about half a percent of their worth in gold. 'At the moment there is a rough balance between supply and demand, when you get new people wanting it then you will see the price move up. When the price fell below $300 many marginal mines closed. It will be difficult to get supply up; you can't just restart mines. There will be a time lag.'

Murrin has also been trading the gold stocks. Typically the stocks are an early warning system for the bullion price. He bought the South African mine Gold Fields in February 2002 as a precursor to buying the metal in December of that year. He paid $7.50 per share for his stake and later sold the shares at around $12. Murrin says the trend for gold miners to abandon forward selling is another strong positive for the bullion price. The slide in the dollar has left the miners preoccupied with another problem, the currencies: 'In South Africa in particular, the rising Rand has the miners more concerned about hedging their currency risks than anything else.'

The gold bugs that fear central bank selling will suppress the price. They worry about manipulation of the market and point to the world's central banks as the most likely source of new supply. Back in September 1999, the major European central banks signed the Washington Agreement restraining their selling of gold and restating that 'gold will remain an important element of monetary reserves'. The day after the agreement the US and Japan both said they would pursue similar restraint. At the time of the Washington Agreement the participating banks reportedly held just under 16000 tonnes or 50% of the world's official gold holdings. With the Washington agreement on central bank selling of gold due for renewal in 2004, does Murrin fear that the bullion price over the rest of the decade could be brought down by a flood of supply from central bank sales?

Murrin suggests that the conspiracy theorists make a mental adjustment and recognise the central banks as but one more player in the market. Their activities in the gold market should be viewed in that light. 'I think they have sold a lot already and I think many of them will realise they have been selling at the wrong price. They may have extra knowledge, but they are still just a bigger market participant, they're part of the collective psychology of the market.'

WESTERN EQUITY MARKETS

If Murrin sees dark days ahead for Western equity markets, when will Western investors feel comfortable again buying their own equity markets? The short answer, says Murrin, is probably not for some years. His expectation is that 2008–2009 will mark a low for these markets. He says that a process of reassessment is still taking place about the role of equity in financing the future. It may not be grabbing headlines but it is changing long-term investment decisions.

> 'The man on the street was led to believe if he worked hard and saved and worked to 65 his pension would be assured. That would be a fairly unique situation in history but that is what he was told and it all looked good until the year 2000. Everyone was so invested in this rally that governments and insurance companies perpetuated this belief that you got security through equity. Then we woke up and realised these shares are just like anything else, they can go up and they can go down. That is why you now see all this questioning. Take any business that had massive increases in the value of its equity during that period, it is likely that if you looked harder there would be some problems – it spilled over into everything, corporate governance, equity research and so on.'

Murrin believes that there will be significant changes in the way businesses and the markets operate in the West over the coming decade. Part of that long-term story will be about regaining investor trust. The comparison is Japan where it has taken more than a decade to wring out much of the excess of the boom times of the mid-1980s. Local investors are only slowly returning to the equity market after the banking and property scandals that marked the collapse in values. Ironically, in Japan it is the locals that are slow to follow the foreigners back into their own market. That will be a feature of Western markets when the coming bear market has done its work. 'By the time the lows are in place in 2008–2009, most people will have their money out of traditional long-only pension funds. They will be in absolute return funds or alternative structures. That is probably the time when you will want to do the opposite.'

Murrin says investors who are complacent about the coming bear phase for Western markets are mistaking the US authority's fiscal and monetary stimulus as a new bull cycle. The markets' rallies since March 2003 are part of an unfolding process that takes markets lower. He feels that 2003 was about being in a holding pattern after the band-aid had been applied. The Federal Reserve had watched and learned from the failure of the Bank of Japan and Ministry of Finance to sufficiently ease monetary policy in the early years of that country's deflationary cycle. If his timing is correct the US markets will follow the same pattern as Japan. After an initial fall, the Nikkei saw two years of sideways trading, from mid-1990 to 1992, before heading lower again. When that next major leg-down in US markets starts, Murrin thinks the US authorities will have a sense of helplessness at how to respond.

WHERE DO BONDS FIT?

Where the environment is negative for Western equity markets, will bonds be the beneficiary? Murrin is looking for money to find its way back into government bonds as the equity market picture deteriorates. The Emergent group made money from selling bonds in 2003 as the market experienced a sharp fall in value. He says that the US bond cycle is indicating that a 6–8 year correction is due, although this time the sell-off was delayed two and a half years because of declining interest rates.

Murrin is forecasting the S&P 500 to peak at around 1200 by the end of 2005. There will then be a major deflationary decline into 2009, and in deflation one of the safest places to be is in government bonds. The US government makes a fixed coupon payment on Treasuries every year and that will become worth more as prices in the economy fall. Murrin anticipates a rally in bond prices, underpinned by central bank policy to keep interest rates low. That will find support from money managers who are under-invested in treasuries because they were convinced an economic recovery was underway.

Emerging market corporate debt may also perform in this environment as these economies see a pick-up in growth under Murrin's Roadmap. A word of warning, however, on Western corporate debt. In deflation, debt payments become a heavier burden, and in an environment where companies could go bankrupt the risk of default is likely to rise.

END OF EMPIRE

If Murrin's deflationary decade comes to pass he thinks the Dow will be closer to 4000 by 2009 than it is to 11000. Murrin says investors wedded to the '90s idea that the US can continue to be the world's engine of growth need to think again. His most pessimistic scenario envisages this decade as marking not just a 70-year peak for the US, but the peak for the English language empire and its influence on the world. That will hasten the trend of America becoming isolationist.

Murrin believes that we are at a critical transition point in the relationships between Asia, Europe and the United States. The clincher is whether China is on a sustainable growth path. He believes economic growth will bring with it a new self-confidence on the world stage. 'China is evolving finally as a real economic powerhouse, and the history of nations indicates that new-found economic confidence will bring with it a desire to play a greater role in world affairs.' A resurgent Japan will provide Asia with two systems that will increasingly compete for pre-eminence. Murrin expects that competition will find expression in the traditional manner, an escalation of meaningful military competition or, in other words, an arms race. For the best guess of the consequences of that for the world, Murrin says we should think about Britain's waning ability to control events outside its borders as the British Empire gave way to the ascendancy of the American system.

Murrin thinks the the battle to control the distribution of nuclear technology will be costly and only hasten a decline in the US's dominance of world events. Increasingly, the West's relationships with emerging nations will be framed by the issue of proliferation. The dilemma is how to respond to potential aggression where the risks of getting it wrong are huge. For investors, that offers opportunities in the emerging world, against the backdrop of struggling Western financial markets.

4
Philip Manduca:
The Coming Crisis

'Put half your savings in gold. Don't measure your net worth based on the value of your house. And, work very, very hard for as long as you can because you need to generate income.'

It is 1990. The world feels an uncertain place: Iraq has invaded Kuwait; barely months earlier China is condemned by the international community for killing students in Tiananmen Square; and all across Europe countries from either side of the Iron Curtain are trying to understand the implications of the end of the cold war. The collapse of the Berlin Wall in the previous year brought to a close 28 years of division in the German city and marked a major landmark in the opening up of Eastern Europe for business.

In London, Philip Manduca is set to retire from a life in the financial markets. He is just 31 years old but is already probably among the highest paid in the City, roaring around town in his company-paid-for Ferrari. In under a decade he has made enough money in the derivatives business to walk away and, attracted by the new opportunities in Eastern Europe, has a strong conviction that it is time he tried his hand at being a businessman. Looking back, Manduca is philosophical about the ambitious young man who thought he was going to put major deals together. 'I was someone who had an overblown ego, and probably thought they were better than they were and thought they knew considerably more than they probably did.'

He quit his job and decided to go travelling. Manduca had a cheque-book and desire to find out what opportunities were opening up in the emerging world. He calls the three and half years he spent travelling the world looking for deals, the best practical MBA he could have taken. The experience was certainly colourful.

In Russia he held intense negotiations with the World Chess Champion Garry Kasparov. Kasparov was on a high, fresh from his 1990 victory over old rival Anatoly Karpov. This secured for him the world title and Manduca hoped to sign the chess genius to his management agency. With a bit of fast talking Kasparov was persuaded of the advantages. Manduca says he told Kasparov, 'you are brighter and better looking than me, but I am richer than you, Garry'. After a few moments contemplating the comment a hand was extended and they shook on the deal.

In Panama, Manduca says street riots broke out against him after he tried to buy a piece of land for building enclosed secure resorts. The idea was to build tax havens for rich Americans. Panama appeared to be a logical location with its geographical proximity and fine climate. The private equity deal he was trying to put together was for estates of luxury resorts built to plan for the world's wealthy. The arrangement didn't sit too comfortably with the locals who didn't want to live next door to secure-gated luxury estates.

Manduca says, with hindsight, lots of deals got talked about at the time, but not too many ultimately got done. The experience, though, left an indelible impression about the difference between businessmen who create wealth, and financiers and money managers who don't. 'I was learning about how real businessmen talk, as opposed to how we in the financial community that manage money think of ourselves as businessmen. Ultimately, we're just processors and what I call money pushers rather than money creators.'

OUT OF RETIREMENT

Manduca took the lesson back to the UK in 1993, setting up his own global macro hedge fund business Sant Cassia Investment Management. He may not have been the best businessman, but the experience guided his first foray into the world of hedge funds. The brief business career taught him to seek out the new and original. The new in asset management terms were the emerging markets. For so long considered a financial black hole where risk capital was ventured and lost, in the early 1990's the model was changing. He saw it could be the niche that would draw in return-hungry investors.

A hedge fund could compete with the large asset management companies if the offering was unique. Manduca created a fund that invested using a top-down global macro-economic approach. The fund would invest in fixed income or equities anywhere in the world. Today there are thousands of hedge funds that have the same remit, back in 1993 the concept was still exotic.

> 'My rationale was this, if I can only do what Barclays do then who are investors going to invest with? It surely won't be me. So I diversified the business into Emerging Europe which was based on the idea of arbitrage. The world was globalising and drawing in. There was an interesting arbitrage opportunity between Western and Eastern Europe, the same as we saw between Western and Eastern Germany.'

The Panama episode had demonstrated the importance of that other golden rule for exploiting business opportunities: timing. In Panama the timing was clearly wrong. But in 1990 it seemed that the time for emerging markets had arrived. Manduca figured that the strong geopolitical impetus for emerging Europe and Asia to engage economically with the developed world would only push up valuations. He says that unlike the stop–go investment that had characterised previous periods of optimism for the emerging world, this time it seemed different. It was 'an emergent play that appeared to have longevity'.

In 1989 the US Treasury Secretary, Nicholas Brady, had proposed a raft of changes to the way less-developed countries raised money from international markets. Instead of the tough love approach that had characterised debt support through the 1980s, countries were told there was an alternative. The Brady programme created credible bonds issued by governments and underwritten by the IMF and World Bank. Countries in Latin America, Asia and Eastern Europe all signed up for the new Brady bonds. The bonds were tied to promises about economic reforms and kick started the flow of new cash into emerging markets. By 1994 Brady bond trading accounted for around two-thirds of all emerging market debt traded.

The timing of Manduca's new hedge fund was prescient. After a brief hiccup in 1994, global equity markets began rising steadily. Emerging markets benefited from tens of billions of dollars flowing in from the new debt programme, and the overall confidence it created in the safety of new investments.

Manduca bolstered the fund's emerging Europe skills by combining the new company with another firm strong on research in the East. The other company already had analysts on the ground in Russia, Poland, the Czech Republic and the Ukraine. The group picked up a new name, Eldon Capital Management. The firms main product, the 'New Capital Markets Fund' picked up the top ratings from the Micropal fund rating service in 1995 and 1997. It was first in both years for the Eastern Europe category.

THE RUSSIAN CRISIS

Manduca's group appeared to be growing nicely on the flow of money into the emerging markets. Aeroplanes landing in Asian or Eastern European cities were full of Western bankers and financiers looking for projects to buy or invest in. The boom times continued for Manduca's company until Russia imploded.

As with so many other hedge fund companies invested in Emerging Europe in 1998, Russia was to prove to be the group's undoing. Calculated in dollars the Russian stock market had run up almost 150% in 1997. The IMF was pouring money into the country to support the efforts of reformers to remodel the economy along capitalist lines. International investors were buying short-term government debt, or GKOs, which paid an annual interest of 40%. But by the middle of 1998 Russia was starting to look sick. The stock market had already fallen heavily and there was growing pressure on the government to devalue the rouble. The shock for investors came on

17 August of that year when the Russian Prime Minister, Sergei Kiriyenko, announced that the rouble would be devalued and the government would not honour its GKO payments.

The default on the government's debt hit Manduca's group like a hammer blow. Eldon had $100 million invested in Russia in 1998, a significant part of the group's capital. The losses suffered in Russia would not be survivable for the fund. 'Clearly it was going to be difficult to raise assets at the time of the GKO market crisis. Unlike plenty of other funds we didn't go bust, but it wasn't commercially viable to carry on operating.' The group was wound up. The Russian meltdown went on to become the catalyst for the collapse of Long Term Capital Management, the hedge fund that attracted media attention for its high quotient of PhD's. The event cost Western investment banks billions of dollars and raised fears of a systemic threat to the international financial system.

Manduca says there is a message in the experience that he carries with him today. He says it is more relevant now than at any time since the Russian debt crisis. Perceived risk in investing rarely accounts for the real risk involved in holding paper assets. 'Don't go through life believing the ground floor is the lowest point you can fall to, because the ground floor isn't the bottom floor. I think most people don't realise that there are many floors below ground; ground level is only the nearest point to stability.'

In 1998, most people who invested in Russia were expecting a rouble devaluation. That was becoming the consensus, but few were troubled because they believed a devaluation was survivable. But the devaluation came with a debt default and a government edict to local banks not to honour foreign exchange contracts for a month. 'Suddenly the Russian government had demonstrated that the ground floor was just a brief stopping point on the way to the basement.'

Manduca says the group had put too much of its cash into the Russian market – an early weakness in risk control. 'It was a mistake that I will not do again. We got trapped in a single country and that was bad for business.' There is a strain of investment theory that says where there is a strong country or sector theme a portfolio ought to be concentrated in that theme to get the largest capital gains. Manduca takes a different view. The Russian experience taught him a lesson about the virtues of diversification, and he says that while events like the Russian default do not happen often they are of sufficient magnitude to cast doubt on the concentrated portfolio theory. The Russian experience also reinforced the point that if things can go wrong in financial markets they will. Investors thought the rouble devaluation was a calculated risk but few had recognised the likelihood of a government enforced debt default.

NEW FUND

Today, Manduca is several years into the launch of a new hedge fund group, Titanium Capital. Titanium runs $350 million in several products covering emerging markets, Commodities, Global Event Arbitrage, and has a Long/Short European Fund. He manages the business and gives guidance on strategy rather than making the day-to-day investment decisions. Those are left to a team of eight: five fund managers and a small team of three researchers. The year 2003 proved to be a bruising encounter with the markets for the European Fund which only rose 7% due to the group's reluctance to chase the March rally. Typical of absolute return hedge funds, the group has a focus on preserving capital. On a three-year record Manduca says the fund has annualised at just under 20%. An indication that the management style was effective at producing gains through the 2000–03 bear market.

He describes the 2003 rally as momentum money buying 'crap stocks', where valuations were poor but money was readily available and the opportunity cost low. He says promiscuous professional investors were willing to invest on the expectation that they could still exit the market and leave the stocks in the hands of the retail investor if the market started to go down. He says the percentage gains for some funds in 2003 will have made their managers look like heroes, but the intelligent investor needs to look beyond the headline figures. The game is weighted, he argues, to encourage the fund managers to take on more risk. Manduca stresses that return is, of course, important but the basic rule of minimising risk to the assets under management while maximising return remains all important. Manduca argues that by chasing the momentum some investors will have lost sight of important risk control in their portfolio.

Manduca describes his own investment approach as top-down and valuation driven. He doesn't trade markets but looks for strategic opportunities or themes; the focus is on finding events or situations that lead to a change in valuations. That outlook drove his decision to launch his second hedge fund company. He believes the bigger market environment is right for fund managers that are capable of doing more than buy and hold stocks. The last bear market made more of that raw talent available.

> 'Good managers were being let go by the big investment banks. The other source of managers, single-man hedge fund boutiques were also offering interesting opportunities. Many of them just wouldn't make it – they could invest money they just didn't know how to run their own business.'

A decade in hedge funds, says Manduca, has demonstrated to him that they need three things to survive and prosper: a good business manager; a great stock picker or pickers; and a portfolio manager with a command of the current risk profile. From an investment standpoint the combination of talents should be fleet of foot, recognising 'you cannot rely on any trend or sustained trend to make money'. The new business was set up on the view that future market conditions would fuel the drift away from passively invested or indexed money. Manduca sees the hedge fund industry continuing to pick up mandates to manage money from insurance companies, pension funds and wealthy individuals as the focus switches from 'relative' return benchmarks to 'absolute' return. The alternative asset management business should benefit, and so, believes Manduca, will long-only hedge funds that can go to 100% cash depending on the state of the markets.

'There has to be evolution in the asset management world, alternative products mean that if you are making money you are right: there is no alternative! Being lower, but still better than the index, is no longer good enough.'

BEAR MARKET DENIAL

Manduca believes the rally off the lows of the last bear market should be viewed in the context of a market in denial. He argues that the broadly positive environment for markets from the early 1980s has distorted the attitude of investors. It has engendered a mindset that sees indices steadily rising as the natural state of affairs, and market sell-offs as anomalies. As he describes it, investors have a fundamentally positive expectation ahead of every trading day, borne by years of gains. Rising expectations have created a need for markets to go higher and a fear that they may fall. That attitude, which he sees across the investment community, has clouded judgement about the current underlying state of the market.

In January 2004 Manduca acknowledged that the rally through 2003 could continue because of the weight of money being added to the markets. But, complacent investors should bear in mind the three forces that are sustaining ever higher equity market gains:

1.　　95% of market professionals can only buy. The investment industry is dependent on rising markets. The continued employment of brokers, analysts, and fund managers depends on bull markets. Their wages, commissions and bonuses are tied to equity markets. If they stop buying the market they will slowly lose their jobs, 'everybody wakes up hoping the market is going up and, secondly, fearing it might go down'.

2.　　1% interest rates in the US, are incredibly simulative for asset prices. With money this cheap the opportunity cost is low. It appears foolish not to be trying to get a higher return by buying stocks.

3.　　The cost of financing at between 3 and 4% is encouraging tear-away consumption. Those rates also bring the small investor back into the financial markets looking for a bet, or into the property market where they are chasing prices higher.

Manduca questions the sustainability of these forces and argues these are not healthy reasons to risk capital. They are not a statement on the strength of the underlying economy, and, says Manduca, while markets and the economy can operate in isolation for some time, the former must ultimately come to reflect the latter. It requires very bad news to negate the effect of one, let alone all three of the positive forces.

When the psychology of the market appears to be to deny the hazards involved with buying any financial product, investors should appreciate that risks are rising.

Manduca marvel's at how quickly investors forget the financial community's inability to cope with sharply falling asset prices. He says that the same mindset caused the failure of most professional money managers to deal with the downturn in 2000. People didn't want to believe that it could be a two-way market, and they weren't trained to deal with it. 'A typical 35-year-old fund manager had never experienced a market like it, which is why their performance was poor.'

Manduca says that even in the hedge fund industry, which is supposedly better equipped to manage bear markets because they can operate more easily on the short side, the general standard of returns was also low. So the bear market did teach money managers a painful lesson about what a bear market feels like. Unfortunately, he argues, there is still denial about what the bear market is signalling. Much like the tremors that precede a powerful earthquake, Manduca views the 2000–03 meltdown as an early warning signal of a bigger breakdown to come.

He views the compression in investor outlook as similarly misleading when it comes to forecasting the 5- to 10-year trend for Western stock markets. To illustrate the point Manduca suggests looking at a longer five-year time-frame and viewing the rally off the lows through 2003 in that context. His concern is that investors have locked on to a short-term time-frame, purchasing equities relative to their three-or six-month performance rather than looking at their value over 1, 3 or 5 years. He says every investor must ask some basic questions about the bull market valuations that were achieved before the sell-off. Were they valuations with integrity? Were highs achieved due to the underlying dynamism of the business models, or purely through cash-driven momentum? And how comfortable are investors with the market reference points they're using to understand current valuations?

Manduca believes that investors are too focused on 'narrow realities', and that is pushing them to take on greater risks to find the returns they remember making in the 1990s. Because of low interest rates, 'money has pushed risk rates down to the point where you have a contraction of the spread between first world and emerging world assets. These spreads have narrowed considerably.' The spread of emerging debt over US government bonds is a standard measure of how likely the market thinks the risk is of a default. The narrower the spread, the lower the perceived risk. Manduca cites South Africa as an example, where money has continued to flow into the Rand seeking double-digit returns from an economy with high interest rates. That money, he thinks, would have been more discerning five years ago, avoiding the potential illiquidity of South African markets. 'I am not saying they will lose money in South Africa. But if the lights go out tomorrow you are done. You can't get out of the market and exchange controls will be imposed overnight.'

Manduca says for around 6% returns above underlying US government bonds (the spread at the time of the interview) investors are not being properly compensated now for the risk that they are taking on. While he doesn't see any specific near-term threat to cash parked in South Africa, he says the low return that investors are prepared to accept for the risk involved is yet again an example of investors in bear market denial.

REASSERTION OF RATIONAL VALUE?

There is a valuation trick economics Professors like to play on their students. If an asset has a rational or 'real' value for something at one price in the equity market today, why did it have a different price yesterday? Has so much changed in 24 hours that it is worth more or less in such a short time frame? It sums up the problem fund managers face every day trying to decide what a stock is worth.

Manduca says the current dilemma is in trying 'to measure value in the midst of volatility. You need a stable market to get a sense of where the consensus measure of value is and in this volatility the consensus is never there long enough.'

This is especially relevant to analysis of companies that compete at a global level. Manduca says there is so much change in industries and across markets that it is difficult to just look at a company's business and decide what it is worth on a simple sum of the parts valuation.

> 'I asked my fund manager the other day what sector does the French stock Sagem belong to. Is it a tech stock? Is it a mobile handset company? It does a multiplicity of things most of which it is not known for; it sells a few handsets which make up 30% of its business. You then have to ask: Is it going to compete with Chinese handsets? Is it a takeover target? Would the French protect it? And so on. There are so many questions because we are in a period of change and that is a very hard concept for the human mind to deal with.'

The globalisation story is also making top-down analysis problematic. Trying to understand the importance of what is happening in China or India , says Manduca, will defeat most people. 'What do people really know about the tensions inside these markets? Look at Japan, who really knows whether it is recovering or not? When it comes to trying to analyse stocks in this world there is very little science out there.'

Manduca says that such periods in history require long-term investors to step back and take a broader sweep of the markets. 'The things that everybody should be talking about are the big time-frames, but of course the markets have gone to a short-term view of the world.' The shock will come for investors when the market decides to reassert rational value measures. Without the continued application of the fiscal and monetary stimulus provided by Western governments and central banks, will equity markets hold on to current prices? Manduca thinks not.

OUTLOOK

Manduca takes the honours for being the most bearish Maverick in this book. Wherever he looks he sees only reasons to be worried about the outlook for the next 10 years for Western economies and investors. He believes standards of living in the West are going to decline. In order of severity, continental Europe will see the greatest fall-off, the UK will see a less severe decline and the United States will weather the pressures the best. The investment community, he insists, is sleep walking into a decade of turbulence for financial services.

Does that mean a long-term bear market for stocks? Not necessarily, says Manduca; it will be damaging enough if the market does nothing but trend sideways for several years to come. If the markets are static, he says, that'll be equally devastating for people's expectations and lifestyles. And this is the essence of Manduca's contention that markets don't have to go down before people feel bad; they just have to go nowhere. Because Western consumers have lifestyles that are geared to rising bonuses, salary increases and luxuries like foreign travel and new cars, a bear market for individuals is not solely about stock markets going down, it is about a contraction in lifestyles.

The alternative is for everyone to cut back spending or work harder to sustain the same level of consumption. A fundamental change underway in market and economic conditions will take its toll on societies. In the 10 years prior to the bear market, steadily rising stock prices and rising property values created asset price wealth. The next 10 years will see no such phenomena.

Manduca cites as evidence the current low interest rate environment, under-funded pensions and longer life expectancy. All will test the individual investor over the next decade as they put pressure on equity values. His concerns about valuations within the stock and property markets, and the size of personal debt in Western economies, make him wary of seeing the markets as a solution to the wealth dilemma.

Manduca believes that many people are already witnessing a lifestyle recession. To understand this concept, individuals should do their own lifestyle test. In terms of income and leisure time, is the quality much better than it was five years ago? He points to the life quality compression he sees especially in the UK, where in much of the country outside London conditions haven't improved for the broad body of the population. Manduca points out that in some areas the infrastructure hasn't developed; in fact he claims there is evidence that transport systems and services are actually worse. Even in London there is evidence for him that, while incomes may appear to be holding steady, real quality of life is declining. Working hours are lengthening, real disposable income is declining and leisure time is being reduced.

Manduca's solution for the depression in lifestyles he is forecasting over the next decade is simple. Everyone concerned about their financial health must begin saving more. We should all be saving hard to sustain our lifestyles, but his fear is that we are not.

> 'People extrapolate rates of return based on their personal history. In the 50s it was low single digit, in the 80s it was 10–20%, today people talk about their required rate of return being about 10%. The only way to get that is to take some risks. The fear is that you wake up in your 40s or 50s without enough capital to live on, unproductive, and without a job. If you are earning 1% on your savings that isn't enough. That is when capital overnight becomes income.'

'ME TOO'

Manduca's short-hand for deflation in the business world is 'me too'. His conclusion is that there are few real innovations on the horizon within technology, or, more broadly, society, to drive the next significant profits cycle for the global economy. When I suggest that it may be premature to call the end of innovation, he goes on to explain that the point is more about the ability of businesses to exploit monopolistic advantage for superior profits. 'Of course there is more innovation going on today than ever before, by a huge quantum leap. The innovation is global but that innovation can be copied and it is not monopolised, which means profit margins are not extracted for very long.'

Within his own industry Manduca already detects signs of the deflation that will undermine the profit growth story for financial assets.

> 'Take a look at every single sector and you will see there is huge competition, even hedge fund managers tell me there are no margins, the new guy on the block has to be prepared to subsidise his way into the industry. So you have got rising costs and low margins while shareholders are demanding higher profits at the expense of reinvestment and growth.'

Manduca illustrates the point with an anecdote about the financial services industry. If you were a broker dealer in the early 1980s, access to information gave you an enormous premium over rivals and other market participants. At the time only some brokers had Telerate terminals, and other information providers like Reuters still only displayed prices on commodities and currencies rather than also covering bonds and equities. Charts were not readily available, graphics were not strong, and only the prime dealers would know what the Federal Reserve operations were that would move the bond market. Information was transferred between market participants on a relationship basis rather than via clever Information Technology.

Today that information advantage has been all but removed, and market prices or central bank decisions are disseminated at the speed it takes to travel through the fibre-optic cables. Manduca says that beyond the financial industry, which has also had profound effects on the specialist information, it is the providers themselves who must compete with a plethora of internet-based low-cost rivals.

Often where newcomers want to enter the market, Manduca says they may have to be prepared to subsidise their way into the industry. Even in a relatively new business like semiconductor manufacturing, some companies have had to produce chips below cost to gain or retain market share. Manduca says the same is true across the financial services industry where new players may have to reduce fees and offer preferential business terms to secure investment mandates. He doesn't see any foreseeable change in that at either a big or small business level.

This deflation is helping to drive down wages and will ultimately have an effect on Western employment. Where producers have a limited ability to enforce pricing power on consumers, the increased trend will be for costs to be reduced by migrating

Western labour to cheaper emerging markets. Manduca says this will impinge on all of us, driving down the standards of living in the West; the future will be bleaker because Western economies will not be generating the same amount of wealth per capita.

Are there any sectors of Western economies that will be in better shape? Manduca makes the point that today real inflation is to be found only in the public economy, or in the provision of government services. This is the one area that is still privy to monopoly provision.

FINANCIAL PRESERVATION

After a decade of excessive consumption fuelled by credit, Manduca says the next decade will be characterised by financial preservation. Fortunately, he argues that for the thrill seekers and the materialistic there are few horizons left to drive spending. The fascination factor of new experiences has grown a little weary. People have bought the second or third car, he says, and those who have sought a Caribbean holiday or skiing adventure, have probably had it already. This is the opportunity then for Western consumers to wean themselves off debt and start to rebuild their personal balance sheets.

Among the seriously wealthy Manduca says there is a lot of searching for bargain business deals going on, but very few are being done. The ratio of talk to deals is at an all time high. For instance, within the Private Equity world actual deals done in 2003 were a tiny percentage of the deal flow in the 1990s. The lesson to be drawn from this, says Manduca, is that the high-net worth individuals who run pools of 'smart' money are already in capital preservation mode. If the small investors can take anything away from this it is that they should be doing the same thing.

BACKGROUND

Of Maltese origins Manduca is one of four brothers, three of whom have found careers in the financial markets. Manduca is the only one to have specialised in the hedge fund world. I suggest to him having brothers working in the same industry must have created a very competitive streak. Manduca says with a smile that it made all of them aware that there is such a thing as brand risk. Inevitably, they would all have to be protective of the family name to ensure that they didn't make life more difficult for each other.

His father moved to Britain in the 1950s, and the young Philip grew up in an English culture but with an understanding that he was still considered by some in his host community as an outsider. Manduca says that mattered in the UK of the 1950s but the positive side was it allowed him to watch and observe the English at work and play. When it came to taking his first job in the City the overhang of class discrimination and prejudice was part of the fault lines Manduca identified as a weakness in the British. He says, pointedly, that the same problems of complacency and lack of vision meant that by 1993 there was not one major British investment bank left in the City.

Manduca began his career in the commodity markets in 1979. Upon leaving university he weighed his opportunities between entering the insurance business or commodities broking. Commodities had enjoyed a boom and the prospect of better income won through. In the winter of that year he joined a sugar broker. Ultimately, timing was against him, as both the insurance and commodity business were about to enter a 20-year decline.

Manduca, though, wouldn't be in the industry long enough to see the bear market assert itself. It wasn't long before he became frustrated with distortions in the supply and demand for sugar that seemed to go with the territory. 'Within a year of being in the commodities business I had come to the conclusion that I couldn't recommend the product to a client when, overnight, some banana republic dictator could change the rules.' Manduca also found the working environment difficult. Competitive by nature, it was hard to accept that promotion prospects were still tied to family background or seniority. He wanted to work in an industry that paid according to results and not connections or a history of military service, at the time a feature of 'old city' values.

Fortunately, for Manduca his arrival in the City coincided with deregulation of the London Stock Exchange. Announced in 1983 the financial system reforms would bring the major American banks to London. Weighed down with strong dollars and the bull market of the second Reagan term in office, they were in the mood to buy. Prior to 1983 London had had little appeal to the Americans. In the city they were quite happy for that status quo to be maintained, but the Thatcher-driven revolution in financial services changed that, and stock market deregulation made London attractive. Just 22 years old, Manduca was ready to turn his back on commodities and throw his lot in with the Americans. He saw an opportunity at Merrill Lynch and considered him self very fortunate to land the job. He went to Merrills on the tidy sum of £3500 a year.

The job switch was to be the making of his career. His new position put him in a team specialising in bringing financial futures contracts to Europe. It was 1980, just two years away from the establishment of the London Financial Futures and Options Exchange (LIFFE) and the removal of foreign exchange controls in the UK. Manduca's timing was impeccable. He describes hitting the city in a supped-up formula one car, at a time when there was very little local experience the derivatives market, and age didn't count against you. United with talent brought to London from the United States, Manduca and his colleagues would be among a select group just starting to offer financial futures products outside of the United States. By 1989, he says he was probably one of the highest paid individuals in the City, running around in a Ferrari supplied as a company car.

That decade saw Manduca transit through the American investment houses. He moved from Merrill Lynch to Kidder Peabody and then on to the English Mercantile companies. By the summer of 1987 he was working for a Japanese bank. By that point he says they were the only game left in town, meaning they were the only companies flush with enough cash from the great Japanese equity bull market willing to pay the inflated salaries. As it happened, that move preceded the start of the Japanese market crash by just a few months. With opportunistic timing Manduca was able to sell on the business he had created to the Japanese, taking the decision at the age of 31 to retire.

He says that, by then, he had become disillusioned by the thought of working for large companies. After a decade of witnessing the inefficiencies in large investment houses he wanted out. Manduca had witnessed a decade where the old City was dying and in its place were emerging new American and Japanese investment banks. They were well financed and willing to pay for access to local talent in a niche sector of the industry. It had made his fortune.

WORK HARD, PLAY HARD

The golf course, beloved by the business community as that other board room for discussing deals, is where most of Manduca's leisure time is spent. He has taken his winning approach from other areas of life into his golf game and plays off a very respectable handicap of four. His commitment to the game, and it must be said his money, have allowed him to play alongside the world's top players. Along with Nick Price, Darren Clark and Justin Rose, Manduca has achieved his lifetime dream of playing with Nick Faldo.

Manduca is an intense man. Of medium build and height, he talks quickly with an edge of determination to his voice. He has an emphatic delivery, which rises in volume when he wishes to stress a point or reinforce an argument. Manduca's smiles flash quickly and unexpectedly across his tanned face, and leave in the same manner. He holds it as an article of faith that anyone who wants to be rich only needs to properly dedicate themselves to that goal with hard work.

Golf, ironically, is the one area that continues to frustrate the aggressive tack he takes to business. 'If you are highly aggressive in business you will probably win, if you take the same approach to golf you'll lose for sure. You have to walk on to the golf course relaxed.' Manduca is one of the few amateur golfers who have consulted a sports psychologist to improve their game, a mark of the seriousness with which he undertakes any endeavour, even when it is meant to be for leisure.

THE GLOBALISATION DILEMMA

The years spent investing in emerging markets has left Manduca with a number of firm ideas about the outlook for globalisation, and the success of investing in certain markets over the next decade. He suggests that investors should think very hard about the emerging markets they choose to trust with their cash. His view is that China and India represent a much better risk than Russia or Eastern Europe.

Manduca prefaces his comments by saying these are 'big generalisations, but are issues people should think about'. He believes the legacy of communism in Eastern Europe has left a deep-seated culture that 'has no genuine belief in tomorrow. The attitude is short-term and those countries' politicians and businessmen do not invest in relationships.' The counterpoint he suggests is to be found in India and China where there is a long tradition of building relationships, and the experiments in communism or socialism have never removed the basic view that there is a tomorrow and it is worth investing in.

There is also, he says, a worrying mismatch between investors expected returns from emerging markets and the growth and maturity of the underlying economies. Again, he stresses, there is an element of generalisation in the message. 'Because investments in the emerging world tend to generate a return over a long time-frame they are better suited to investing through private equity rather than buying publicly listed vehicles.' He says events like the Asian currency crisis exposed the weakness of management in many countries. It showed the danger of investing over a short time-frame in markets ramped by speculative money.

Manduca says that any investor looking at Russia has to understand the current strategic dynamic facing the Russian leadership; do they cooperate with the United States or do they compete? They have significant oil and gas reserves, and he thinks they will work with Western oil companies to exploit that because of a short-term desire to get rich. He says, however, that he is not investing in Russia currently and believes there are easier and less risky places to put money. He thinks the medium-term issue for Russian–US relations and stability for Russian markets revolves around the outcome of events in the Middle East. Manduca suggests that instability emanating from Saudi Arabia will keep Russian cooperation high on the US State Department's wish list.

THE MIDDLE EAST AND AMERICA

Manduca believes that the invasion of Iraq by US-led forces was a distraction from what is essentially a story about Saudi Arabia, and a doomed US attempt to dominate the Middle East oil market. Manduca says America is taking one step forward to secure oil resources, but it will turn into a backward leap for America's presence on the world stage. Ultimately this entanglement in the Middle East will lead to a vote back home for Fortress America – a trend he thinks is already underway. 'In 5 to 10 years that theme will rule America's relations with the rest of the world, the average American will see little need to engage.'

He says trade wars are inevitable and will be part of America's withdrawal from a free international trading system. The pressure will be domestic, driven by discontented labour that equates trade tariffs with job protection. Where 90% of the population don't own a passport there will be little concern about the consequences of destructive trade policies on other countries around the world. Incidentally, the experience of trying to operate in Latin America gave him a peculiar take on Pax Americana, and an enduring view that, unlike other empires created by the British or Spanish, Americans look inwards and take on expansion with a view to always returning back home. As it applies to the US's current role as international policeman, Manduca believes that America – unlike Europeans who seek a global role on the world stage – will probably retreat into itself in times of domestic stress or difficulty.

INVESTMENT INDUSTRY OUTLOOK

Manduca has now set up two hedge fund businesses, and unsurprisingly only sees their role in the financial services industry growing. He says as traditional long-only asset management businesses get sold-off or broken up, many more medium-sized alternative asset management companies, or hedge funds, will evolve to take the money. Small investors, says Manduca, must be aware of this trend and think about where they can also use it to their advantage.

Already Manduca sees movement in the hedge fund community to make products more mainstream. Part of that is about bulking-up groups to provide investment scale. To do that, he says, single product hedge fund companies are starting to transpose themselves into multiple product hedge funds with a multiplicity of strategies under one roof. The key is to offer a range of managers with a range of products to fill the vacuum left by the long industry funds. This trend will grow as over the decade the financial services sector fights to hold on to a shrinking business. The demographics in Western economies, he says, will run against the industry as pensions start to be spent and workers have less money to save. 'I think the financial services industry has been slow to adjust. I think there has been a gap in what the financial services industry has done and what the markets have done; the long-only industry is toast!'

Manduca says it will be increasingly important for the hedge funds to differentiate their offerings to attract new funds, and the same search for star money managers that has characterised the traditional fund management business will appear among the hedge fund community as the industry takes on a higher public profile.

OPPORTUNITY

Against the misery of the world in which Manduca sees investors doing battle over the next decade, there are a couple of plays that he feels are potentially strong enough stories to keep money invested.

He likes strong brands and believes that the best can still generate good value in a bear market. If the world is facing recessionary conditions, brands stand out because they bring comfort in difficult times. Again, Manduca returns to the theme of monopolistic suppliers, and says that brands with strong consumer loyalty will be among the few products that can enforce pricing power. He advises investors to look at the emerging markets in Asia and Europe to find the established brands that are gaining a foothold. The notion of brand is more commonly understood in the context of luxury goods. Manduca is using it in a much broader context of products and services, and investors must do the same.

Interestingly, given his concerns about the outlook for consumer financial health, Manduca likes the banking sector. It is their position as conduits of cash to other parts of the world that are growing that keeps him optimistic. 'Banking is a great sector because it has custody, which is very important. The banks will be recycling money into China and into Asia more generally. Just look at the current figures for foreign direct investment.' He says that the truly global business banks are a better risk than domestic Western banks. Top tier global banks that have the strength to weather non-performing loan problems are preferred, and Manduca mentions HSBC as one of the better examples. In this sector he is looking at the survivors, those that can come through any weakness across Western economies in good shape.

WATCH MICRO-CAPS

Manduca watches small cap companies for early business trends – that is, companies that have a value or turnover of less than $50 million. He pinpoints these smaller companies as the early warning systems that are always at the leading edge of discoveries in new technologies or must-have products.

As investments they are difficult to access, and most fund managers are unable to invest in them because of their size. Beyond the problem of liquidity, they are also by nature not easy to research. The company managers do not have the time or money to cultivate investor interest. They may be off most fund manager's radar screens, but, says Manduca, diligent small private investors may find it a profitable area of research. It is within this dynamic entrepreneurial environment that Manduca looks for confirmation of trends that may become the investment stories in future years. He suggests that investors who are willing to seek out 'early' fundamental stories should look to this sector of the economy for their edge.

Ideally, Manduca would like to seed money into micro-caps in the emerging world. There is a revolution taking place in low-cost innovation in the emerging economies. But he recognises that the strategy is fraught with danger. You may need to invest in 10, to find two that can survive and prosper. 'The ones that do go bust will be a problem because they will take your money with them. You won't be able to get it out fast enough.' The dilemma then is whether to put more cash into the survivors. Their size constrains the investment they can take and their life-span as small companies may be limited. Once they attract the attention of larger players a buy-out may be the ultimate end-game, closing out the investment opportunity.

GOLD

Gold is the one investment Manduca has been comfortable about putting money into for some years now. After correctly calling the end of 2003 target above $400 an ounce he is expecting the price to rise to $500 an ounce in 2004. He doesn't rule out $600 depending on the weakness in the US dollar. He believes that gold offers the one significant refuge in his downbeat outlook. 'Put more than half your savings in gold. Probably the best place is gold shares, and Newmont Mining would be the obvious choice as it is one of the largest capitalised companies. Even buying bullion, if you can manage it, will turn out to be a good choice.'

The reflation of the US economy is the best argument for buying gold, says Manduca, whether it succeeds or not in preventing the US economy slipping back into recession. The Federal Reserve is more concerned about the risks to recovery and deflation, which means there will be little or no tightening in interest rates through 2004. Sceptical of the motivations of politicians, he thinks that US Republicans and President Bush will do what they feel is necessary to hold on to power, and if that means printing money and devaluing the dollar, so be it. 'Guess what the response of those that rule will be, they will print as much money as they possibly can to reflate the economy. It is no coincidence that over the last few years we have had the biggest reflation story this generation.'

Manduca believes that the devaluation of the dollar will be a long-term story that supports gold. Apart from being a recognised store of value, the most important thing about gold is that it has no debt attached to it. Gold, unlike property or shares, is debt free. Manduca urges people not to measure their wealth in property, and if his outlook comes to pass property values in the UK and the US will fall heavily.

COMMODITY STRENGTH

Investors should participate in the short-term bull market for commodities because production is 'kicking back in as China and India suck in commodities reversing a 20-year bear market for these raw materials'. The bull market will last as long as mothballed plants and abandoned mines are brought back into production.

Commodity prices are not going up, says Manduca, because of better growth rates in the US or inflation. 'It is to do with the fact that you have got huge resource-hungry economies in India and China, and to a lesser extent other economies in Asia that are benefiting.' The trade ratios in Asia show that the region is a net importer from that part of the world and Asia will continue to enjoy growth on the back of China.

Manduca says that investors need to be cautious about extrapolating rising commodity prices as bullish for Western company profits. 'This is not about Western demand-pull for commodity markets, because we don't have growth here we won't get inflation. Ask the question, why aren't rising raw materials prices driving up prices on the High Street? The companies are absorbing any rising costs because they know there is consumer resistance to paying up, which means that corporate margins will continue to be squeezed.'

CURRENCIES

The dollar, despite its nascent weakness, remains favoured. Manduca suggests the Chinese renmimbi might be the most attractive currency to hold on a medium term view, but its lack of convertibility rules it out as a viable choice. However promiscuous the US authorities are in printing dollars, Manduca still thinks its reserve status, and the size of the economy it is tied to, offers some security.

Sceptical about the Euro, Manduca acknowledges that it is the currency Europeans must hold, but he dislikes the fundamentals. He is also deeply cynical about the political union. He suspects ultimately that the economic stagnation in the bloc's two largest economies will cause the Europeans to act by increasing the money supply. 'I do believe one of the things they could flirt with in a bid to preserve the Union is to print euros, if you look at the numbers there were already signs that the money supply was rising before the dollar started to weaken.'

Manduca cites labour rigidity as a considerable problem that limits his enthusiasm on growth prospects for Europe. He fears that the more insidious face of labour rigidity is growing calls for immigration control that will hold back continental economies. He also views the immigration dynamic as different for the US and Europe. Where migrant labour moves to the US it is driven by ambition and encouraged by the culture of entrepreneurship. This has helped to foster a diverse ethnic workforce engaged in the American dream of turning rags to riches. By contrast, he sees immigrants who arrive in European countries being put on government benefits and not welcomed into the broader labour pool. Given the declining populations in many European countries it is an attitude that should be changing. This, Manduca says, creates a different motivation for people to cross borders in Europe and the United States. In the US immigrants join a dynamic labour force; in Europe they heighten racial tensions and foster a fortress Europe mentality.

FINAL WORDS...

Manduca says that the key to surviving the decade he envisions is to diversify wealth carefully. In the UK in particular people must not measure themselves by the wealth in their property. Property is tied to debt and is ultimately vulnerable to a weak economic environment. Any investors also employed in the financial services industry must think hard about spreading their risks away from the financial markets.

Trying to call short-term market direction is a mug's game that will not enrich your financial health. Manduca's view is that there are few market participants gifted with the trading skills to consistently make money from the right directional calls. The primary trend he says is still bearish, and even if stocks appear to be well supported it is just a question of timing before the selling starts.

If you are able to make high single-digit returns from investments in the next few years you should be very happy, says Manduca. Otherwise, 'work very hard, and for as long as you can because you need to generate income'.

Part II
TECHNICAL TRADERS

5
Chris Locke: Elliott Wave and the Planets

'We have had the Tulip bubble and other manias over the years. It is curious that they happen over and over again, we do not learn from the experience. Look at the tech bubble it was just the latest example.'

Chris Locke is mildly concerned. It is September 2003, and Locke is worried that the date is connected to a stock market crash that took place 119 years ago. The week of our interview has an important connection to General Ulysses Grant's Last Panic of 1884. The panic in the market in that year was caused by falling railway stock prices. Gradual selling turned into a rout eventually causing financial loss to the US President. General Ulysses Grant was a partner in a financial company called Grant and Ward that went bust in the crash. What does this have to do with 2003? Quite a lot says Locke.

Locke is a technical analyst. He has a trading system based on three decades of experience operating in the commodity markets. He uses price charts to assess entry and exit levels for trades, and the price patterns to confirm the timing. When he opens a position he runs close stops and uses careful money management techniques to limit losses. All of this is standard fare for any trader in the commodity or financial futures markets. What differentiates him from other traders or technical analysts is his belief in the influence of non-financial causes on market activity.

Technical analysis is a measure of crowd behaviour represented by a price line. The basis of all technical analysis is the belief in recurrent patterns that can be exploited to predict the future direction of prices. Underlying these patterns is the idea that they represent the collective action, or psychology of the market. The market is a collection of individuals all acting in their own interests, but also reacting to the feedback from the market. If human nature doesn't change, say the chartists, the behaviour of individuals and their inputs and reaction to the market feedback should be predictable.

Locke has taken the next step. If buying stocks, currencies or commodities is about how humans behave in market situations, why not also look at the bigger external influences. And they don't get much bigger than the planets. It is the quest for the holy grail of investing – a technique that works in all market conditions that has pushed Locke further and further towards what many would view as the fringes of credible investment analysis. Most of his trading is based on chart analysis that would be familiar to any trader with a passing knowledge of Elliott Wave theory and basic technical tools. The planetary aspect is an overlay. It is an attempt to find a larger logic to the pattern of financial market behaviour.

His starting point was the observation that market events repeat. Locke has witnessed a lot of market cycles in his 30-year career. He is convinced that the herd-like behaviour of traders and investors, fuelled by greed and fear, is one constant that can be relied upon. 'Think about how groups behave. We have had the Tulip bubble and other manias over the years. It is curious that they happen over and over again, but we do not learn from the experience. Look at the tech bubble; it was just the latest example.' Locke wanted to get a better understanding of why there is repetition and whether it could be predicted. He found Elliott Wave useful, but also frustrating. The theory uses an eight-wave pattern to forecast the direction for prices. But the subjective nature of wave counting sent him in search of other influences on group behaviour. It wasn't long before Locke was reading extensively about other chartists like W.D. Gann who had views on environmental forces and the influence of the planets on the human condition. 'History repeats itself, and, like the moon affects the tides, the planets affect human behaviour in cycles.'

In the event, September 2003 passed without any serious problem for the markets. Locke didn't stop his trading activities, but decided to exercise extra caution during those weeks. The date, however, remains a relevant marker. As with all dates highlighted by his planetary work, if nothing happens on a particular date 'we then move forward to the next date which could be of bigger consequence'. He has a whole calendar of dates for this year and years to come which have connections with historic panics and market high and low points. He believes that there may be significant market sentiment turns on these dates. They may be either generated within the markets or caused by external events changing the market's direction, such as a terrorist act or corporate scandal. The analysis can't determine the nature of the event but signposts that it is due because of the position of planets at the time.

THE SPIRAL CALENDAR

The starting point for Locke's astral research is the Spiral Calendar (SC). This is a model created by former stock option pit-trader Christopher Carolan. To understand how Locke uses the planetary influences to interpret the markets it is necessary to explain how the SC was created.

Carolan was working in a trading pit in the Pacific Exchange in San Francisco during the 1987 market crash. He made two observations: firstly, the pit traders at times of high emotion behave as a crowd and discard individual action counter to the group; and, secondly, the charts for the DJIA in 1987 and for the crash of 1929 were almost identical – almost, but not quite, as the pattern appeared to be out of lock-step by 9 or 10 days.

This bothered him. Why should two groups of individual traders separated by a generation behave in the same way? Why, when most were facing their first market panic, would the traders in 1987 perform with identical greed and fear to the traders in 1929? The price patterns were almost the same, but for the difference of 9 to 10 days. Why weren't they identical? After messing around with some ideas he finally found his answer by rebasing the calendar to a lunar year of 354 days rather than the 365-day year based on the Gregorian calendar we commonly use. The rebasing removed the discrepancy and the charts aligned.

He figured that if working to a lunar calendar solved the discrepancy in the patterns, it might also hold the key as to why the behaviour of the traders 58 years apart was the same. Carolan thought he had his answer: 'The phases of the moon provided the rhythms of greed and fear by which they bought and sold.' He went on to count the number of new moons that occurred during the 58 years that separated the two market crashes. That number worked out at 717. Was this number significant in its own right?

Carolan looked for help from the mathematical birthplace of technical analysis, the series of numbers recognised by Leonardo Fibonacci. After the first, each Fibonacci number is the total of the previous two. The peculiar properties of Fibonacci numbers are beyond the scope of this book, but the series of numbers have caused fascination since they were discovered because the mathematical relationships between them crop up in nature. Spiral galaxies apparently are designed along these lines. The point to make here is that Carolan found his match in the square root of the 29th number in the Fibonacci sequence. Punching some keys on the calculator revealed that the square root of 514 229 is 717.0976.

Was this a bizarre coincidence or had Carolan uncovered a connection between two market crashes and the number of new moons? Was he one step closer to establishing a mathematical system tied to the moon's rotations that could predict stock market behaviour? In Carolan's mind it was clear. About 5000 years ago the ancient Mesopotamians had recognised the influence of the sun and moon on man. Why should there not be an influence now? He set about creating a revised calendar based on the lunar model of time, and earmarked specific dates across the decades that had meaning for financial markets. This is how Carolan sums up his conclusions: 'People make investment mistake when they behave emotionally. The Spiral Calendar demonstrates that this emotional behaviour occurs *en masse*, and that these irrational time periods are cyclically linked.'

Carolan went on to create a methodology for calculating which SC dates would have important connections:

1.   Take the start date of a panic or event.
2.   Take the Fibonacci sequence 1, 3, 5, 8, 13, 21, 34, ...
3.   Square root each Fibonacci sequence.
4.   Multiply the number by 29.5 for the Lunar days in each month.
5.   Name each calculated date F2, F3, F4, F5, F6, F7, . . . , F33 for ease of
      reference.

The SC seems to suggest that highly emotional events in the past generate related
highly emotional events in the future in a mathematically calculable series. Its influence is not limited to financial markets, but the events can happen in and out of
markets. Followers like Locke say accuracy is generally found within 3 calendar days
over periods as long as 245 years. 'The Spiral Calendar is an integral part of my
overall analysis. It is rather complex in its nature but can be exceedingly accurate and
complements all my other work. I use my own spreadsheet to formulate it.'

Locke says his experience with using the system of dates has shown that major
highs and lows in the stock market are driven by SC intervals to previous panics.
He continued to be concerned about the duration of the US equity market rally in
the summer of 2003 because he could see connections to bearish dates. 'This last
summer has certainly been interesting because the market has shown four very valid
SC intervals on the highs of 17/6/03, 14/7/03, 31/7/03 and 8/9/03, 13/10/03, 15/12/03,
4/1/03 and then beat them all.' He believes the market may not have been affected
because there is an even larger SC idea out there dragging the market to it. Figure 5.1
shows the SC dates through the second half of 2003, and the underlying behaviour of
the market.

Figure 5.1   SC dates through the second half of 2003.

If that is so, he says, there is still a case that can be made from the Calendar to explain the positive market.

> 'The bullish take is to compare the S&P 500 now to the S&P 20 years ago, and the full 20-year Jupiter–Saturn cycle. If we move the periods over a little we can get a pretty good match. This would also indicate that a top is nearby and the theory of this comparison would be that the market corrects in the first half of 2004 before moving higher again. However, even if this is a bullish outcome basis the early 1980s comparison, we should still see 2004 as a consolidation year basis this pattern.'

CYCLES THAT COUNT

Cycles are not new to investment theory. It is widely accepted that economies behave in cycles, essentially they have a growth phase and then they slow down. During the respite the seeds are sown for the next growth phase and so the cycle completes. The difficult part is working out whether there is a specific time period that can be applied to stock prices that has predictive value.

Financial textbooks are sprinkled with cycle theories. Most readers will have at least heard of the work of Russian economist Kondratieff, who claimed that economies and markets move in 48- to 60-year waves or cycles. Then there are the shorter periods, discussed in the work of Charles Dow that were built upon for Elliott Wave theory.

Locke's research and the work of Christopher Carolan and another 'pupil' Roy Fellars have led to the creation of a number of time-frames he considers important reference points for extreme investor behaviour:

- *84 years*. The largest cycle based on Uranus and its Sun orbit. It connected US market highs of 1835 and 1919.
- *58 years*. Based on the 717 new moons observed by Christopher Carolan as connecting the crashes of 1929 and 1987.
- *29.5 years*. The Saturn cycle. The time it takes Saturn to revolve around the Sun. Currently interesting for commodities – refers back to the 1970s a period of booming commodity prices.
- *20 years*. The Jupiter–Saturn cycle, with a half cycle of 10 years. This is the source of bearish comparisons with the Dow and the Nikkei (1989 vs 1999). Or a straight comparisons with the US 10 and 20 years ago, which is bullish.
- *4 years*. Perhaps the most commonly accepted short-cycle period. Recognised as a traditional business cycle with two up years, and two down years. It has been utilised by Dow theorists and other technical analysis for many years.
- *29.5 days*. The Lunar cycle, or the time it takes for the Moon to rotate around the Earth. Used for investment timing around the new Moon or full Moon periods.

Users of these cycles to identify market activity watch the start and finish of the cycles for indicating highs and lows of market emotion. The periods in between are also relevant to the analysis. They represent the build up to and the ebbing away from those key points.

TRADING TOOL KIT

Intrigued by the possibilities in astral research, Locke is reading more deeply into the subject. The process of investing his own cash has only increased his conviction that there is enough that is effective to justify continuing more work in this field. His current belief is such that he no longer places a trade without being aware of the astral overlay.

Locke supplements this research work with charting Elliott Wave patterns – the series of eight waves that Elliott practitioners claim to see in all price charts. The pattern is characterised by a series of five up moves and three down moves. The eight-wave pattern is repeated across time-frames from the Grand Cycle of 150–200 years that Charles Elliott identified down to daily price fluctuations. Locke is wary of the subjective nature of wave counting but hasn't found a system that works better, in calling turns in the trend. 'It is the basis of my work mainly because it is contrary to the main thought at the time. We know that when everyone is bullish it means they have already bought and when everyone is bearish they have already sold. It is not popular with the crowd because positions mostly are at the opposite extreme of where the crowd is.'

Is there any conflict between the SC and Elliott Wave? Locke believes not; the two cycle systems are analogous. He says it is a question of interpretation. 'As in all Technical and Fundamental analysis you can find an analyst reading the same picture bullish at the same time as one finds the picture bearish.'

In addition to Elliott Wave, Locke uses a collection of technical indicators to forecast trends. A favourite is a combination of 40- and 200-day Exponential Averages to determine intermediate and long-term trends, depending on whether he is taking a daily or weekly chart. On shorter time-frames he uses smaller simple Moving Averages, a 72-day MA for direction, and 23- or 50-day Exponential Averages.

Locke will also pull up a Relative Strength Indicator on short-term charts. This shows how the target index has been performing relative to other markets, or assets. He will also draw in Bollinger Bands, a pair of lines marked in either side of an average to show a trend channel. Locke finds these useful on intra-day charts. But he says the most useful tool he uses on the daily and weekly picture is the difference of two Moving Averages. He will run these across three different time-scales. They help to identify bullish or bearish divergence and completion of the fifth Elliott Wave. This is the final wave before the three correction waves.

CALLING THE TURNS

The process Locke uses for market forecasting is a very complicated blend of Elliott Wave counting and astral overlay. He is also heavily influenced by the writings of

W.D. Gann, an American trader who was active in the commodity and equity markets in the first half of the twentieth century. Gann believed in the repetition of history and wrote extensively on how markets could be predicted with price and time analysis.

To investors who believe a share price is only determined by a company's earnings, Locke's process is fanciful nonsense. To think the Moon could affect the decision a person makes today about whether to buy a stock or market appears on the face of it quite absurd. He is the first to acknowledge that discussion of the planetary aspect of his work doesn't go down well with everyone. He gets a better reception from other believers or traders with an open mind.

Wherever feelings lie on the issue, Locke has demonstrated the ability over the last four years to make tradable calls on market turns. The record hasn't been 100%, but the evidence suggests that he is either a very gifted gut trader, or his forecasting tools work, or, more likely, a combination of the two.

I first spoke with Locke in the autumn of 2000. Television stations get a lot of e-mail and much of it gets deleted fairly quickly, but Locke's correspondence was very different as it presented a cogent, albeit complicated analysis of the markets. It differed from the body of financial research written in that the forecasts were day specific, and predicted the degree of the move expected. After several months of receiving his mails I called him and persuaded him to go on air with his work.

What follows is a run through of turns Locke called over the last four years, with the previously unseen commentaries that were sent to me ahead of his weekly interviews:

Soybeans

Locke is extremely positive on the outlook for the soft commodity markets over coming years. At the end of 2002 he was calling a major move in the Soybean price for full year 2003. He was rewarded with a 1600% gain by the time of option expiry at the end of 2003.

31 December 2002. Tip for 2003 commodities?... Out of money call options at some stage on November 2003 Beans and December 2003 Wheat. Implied seasonals are near their lowest level into March. Hopefully end January will be near a reasonable entry level. For example Nov 620/640 Bean calls... or debit spreads (limited risk strategies).

Gold

In January 2001 with gold at around $265 an ounce and the bear market low, Locke began to recommend a long-term buying opportunity. In April 2001, after charting what he was sure was a long-term bottom in the Gold price, Locke again suggested taking long positions. He then traded in and out as the price consolidated above $350. Below are the three calls he made in January 2001.

18 January 2001. Nymex Crude Oil rallied into resistance just above 30 . . . new lows soon . . . GOLDGOLDGOLD . . . ah . . . the sleeping Giant . . . watch closely this one.

19 January 2001. Crude resistance here . . . new lows soon . . . Gold . . . the sleeping Giant . . . watch that . . . I expect sharp move soon towards 300.

More in depth later because THIS WILL BE AN IMPORTANT FEW DAYS on how we will unfold from here.

21 January 2001. GOLD . . . Still the sleeping giant . . . BUYBUYBUY.

Bonds

Locke is looking for the bond market to make a major high in the middle of 2003. The market subsequently sold off sharply in one of the largest moves seen over a matter of weeks.

24 June 2003. I know it is hard to believe but we have all the signs that the bull move on long-term bonds from the lows from 2000 is coming to an end, or at least is entering a multi-week correction. The US Treasury 10-year notes weekly chart shows a clear 5 wave structure complete with the last bull leg from lows early in 2002 also supporting a 5 wave structure.

Notice weekly stochastics turning lower. Initial targets downside are the weekly averages near 113 with potential to move down to 102–103 at the 4th wave of a larger degree. Only new highs would prolong the rally but, as I said, I suspect we have at least a multi-week correction from here. The 10-year German Bunds weekly chart shows that the market has topped so far at the 1.382% Fibonacci extension level from the bull move beginning in 2000. With the key downside weekly reversals in place last Friday it is looking like a multi-week pullback has begun to shake out the weak longs down towards 112.50 initially.

Equities

Locke was looking for a turn in market fortunes ahead of the 12 March 2003 low. This proved to be the major turning point for European markets. It signalled the start of a very strong rally throughout 2003.

February 2003. Good morning Geoff. Indices . . . on FULL ALERT for a tradable low from here on . . . Cycles into March lows. 10 March +/− for the 3-month cycle turning point. 17 March for the yearly cycle turning point. The point turn on the yearly cycle could extend a little more time through. What does this mean? I expect to see a rally from this low (and I think that low is between now and 10% lower) up well into May . . . similar to March 2001. . . . Last year we saw a high in this period (1173). . . . We are near or at all levels I have mentioned as targets the past months for European Indices.

Locke also made very accurate calls on the direction of the Euro and Yen. He plotted his expectation from 2002 and into 2003 that both currencies would make major moves higher against the US dollar. The stronger yen remains one of Locke's most confident calls, at least for the rest of 2004 and possibly beyond.

I am alert to the danger here in emphasising the good at the risk of misleading investors about the bad. Locke doesn't get them all right, and there is a world of difference between showing with hindsight that the forecast was correct, and being able to trade every twist and turn at the time.

S&P 500

Locke thinks that with the benefit of hindsight he may have relied too heavily on the bearish count in his Elliott Wave analysis. He called the March low with great accuracy, but felt the selling could return. His SC dates were not accurate in calling a change in the bullish trend. Locke knew the move above his technical resistance at 965 was important and the market should extend towards 1020, but he remained bearish on the outlook. For the rest of 2003 the S&P never looked back at 965. He mentions a significant event expected on 29 July. In the event the day passed without note.

June 2003. The consolidation I was expecting in May as I mentioned past 2 weeks did not transpire after the expected run up from March and we just extended the gains. HOWEVER, the date 29 July looms fast. This date I have mentioned since the beginning of the year. I am convinced it's a deep point in the market despite being asked whether it is an inversion. THIS DAY IS CONNECTING THE DEEPEST POINTS OF 1929 AND 1987 MATHEMATICALLY WITH THE NEXT DATE ON THE SPIRAL AT 29 JULY 1987. It is also connecting major events from 1945. The first spiral those 2 dates were lows. Therefore the probability is that 29 July will be a deep point.

PUTTING THEORY INTO PRACTICE

Locke's analysis builds up layer upon layer of cycle work. What follows is a simple example of the stages he goes through to reach the conclusions that guide his forecasts. The charts show the development of the Soybean price based on planetary work, Elliott Wave, Gann and seasonals:

1.   The 29.5-year Saturn cycle suggests that Soybeans/commodities in general are starting a long-term bull phase similar to the 1970s. Bottoms 1940, 1969 and 1999 (Figure 5.2). In addition the Jupiter–Uranus cycle highlighted a shorter-term low in 1999 (not shown).

2.   Once Locke has identified the long-term low cycle period, he looks for the shorter-term cycles. The first is the 4-year cycle turns highlighted on Figure 5.3. He knows a low is due in 1999 – the cycle, he says, is predetermined.

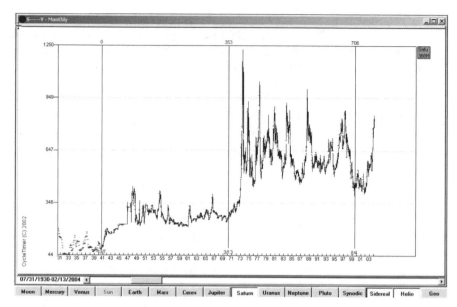

Figure 5.2   The 29.5-year Saturn cycle.
Source: CycleTimer. Reproduced by permission of Bradley F. Cowan

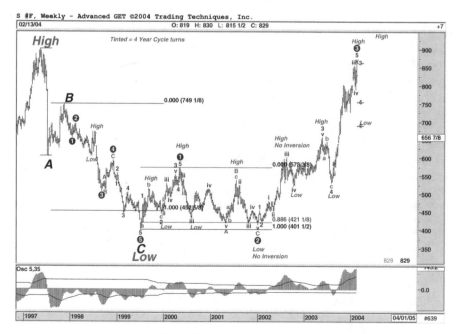

Figure 5.3   A four-year cycle.

These cycle patterns repeat through life from large cycles to minute. It's a question of identifying the fixed turn windows. He says there can be inversions at certain times, but mostly guessing can be eliminated using other tools at hand.

3.   Locke searches for the completion of an Elliott Wave sequence. He finds it, 'The completion of a 5 wave C was evident, with a bullish divergence oscillator into the 1999 low where also wave C was almost equal to wave A. BINGO.'

4.   Now the bull begins in an expected 5 wave up sequence. The 4-year turns continue. Locke matches the E wave with other cycles. 'Currently prices are in a 4-year point high cycle due. I know there is a good chance of another wave 5 high once the correction into May $+/-$ is over because of the oscillator at new highs; no bear divergence as of this writing on the weekly chart.'

5.   Locke matches up the one-year cycles on a daily chart. 'From the July 2002 lows (identified on previous chart as a smaller wave 4) there are 5 waves up on the daily chart to complete possible larger wave 3 also shown on Figure 5.2 with bear divergence. Also a 1-year cycle turn point is due at this time of writing (Figure 5.4). Therefore I look for possible completion of larger wave 3 in February 2003 with a wave 4 correction into May 2003. This is all forecasted. As time moves on I would make changes to the forecast if necessary.'

6.   Once he has identified the possible shorter-term cycles he looks for a 'seasonal' pattern to fit the recent past and project into the future. This pattern

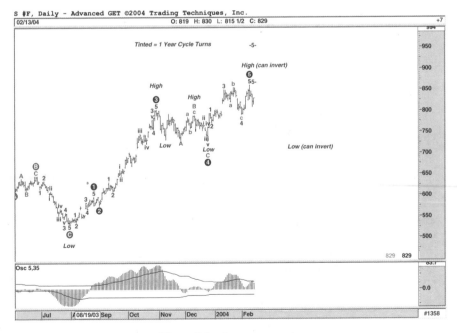

Figure 5.4 A one-year cycle.

Figure 5.5   An inverted seasonal cycle.

may even be an inverted seasonal cycle such as in Figure 5.5. There are much shorter-term cycles such as the 4-month cycle. The sequence repeats every 4 months. There are even cycles into 4-day periods, but have been left out of the analysis to avoid complicating the picture.

7.   Finally, Locke goes back to the big cycle picture to locate turns going forward (Figure 5.6).

APPROACHING A TRADE

The clearest way to describe how Locke trades his forecasts is to walk through a trade made on the S&P 500. Remember, he is aiming to take a position at the start of a long-term trend. Obviously, he won't know it is a long-term trend until later, but once he gets confirmation that the trend has begun, he can think about adding to his position. As events unfolded in this example Locke realised that he had traded short into a very major bearish turn for all Western markets. His entry coincides with the S&P coming off its all time high in the year 2000.

First Position

His long-term Elliott Wave count on the S&P in early 2000 suggested a potential top of 5 waves from the 1970s. The fifth wave extended from the lows of 1998 with

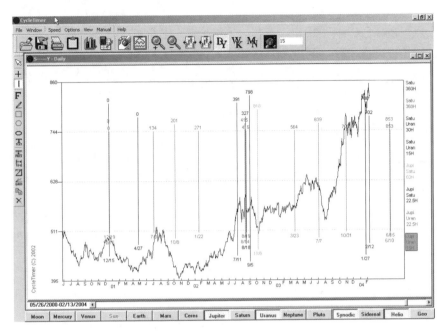

Figure 5.6   Saturn cycles.
Source: CycleTimer. Reproduced by permission of Bradley F. Cowan

sentiment running very high. But Locke figured that momentum in the move was decreasing. The market made a high on 24 March, and a secondary high was made in September 2000. In the secondary high Locke aimed for his first position and shorted the market at 1530 points. To protect himself against the market rising he placed a stop at 1575.

Second Position

The market had been falling for several days. The index breached a technically significant 200-day Moving Average. With the market's fall confirming his analysis, Locke placed a second position and lowered the stop on his first position. The risk was only now in the second position taken. Over the next few days the market rallied to 1480 and moved sideways, holding above the 200 Moving Average, but Locke's short-term Elliott count suggested that it was a smaller wave 4 implying that averages would break. He writes:

> *22 September 2000. There will be no let up today with the selling. If we come in under 1450 December S&P (currently 1442.75) the risk will be a sell off towards 1390 possibly today. Investors have all been all too greedy of late. . . . Buying shares at a p/e over 50 and in some cases over 100 and far more. This will change very quickly.*

The S&P continues to step down through the autumn months before pausing on 12 October to make a short-term low. Locke had charted a break through key 200-day exponential Moving Average levels on 6 October. It is a signal for further weakness:

> **9 October 2000.** *Indices... CHAOS... as forecasted here. TECHS ARE ONLY IN WAVE 3 DAILIES... MORE BIG DOWNSIDE TO COME... S&P... 1450 and 1430 Dec broken. May see small rally here from Friday, but more BIG DOWNSIDE TO COME BEFORE LOWS. You have heard it here this past month!!!*

Locke holds off adding to his shorts. He is still hanging in for the long-term trend trade but is worried about the chance of a pullback. He doesn't want to get caught in the backdraft:

> **12 October 2000.** *Indices as predicted past weeks continue freefall. HOWEVER, maybe nearing time for a correction.... Long Term still exceedingly bearish unless bulls can get S&P Dec back over 1430–1450.*

Locke is fully confident that a major bear market has set in, and sits in shorts. He moves up his stops and looks for opportunities to add shorts on market rallies. The index enjoys a respite from the selling and Locke covers his shorts. The market rallies 100 points into early November. He is dubious about the duration of the rally:

> **1 November 2000.** *INDICES. Are we out of the woods yet? All this exuberance!! TREAT THIS RALLY WITH CAUTION AT THE MOMENT AND TAKE CARE IN THE PICKING OF STOCKS UNTIL WEEKLIES HAVE TAKEN OUT RESIS-TANCE. RISK IS STILL DOWNSIDE AT THE MOMENT IF FAILING HERE.*

Locke waits to remove the covers on his shorts. The S&P makes a short-term high on 2 November and recommences its decline. He looks for further opportunities to short the market.

TRADING LIQUIDITY

Locke is active across a range of different markets. He is happy to trade in commodity, currency, bond and stock markets. What matters most is that the markets exhibit good liquidity. In fact he will trade 'pretty much anything from financials to soft commodities where there is a good liquid contract'. He trades mostly futures contracts on margin, but also options on futures in the soft commodity markets. In equity markets, S&P 500 futures are the main contracts he trades. He uses e-mini's which he can trade electronically from home, and operate like smaller versions of stock index futures contracts used by the major financial houses. Just like futures there is the ability to go long or short, and they come with plenty of leverage.

He doesn't trade much in European markets; occasionally, however, he may take a position on the Dax. The German index has demonstrated a highly volatile correlation with the US markets. On currencies he is active mostly with the euro and yen, but does chart the Swiss franc and the British pound. He will take positions if he can spot a trend building. In the debt markets Locke trades derivatives in the 10-year Bunds, and follows the 30-year Treasury Bonds. He has found that the astral side of his analysis is most effective in the Soybean, Corn and Wheat markets, and with the 30-year bond, the Dow and S&P. Locke has been doing a lot of recent astral work on the Dow, although he recognises the limitations in an index that only follows 30 stocks.

Mostly Locke is a position or swing trader and enters a trade intending to keep it in place for several days or weeks. The game is calling the long-term break-out, or change in trend and riding it for as long as it runs. He says this is where the greatest returns can be made, but it does require some patience and accuracy in calling the turn rather than a false break-out.

That means that he assumes overnight risk on the position, but uses protective stops to limit his losses. Locke doesn't have a hard and fast rule on stops. He thinks it is too mechanistic to apply a 5% or 10% limit, and is a mistake novice traders make. He understands the techniques of the professional pit traders who look for round numbers to push the price around to take out the stop-loss levels. He adjusts his stop positions regularly if the trade is still valid, moving them up on a long trade to secure paper gains. The same approach applies on the shorts.

If he is very confident about the position Locke may be willing to 'hang' in the trade, widening his stops to prevent being taken out by the institutional traders. It takes deep pockets and nerves of steel, but rather than run tight stop-losses and get taken out several times he will ride the volatility. He may wait for several days of weaker closes through a key support level to convince him that the position was wrong. Obviously the losses will be higher, but he says it does mean a clearer run at the gains.

If Locke likes the market, perceiving there to be enough volatility for big percentage moves, he will day trade. But the market must be exceptional, as he believes that most day traders lose money, and the practice will lose its attraction where market volatility has declined. In his opinion, the key to successful day trading is in being able to put yourself in the position of someone on the trading floor in an open outcry environment. Only then can you see how other traders are fading the market – that is, choosing to trade in the opposite direction to a buy or sell signal.

> 'With intra-day trading it doesn't matter what the market trend is, what matters is that you are fading the markets. Like the guys on the floor you are fading the breaks. It is very different technique to swing or position trading.'

When Locke day trades he mostly uses S&P contracts. A very liquid market is important where positions may only be held for several minutes or hours. He prefers not to take very short-term plays on the soft commodity markets because he sees a potential conflict of interest with his position as a broker in the Soybean industry.

MONEY MANAGEMENT

Like any professional trader, Locke takes money management very seriously. He subscribes to the view that it is not the gains that are most important, it is preventing the big losses. Locke follows a basic rule of not putting more than 10% of his cash in any one market. Within that market, if he feels the call is strong enough, he may be willing to put 30% of the allocated cash into one position.

He will stay out of the market if he can't pick out a clear trend on the charts. As he doesn't manage money, he is not required to remain invested or chase profits through very active trading. There are no clients waiting to check their quarterly statement. Locke has built an approach to trading that looks for significant turns, and he would rather sit back and wait for those opportunities than trade every day.

Locke says a lot of his money control comes from the experience of losses down the years, and has taught him to give up on the mistakes early. The bad trades tend to get worse if the position isn't cut quickly. He describes a gut feeling when he thinks the trade could be expensive, and will reverse a trade quickly if it starts to turn sour in his stomach. It's difficult to place a finger on the exact cause; he says trading experience gives him a feel for when trades look right technically but feel wrong psychologically. 'You can be right on the technical points most of the time but if you don't have good money management it can be very costly.'

Locke makes a point of stressing that investors shouldn't confuse careful money management with taking less risk. It is, instead, about balancing the amount traded with the risk at hand. In fact Locke describes himself as an active risk-taker, and says in terms of risk and reward investors can not help taking on large risks if they want to make money. He will build up holdings when position trading, each time testing the idea before venturing another stake. In this way he loses less if the timing is too early or the idea is flawed.

Locke says new investors, particularly those using technical analysis to call markets, must put cash into the market to understand if their system works. Many books for new investors suggest building a model portfolio and running it alongside the market to see whether it is profitable. But he questions the value of any analysis that isn't tested in real trading conditions. He says the process doesn't come close enough to the emotional connection of investors having their own money at risk. He describes his own journey through charts as a process of trial and error where plenty of money was lost along the way. He believes that losing money makes investors spot mistakes and deal with them early, and hopefully teaches them how to prevent such mistakes from happening again. A little money at risk at the beginning also teaches new investors how they respond emotionally, and whether they are cut out for short-term trading or are better suited temperamentally to a system of longer-term position trading.

SOYBEAN, CORN AND COFFEE

Locke's 'real' job is in the soft commodities market as an introducing broker in the Soybean business. His role is to act as intermediary for clients, either buying or selling for a customer, or perhaps swapping contracts for cash. He is constantly checking on contract prices on the Chicago Board of Trade where Soybeans are traded, relaying his chart analysis back to clients and giving advice on the market's tone and direction. It's a high volume low commission business, so Locke cannot afford to make mistakes where he takes positions on his own account.

Mostly his work is simply to act as broker between the growers and the end-users. Several large farmers in Brazil come to him to sell their produce and Locke will transact their business with the buyers on the Chicago commodities exchange. His risk on these occasions is that a party to the transaction will default on a contract leaving him to cover the business. Locke acknowledges that it is a slim risk and so far it has never happened, but he is always awake to the possibility and that is why, through his charting, he seeks constantly to understand the Soybean market and how price changes could inflict financial stress on either party.

There is no difference in his charting approach to the soybeans or financials. By definition, since his work is technical he should be able to find all the information he needs to trade from the chart. The greatest advantage he brings from the commodities side of his trading is a neutral attitude to being short or long the market. In most investors there is a natural psychological inclination to buy the market, which leaves them unable to respond when prices are falling. Locke's background means that he had an early primer in futures trading which is a vital part of the commodities business, and is almost more inclined to sell than buy. 'Commodities traders get their brains reprogrammed to make them look at a market going down as easily as they would a market going up.'

Locke personally finds it easier to make money in bear markets. He says that traders willing to play on the short side need to be alert, particularly to the ends of bull markets and the beginning of bears, where the greatest money is to be made. The problem for most investors, says Locke, is that bear markets tend to come very quickly. When they start to think about shorting the market, half of the move may already have unfolded.

GOLD

As a commodity market specialist Locke has watched gold while other investors allowed the precious metal to drop off the radar screen. Having witnessed its value in periods of both high inflation or market distress, Locke has never written off gold's value as a non-paper store of wealth or an asset perceived as secure in troubled times.

He is bullish on the long-term story for gold and believes technically it could revisit the $800 an ounce level. But there are some caveats. He thinks the ride will be turbulent and the metal must make a convincing high above $400 an ounce by the

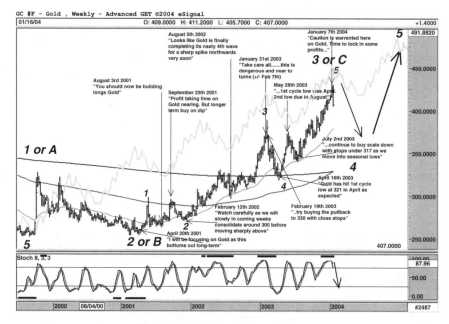

Figure 5.7 Long-term story for gold.
Source: eSignal. www.esignal.com

end of 2004 to confirm the longer-term trend. The US dollar remains important to this story; if it continues to weaken, gold will benefit.

On the downside he sees $327 as an important level. Any breach of that he believes will mark the end of the bull run for gold, with the metal falling back to $250 an ounce. It should be noted that while Locke is a bull on the long-term picture he was shorting the metal at its 2003 highs (Figure 5.7).

OUTLOOK

Locke sees the resurgence in commodity prices continuing for some years. In January 2004, he was starting to spend more time charting copper. He is looking for higher highs through 2004. He sees Coffee as a commodity to watch, and has made corn his play for 2004.

PLANETARY DATES

There are a number of upcoming dates for the remainder of 2004 which Locke believes may have market relevance based on his planetary work. (Further dates are given in Appendix V.)

2004:   02/10/2004   11/10/2004   14/12/2004

GOING PUBLIC

Locke is currently based in the town of Eindhoven in the Netherlands – a country he has made his home since 1985. When we discussed this book he was trading and writing his technical analysis from an office in his home on a quiet street in a suburb of the Dutch town. Locke likes the environment and finds the Dutch have a more relaxed outlook on life than the British or the Americans. It is certainly not for the income tax, he jokes, which used to be 62%. Locke also has a young son in the Netherlands, and he is happy to stay in the country while the boy grows up.

Of average height and heavy build, Locke has a rounded face that flicks swiftly from furrowed brow to beaming smile. He smiles often. In conversation he is self-depreciating, shaking his head at missed opportunities. His hair has thinned at the front showing a lot of tanned forehead; the rest he has closely shaved. He has a thoughtful, almost hesitant manner of speech, pausing briefly before answering questions.

Locke was born in North London and did most of his growing up on the East Coast in Southend on Sea during what he describes as a fairly average middle-class upbringing. His father worked as an export manager for Kleinwort Benson, and Locke junior was expected to follow a well-trodden path from school to University. The 1970s had just started and, ready for a steady three years spent studying Classics and Ancient Greek, Locke was packed off to King's College London.

If he hadn't already displayed the contrarian streak set to become a feature of his market analysis, his parents and the University were just about to discover its existence. A year and a half into the degree course Locke dropped out. He was 19 years old and in love with a Turkish girl he had met in London. The pair left the city for Istanbul and were quickly married. On returning to London in 1973 Locke needed to find work.

He took a job in the back office with stock-jobbing firm Medwin & Lowy. At the time the jobbers had an important position handling the transactions between brokers, and all the shares traded in London went through their books. He was paid £22.50 a week to enter the trades by hand in a large ledger. The firm concentrated on foreign stock, from companies in the US and the Far East. But the timing was poor for these markets, Locke describes those trading days as a disaster. The smart money was going into commodities where the markets were bursting through new highs. He thought he ought to be following the smart money into commodities as well.

In 1976, encouraged by friends who were earning big bonuses, Locke left the world of stocks and shares for a small commodity trading company called DB Mack. It was the owner, Donald Mack, who introduced him to charts. The tools were basic technical analysis and Mack showed him how the patterns for metals and soft commodities could be used to predict future price movements. Locke describes it as good old-fashioned Edwards and Magee style charting. He also remembers the company having a few notable clients at the time, among them Stuart Wheeler who would later make millions founding spread betting firm IG Index, and make headlines donating money to the Conservative party.

Unfortunately, Locke came late to the party for commodity markets. By 1976 the final stages of the great 1970s bull market for commodities was playing itself out. He remains grateful to this day for the grounding in basic Technical Analysis he received from Donald Mack. But as the bull market for commodities started to turn sour, it seemed again to be the right time to move. Locke took the experience he had gained and began trading for himself.

Life continued in that vein for some years until, in 1985, with the end of his first marriage Locke moved to the Netherlands and took up a position in the commodities business of Prudential Bache in Rotterdam. He has stayed in the Netherlands ever since, leaving Prudential Bache to start his own company Oystercatcher Management. He has worked as a trader and broker in the soybean market ever since.

Locke would likely have remained unknown to most people outside of the soybean industry but for his desire to convey his concerns about the coming turn in the late 1990s bull market. Locke is a private man and considers carefully what personal information to reveal. His nascent public profile has surprised no one more than himself. He agonises over the comments he should make to a larger audience, concerned that others might lose money following his research.

FUNDAMENTAL VIEW

Is the fundamental view relevant for a technical analyst? Locke does have a view but tries not to let it influence his chart work. He finds it difficult to be positive on the outlook for the US economy and was concerned about the valuations of US stocks throughout 2003. Arguably his downbeat assessment of medium-term prospects for the US affected his charting through the second half of that year. Locke describes this in his commentaries, underestimating the liquidity pumping that was going on in the US.

Locke subscribes to the school of thought that sees moral hazard in the historically low level of interest rates. He sees only the dangers inherent in trying to reinflate the US economy by encouraging credit expansion. The falling dollar, rising commodity prices and the behaviour of gold, all clearly charted in his wave patterns, gave him cause to be concerned about the equity market outlook over the next few years. He thinks Japanese stocks may offer some safety, where the market has already witnessed a major correction in prices.

Locke suspects that the commodity markets are ultimately correctly signalling a pick-up in inflation in Western economies. His expectation is for real interest rates in the US to rise through 2004, and the government bond markets to go into a greater bear market.

WORK IN PROGRESS

Locke remains troubled by the periods when the analysis has broken down. The summer of 2003 was a difficult experience where he continued to chart a collapse in the bullish trend that never came. Neither his Elliott Wave count nor the Spiral Calendar dates that indicated the need for caution were able to predict the positive trend. Locke had a series of cycle turns due from 6 June through to 29 July, a date he had publicised as marking a significant event for the market. There was no dramatic event on that day, but Locke believes the influence of the cycles was felt turning the S&P flat from the 1015 intra-day high on 18 June into the 6 August lows of 967.

> 'I was out of my shorts from 900 to 950, but the market held the support that was previously the resistance. The sign should have been there for me. Momentum on this run continued to decrease all the way from the June highs. I remained bearish and missed the run up.'

At the time of writing Locke was still long-term bearish on his Elliott Wave count for the US equity markets.

He is doing a lot of research work on inversions of cycles. Locke is frustrated by not being able to clearly decipher whether a turn will invert or not in all periods. He charts these inversions to identify approaching high or low points. He says the inversions happen at a specific time in one particular group of Moon cycles that he follows. He wonders whether it might be caused by non-human trading by a mechanical programme or automatic index funds. He has set himself the task of finding the answer.

Chart work now consumes every waking hour of Locke's life. Even though he works from home and has some flexibility about when he starts his day, he is up early when most people are still sleeping and tends to run long hours. When he is not working on his forecasts he is on the phone to soybean clients, or discussing cycles or wave counts with groups of investors also interested in the astral side of his work. Locke readily admits that he has no hobbies beyond his work and considers reading fiction books a 'waste of time'.

His current study is taking him further away from conventional financial market analysis. Much of this research would be considered esoteric by other technical practitioners, but Locke is undaunted as he has never been greatly influenced by conventional thinking.

Apart from Carolan's work and Locke's own analysis, what else is there to read on the subject? He points me in the direction of 'Trading Chaos', a book by Bill Williams that seeks to explain the markets and the psychology of the markets through non-linearity and chaos theory. Locke suggests as much work by W.D. Gann as it is possible to lay hands on, particularly *Tunnel through the Air* and any work on Gann's Pythagorean square of nine trading tools.

Finally, for the very keen, Locke says that Brad Cowan has a lot of wisdom in his *Four Dimensional Stock Market Structures and Cycles*. Cowan describes how markets move across four dimensions tracing out four-dimensional shapes like a cube or tetrahedron. Locke says the concept is rewarding but does take some work. 'Not for the faint of heart. This book will not be understood the first time around. Persevere. The more times read the clearer it becomes. It opens up the mind to a higher plain of understanding the markets.'

6
Richard Cunningham: Leveraging Up

'Not every trading strategy is successful. In fact, a truism that every trader must confront is that many of the decisions made will be wrong – a large percentage of trades lose money. Risk guidelines act to limit losses by protecting against serious errors in judgement and unexpected market moves.'

Take small bets and trade frequently. Run the stops tight and hold no trade for longer than two weeks. Preferably take an intra-day position and close out before the end of the day, particularly where the stake is two to five times geared. This is the sharp-witted world of the derivatives market and these are some of the basic principles employed by technical analyst and asset management company CEO, Richard Cunningham.

The 33 year old has taken an education in relatively new leveraged products like individual stock futures, exchange traded options and Contracts for Difference (CFDs), and turned it into a money management business. These are early days for Cunningham, his company only became fully licensed in 2001, but in the first year of operation he grew revenues by 170% and doubled the amount of client cash he was running. At the start of 2004, Cunningham Asset Management (CAM) had around $54 million of client money under management, the lion's share of that in the company's Managed Futures Program.

The business operates five managed programs. Two are systematic program trading services which issue automatic buy and sell orders, the other three offer global forex exposure, managed futures and a global macro program. All buy and sell what are commonly known as alternative investment instruments, or derivatives. Typically, leverage is applied across some of the trades, depending on the client's appetite for risk.

Unlike mutual funds, which are pooled investments, Cunningham's clients keep their money in their own brokerage accounts. They sign over permission for his traders to draw on their funds to take positions on their behalf. It is a system of money management more common in the US than in Europe where the traditional Unit Trust model still dominates. For Cunningham the benefit is the greatly reduced cost of administration compared with running a mutual fund business.

Where traditional Unit Trusts predominantly rely on equity markets that are constantly rising, Cunningham is happy to make money on both sides of the market. This is a business that thrives on volatility. Through the latter part of 2003 as equity market volatility declined on Western exchanges, the opposite happened in the currency markets. Cunningham was happy to play the volatility, and makes the point that investors over-exposed in equities could benefit from looking at currency opportunities. It is a market he says that offers some risk advantages where diversification is required. Currency markets are not directly correlated with stock markets.

Trading the short-term derivatives story is not for everyone. But, says Cunningham, after the 2000–2003 bear market there is strong anecdotal evidence that leveraged products are attracting money that would have found its way into stocks. That appears to be driven by two forces: a disappointment with the size of declines in equity markets and a reappraisal of risk, and the desire to generate higher returns than might be expected normally from equity markets.

MAKING TRADES

Cunningham is a trader at heart. His art comes in interpreting technical chart formations and then implementing a trading strategy to take advantage of those patterns. The decline in the dollar has been a dominant theme in the global FX program he offers to clients. The program trades G10 currencies using a large input from technical analysis of both chart patterns and momentum. Its objective is to capture currency trends as they develop over a medium-term time-frame. Typically, the manager will follow technical signals to enter a trade and then reduce positions quickly if the analysis suggests that the trend is reaching exhaustion, or is losing its consistency – in itself a sign that the trend may be failing.

Most of the programs are built on a technical approach to the markets. There is some concession to fundamental factors within the Global Forex Program. For instance, in the case of the dollar Cunningham has had to follow the bigger story of the state of the economy which is perceived as being key to the dollar's direction. Through the best part of 2003 several issues dominated the markets thinking about the US currency. These were: the widening budget deficit, widening current account deficit, falling and low real interest rate yields and slowing GDP. Additionally, certain other Western economies have seen interest rates held relatively steady and, more recently, beginning to rise. That means that the yield spread between the US dollar and the currencies of these other economies has been widening. Cunningham says there are some straightforward conclusions that can be draw from this information which provide a background to the trading.

> 'At its simplest, there are at least 4 reasons NOT to own US dollars and at least one good reason to hold sterling, euros, or, Aussie and New Zealand dollars. Additionally, in spite of the Federal Reserve's rhetoric regarding a strong US dollar policy, it has been generally accepted that the Fed's real agenda has been to facilitate an orderly decline in the buck to help kick-start an export led recovery.'

How do those arguments get turned into an effective trading or investment strategy? Many market participants may anticipate a longer term adjustment in the US dollar, but capitalising on the event (assuming the assumptions are correct) requires a further step. That, in Cunningham's opinion, is an understanding of how the story may play out in the market technically. The obvious response to the pressures on the dollar would be to establish a short position on the dollar versus, say, the euro; but if, on that day, the US dollar starts to rise, the position must be closed because the loss may quickly become unacceptable. Timing is everything, and that is where the technical patterns offer some answers.

Technical analysis covers a range of styles and levels of complexity. Cunningham prefers not to over-analyse the charts, arguing that the addition of tools can obscure the trend rather than make it clearer. 'From our own experience, the danger is that by looking at too many varying inputs such as Bollinger Bands, MACD, Price Oscillators, Relative Strength Indicators and Stochastics, it is all too easy to cloud rather than clarify the outlook.' He says he is happy to evaluate new technical tools as they emerge but on balance there are several simple criteria he uses to detect the trend and time trade entry points. What follows is a step-by-step account of the process Cunningham used for timing a EUR/USD trade.

Figure 6.1 shows the EUR/USD on a daily time horizon. Each bar represents one day of price action.

1.   The first step is to establish the primary trend. Typically, Cunningham says they are looking for at least six months of price action to determine the major trend. Figure 6.1 indicates that the trend is up for the euro.
2.   The next step is to determine the medium (several weeks to 6 months) and short-term trend, or minor trend. In the figure the medium-term trend is still up; the minor trend looks mixed but is beginning to turn positive.
3.   Reviewing the evidence: the fundamentals are in favour of the euro and the three key trends are all positive.
4.   Cunningham places significance on the positioning of the Moving Averages (shown on Figure 6.1). In his consideration, the most important is the slowest Moving Average (MA). The one shown is the 200-day, but he says this is not

Figure 6.1   EUR/USD 27 November 2003.
Source: eSignal. www.esignal.com

necessarily the most appropriate. Depending on the time-frame and the asset, other MAs like the 100-day or 50-day may be considered.

5.   Faster MAs like the 15 and 30 day (shown on the figure) can be used to give clues as to the imminent direction for the market. When the fastest is above the slowest and the inclines are all positive, or pointing upwards in this case, Cunningham says the market is beginning to trend-up, rather than just being in an up-trend, This is an important distinction because trading into a turning trend offers the best opportunity to realise high risk-adjusted returns. In other words, these are the favoured conditions for getting the best return for the least amount of risk.

6.   Everything is looking good for a rewarding trade. But, says Cunningham, there is one more stage to consider. The chart patterns or formations. Over time, certain price patterns repeat and can add to the identification of a positive trade. The analyst's art comes in recognising a true pattern over a false one. There are many complicated formations that excite technical analysts, but Cunningham likes to stick to those that are simple and have proved consistently effective.

'One of the most repetitive and reliable basic patterns is the "double-top". This is exactly as it sounds – the market rallies to a recent new high and then backs off. Several days/weeks later the market rises again to approximately the very same level and then falls off once more. However, the retracement this time is much more material and can even represent the very beginning of a reversal in the prior trend. Therefore, the market is always extremely cautious when prices rise to previous peaks and the inability for the price to move materially higher through such a plateau may be used effectively as a signal to close out positions and await for evidence of another 'assault' and penetration above that ceiling. (Please note that exactly the inverse applies for "double- bottoms".)'

7.   The trend has been charted, the omens are positive and a trade is entered with protective stop-losses.

What if the pattern doesn't confirm the hoped for signs of a new trend? Does the trade get done if any elements are missing? Cunningham says that traders must be patient. He stresses that no trader should be afraid of being out of the market. Under-trading is a virtue, not a flaw. And, he says, traders should also be prepared to buy at a higher level than the exit price of the last position. Psychologically, novice traders can find that an uncomfortable experience, feeling regret that they have missed the move to the higher price.

'It is not a crime to buy at a level higher than you had previously exited the last trade. For example, if and when that double-top is broken and the other inputs justify, it makes a whole lot more sense to buy at a new contract high than to bottom fish. The market is telling you that it wants to move on up, so enjoy the ride. But until it does so stay – away.'

TRADING RULES

Minimising risk dominates Cunningham's investments. Where the contracts he trades in are inherently risky, the use of close stop-loss positions and careful money management protects investors. Regardless of whether the charts or technicals indicate a turn in a trend that would make a losing trade profitable, he will not add to a losing position. He says that chasing losing positions in the hope of buying cheaply before a turn is a sign of hope over experience. 'Not every trading strategy is successful. In fact, a truism that every trader must confront is that many of the decisions made will be wrong – a large percentage of trades lose money. Risk guidelines act to limit losses by protecting against serious errors in judgement and unexpected market moves.'

What marks the best traders out is how they deal with the losing positions. The danger is that one position may be allowed to disproportionately damage the portfolio. Cunningham says that it is easy to get over-confident about a trade and have too much exposure in it. 'Certainly, the losers are what keeps you in check and what keeps the score. I guess from my own experience, from earlier on, the importance of consistent position sizing is a critical lesson learnt to avoid sustaining intolerable loss on a portfolio.' If there is any doubt in Cunningham's mind about the success of a trade, he would rather not open a position than have to subsequently manage an exit.

Cunningham uses a gradual approach in building positions when there is confirmation that a trade is working. The technique minimises the risk of significant losses if the trade turns negative. Even if the technical information and fundamental evidence suggest a positive outcome he wants to make sure that the realisation of a loss will never be too great to digest. 'The key to the rationale is that NOBODY knows when establishing a position whether it will be profitable or not.'

In the case of the dollar, Cunningham worked the theme of dollar weakness from several angles. It is a technique that he uses where one currency is clearly weakening across a range of G10 currencies. After initial gains running a position in EUR/USD he expands the positions out into GBP/USD and maybe also AUD/USD, etc. A number of other currencies are bought against the dollar to exploit the trend. Playing the theme across other currencies also brings the benefit of diversification of risk. The adding of GBP/USD and AUD/USD positions will obviously increase the risk by raising the amount of capital in the portfolio exposed. The useful effect is to reduce the concentration of that risk by diversifying the trade instead of just taking a larger EUR/USD. Again, stop-losses are simultaneously nominated. These mean that the portfolio can be assessed from a 'what if' scenario. If the market turns the opposite way and the stop-losses are taken out, Cunningham knows in advance what the impact will be to the portfolio. He can therefore ensure that he stays within stated risk-parameters.

As time develops, further positions may be added in equal unit sizes, and the stop-losses adjusted when warranted to reduce overall risk to the portfolio. Cunningham says that the ideal scenario arrives when the portfolio is effectively fully positioned and the risk against the stop-losses would actually result in an overall profit to the portfolio, if those stops were taken out. So, the positions may be liquidated when the market finally changes direction, and this liquidation may well result in a profit. Cunningham can choose by using technical analysis whether those same positions may be exited individually or in their entirety when indicators dictate. In this event, he says, it is time to step back and re-evaluate for signs of the next move – which may or may not be in the same direction as previously.

Cunningham does not add any gearing to currency positions. If the market continues to trend he will raise exposure further, but is always mindful of the potential loss to the portfolio if events suddenly turn against those positions. He says it is not necessary or advisable to leverage aggressively in currencies – if the market is trending, a small position can be maintained for longer with a less restrictive stop-loss level.

In Cunningham's other trading programs the attraction for many clients is the addition of leverage. He trades CFDs in the UK both long and short. The leverage may be anywhere between two to five times the amount ventured. Obviously this means that the investor is allowed to control a large position for a relatively small deposit, but that also gears up the potential profit and loss. In CFDs the trading time horizon is quite short term, from intra-day to two to three weeks. The aim is to capture momentum movements in headline stocks which are highly liquid. The risk discipline means that position sizes are limited per stock and positions are cut swiftly. Often if the trade doesn't work as anticipated the position maybe closed at break-even or at a small loss.

CFDs like currencies have a better risk/reward profile where there are clear market trends. In choppy market conditions Cunningham says that traders must watch stop-loss positions carefully and actively cut poor trades. Quite often he will trade the CFD market by looking at relative relationships between stocks, taking a long position in one versus a short position in another; for instance, Barclays versus Standard Chartered. The strategy would be considered 'market neutral' but, as he points out, the actual risk in such a trade is higher than just holding a single long position. This is because the potential loss on a short position is always unlimited. This is not territory for the inexperienced investor and Cunningham says they bespoke their service depending on the risk tolerance of the clients.

STOP-LOSS

Cunningham says derivatives contracts traded in the way he manages them are no more risky that stocks. Because of the awareness that the instruments can be more explosive if not treated with respect, there is a greater focus on risk. He points out that equity investors that lost money through 2000–2003 would have been saved from those losses by running trading stops on all positions. He says the key to running alternative portfolios is building protection into the trades.

As a matter of policy Cunningham enters stop-loss positions on all trades, on all products. The position of the stop tends to be determined by assessment of the market's expectation of what the contract will do and the technical indicators of the size of a move. In most cases the policy is not to put the stop any greater than 6% of the opening transaction price. If the trade is working the stop-loss level will be trailed behind the price. Regardless of fears about the risk of being stopped out and missing a gain, he will not reposition a stop-loss further away from the initial entry point. If the original stop-loss was the correct strategy before the trade was opened, Cunningham will not change it.

There are strict money management rules that he observes to protect investments. Beyond the trade selection there is a big focus on the size of the original position. Some experienced traders argue that this aspect of trading is more important than the actual decisions of what and where to buy and sell. Cunningham takes this part of the trade very seriously. 'What differentiates a gambler and a process-driven money manager or trader is measured money management techniques. For example, within the CAM Global Forex Program, there is a very deliberate definition of a trading unit – or size of each position taken – *before* any positions are established. This is a constant criteria. The only justification for materially changing positions sizes, in my view, is to do with material changes in market volatility – or because of an appreciating/ depreciating portfolio value.'

This establishes the worst case scenario risk to the portfolio. Cunningham repeats the point that no trader can know whether a trade will prove profitable despite their confidence in the analysis. But by putting in place predetermined stop-loss positions he has an instant assessment of what the potential loss to the portfolio will be if the trade turns out to be ill-judged or ill-timed.

'Then, if we are proven wrong, the loss to the portfolio is highly tolerable (typically between 0.2 and 0.5%). This scenario may repeat itself, particularly in markets which become volatile, but even in this event a series of as many as 4 or 5 losers in a row would represent a loss or drawdown on the portfolio of between 0.8 and 2%. This is highly manageable – although it does need to be conceded that if enough losing trades were sustained one after the other the overall loss would eventually become untenable – but it would evolve gradually, over a prolonged period of time.'

Cunningham implements this discipline across the range of different markets he trades in. For instance, in the case of share CFDs the percentage loss permissible on any individual position should be no greater than 7% of the value of that share. The volatility of the market is used to determine the size of positions taken. In periods of extreme market volatility, Cunningham is careful to monitor position sizes to adhere to the stated guidelines on acceptable losses. Again, he stresses that with these risk controls in place there is no reason why the use of derivative instruments should be any more dangerous to financial health than buying stocks.

TECHNICAL ANALYSIS

Cunningham uses technical analysis throughout his investment process. He has no background in traditional fund management and the nature of the products he trades is most suited to a technical approach. He does take note of the fundamental and geopolitical drivers for markets but is less interested in the issues than in the way markets react to them. He doesn't care about the news-flow, but more about the market's reaction to it. If the market doesn't react negatively to bad news, that conveys useful information about market sentiment. It may indicate a positive change in investor perceptions or expectations about the future.

Cunningham writes research pieces for traders, money managers, corporate treasury departments and banks about 10 times a month. Sometimes the analysis will be pure commentary, describing the way the market is unfolding. If he can't see an obvious trend he is conscious of not trying to force one to satisfy paying customers. Other times, if he sees a trading opportunity, he will urge the clients to get into a certain trade before the window of opportunity closes. He provides a technical evaluation as he sees it, but expects the users to have their own sources of fundamental analysis with which to cross-check his views.

The key to using charts, he says, is in letting the price patterns reveal themselves. His tip for amateur chart readers is to stand back and wait for the trends to show themselves, and looking too hard may lead to finding a pattern that isn't really there. When he is troubled by the conclusions he has draw from a pattern he will flip the paper over and look at it from the other side to see whether it validates his view, or casts more doubt.

'Don't over-analyse the chart. Charts are a reference point and they work some times better than others. Charts are about artistry, one man's retracement is another man's trend line. Just using the price line can be self-fulfilling or self-defeating, depending on the environment. The trend should be obvious.'

The charts he says are an emotional barometer of market behaviour. History repeats itself, and the chart patterns are a reflection of a cycle of investor behaviour. Higher highs are achieved because investors that missed out yesterday are buying the market today. When lower lows are taking the price south, that reflects the last worried investor leaving the trade.

Cunningham says that all serious market participants look at the charts and are working off the same data. That in itself should command caution when it comes to trading off a pattern. The greatest risk comes in buying a break-out too early and finding it is a false break that retraces taking investors money in the process. Other inputs like volume and momentum must be used in conjunction with the price pattern to confirm the break-out. A good way that is also used by the professionals to cross-check sentiment is to look at traders' reports in the derivative markets. For instance, the Put/Call ratio in the options market shows how optimistic or pessimistic options traders may feel. A word to the wise for new investors, the results are often used for contrarian market timing on the basis that options traders are not very good judges of market turns.

BACKGROUND

Cunningham operates his business in a building deep in the Surrey countryside. The converted house shares the site with a company that mints commemorative coins, and is run by his wife. A discrete white-painted sign on the building indicates the offices of CAMplc, but there is little beyond that to describe the nature of the business being conducted inside. Forget the brass nameplates, glass and chrome receptions, or the surly security desks of city of London-based financial institutions. This is money management carried out with a close eye on cost overheads. 'So many hedge funds want an office in Mayfair and a room full of Bloomberg terminals. You could easily throw a million pounds at a new boutique investment business, but that is not what we are doing. We have none of the excesses of the asset management industry.'

Cunningham's attitude reflects a business more concerned about trading the markets than what clients think of the décor. Inside the building the colour scheme is simple; everything is white. Big windows let in plenty of light, which reflects off the white-painted walls and ceiling, giving a slightly stark feel. The small staff of eight work from a single, large room on the ground floor. The office is set up as a mini-dealing room, equipped with several television sets permanently tuned to news and business channels. The traders have their own positions at desks crowded with computer screens continually updating with live market data. Any remaining space is taken by telephones, research papers or the clutter of pen holders and business card files typical of any office. Like all busy trading areas, the room is untidy and has few concessions to comfort. There is a water dispenser in one corner, but the traders have to make their own coffee and tea in a kitchen in a neighbouring room.

Cunningham moves between the desks in a blue shirt and light grey suit, checking on positions or discussing the latest market news. He always wears a shirt and tie, and most of the traders are similarly dressed in business attire, although one or two have dispensed with ties. He looks strikingly younger than his early thirties would suggest. He has a boyish oval face topped with a neat cut of light brown hair. The sides are short over the ears and the front combed back away from the forehead. It is a conservative, straightforward look. He is a little under average height and that adds to the impression of youth. The atmosphere in the office is easy-going, but there is the same underlying twitchiness that marks out trading rooms the world over. Conversations are punctuated with quick glances at screens, someone is always on a phone, and there is invariably another one ringing. The restless energy waits for a news story, or an economic data release that may galvanise the room into a flurry of action. As short-term trend traders, his team are particularly focused on exploiting events or stories that could cause a turn in the market direction.

Cunningham dropped out of Reading University just seven months into an economics degree. Disenchanted with the slow pace of learning he was hungry to start earning a wage; as he describes it, he felt he was wasting time with the academic work. A spell working for Robert Maxwell followed selling advertising space. It taught Cunningham some useful skills about presentation and selling but he couldn't see a career in it. He also couldn't see how it was going to make him too much money, the reason he had given up his university education. Fortunately friends and family that had connections with the financial industry suggested he take a look at an area of the market that seemed to be growing quickly: derivatives.

He got his break with Tullet and Tokyo in 1992. The company was and still is active in the currency markets and took him on as a trainee institutional broker. Cunningham enjoyed his time there and found the stimulation that had been lacking in his degree course. 'It was a really good place to learn about the industry. It was well paid, and a colourful place to work.' After a spell in equity options, he was transferred to the floor of the London Futures Exchange (LIFFE) where he managed the UK interest rate division of the company's London operations. He took his experience to Refco Overseas in 1997 and helped to establish a European interest rate business that dealt primarily with investment banks and hedge funds.

Cunningham was making good money and doing plenty of business at Refco but he was also aware that changes were afoot in the small investor market. The internet was providing a painless way into the derivatives market for the retail investor. 'Up until that point it wasn't so common to find people trading on a margin or trading a futures account, but there was this growing interest in the retail market. Before that it had been a wholesale institutional business.' In 2000 he left the LIFFE floor to co-found a new company which aimed to offer products to this growing band of speculators.

As Dealing Director at Halewood International Futures he would advise retail and institutional clients on trading and risk. His particular area of focus was on equity CFDs.

The new companies offering CFDs and Spread-Betting services were surprised to find that the equity bear market was doing little to put off customers. In fact, dissatisfaction with equity brokers and traditional stock investments was pushing the more ambitious investors to look at the new derivative products on offer. What they found were instruments, unlike stocks, on which they didn't have to pay UK stamp duty. They could also gear up their bets to take a position perhaps 10 times bigger than would be possible with stocks.

Cunningham figured that if he could start a business once with colleagues, he could do it again on his own. Late in 2001 CAMplc officially opened its doors to clients with a staff of three. With a conservative business plan and just £70 000 in set-up capital he was ready to deal. 'People think I am young to have started a business like this, but, like trading, you can't be scared of losing money or failing. If you avoid risk, what you've got is all you'll ever have. It is an attitude of mind, you have to take a risk to go somewhere.'

TRADING WITHOUT EMOTION

Two of the managed programs Cunningham offers are 100% systematic. The programs are designed to throw out a buy or sell signal which is then executed regardless of external factors like the traders' concern about market conditions. In simple terms they operate by monitoring stock index price levels. When these prices reach predetermined targets the program carries out a trade. The programs are written to operate strictly on price information. For instance, the US managed index futures system has been designed on the basis of historical data running back 17 years. The system has been back tested on the data to ensure that it performs effectively in current market conditions.

These systems take no account of fundamental information about earnings or growth prospects, they are purely technical. Although some variables, such as the level of interest rates or currencies, could be written into them, they are not. The program could be considered blind in that it doesn't register geopolitical events or changes in government policies. But fans of program trading, like Cunningham, say that is exactly what makes them attractive; they exclude extraneous noise and react to the most important variable; changes in price.

> 'Whilst it may be seen as unwise to ignore information of obvious value related to political or economic developments, the disadvantage of this approach is far outweighed by the advantage of the discipline that rigorously following the systems instills. The systems will often generate significant profits by holding on to positions for much longer than conventional wisdom would suggest.'

The programs also decide the size of the position taken and respond to the success of the trade. If the trade becomes profitable the position size is likely to increase as the program suggests adding capital. Cunningham says that in both programs trading is typically inactive, and positions may be established or exited between 5 and 35 times a year.

It is an area of the business he is concentrating on developing, convinced of the benefits of trading systems that remove the human element. 'Discipline is the biggest problem most traders have. I want to negate the emotional element as much as possible and you can do that with a purely technical trading platform.' Program trading is a growing business and has moved forward immeasurably from the 1987 crash where is was blamed for hastening the US market's decline. When placing a trade in the US there is a good chance a computer program is on the other side. The New York Stock Exchange's own data indicates regular weekly trading done by programs is 40% of the total volume transacted.

Cunningham's US Index Program, which is designed to capitalise on medium-term trends on the S&P 500 and the Russell 2000 stock indices in the US returned 20% in 2003 and just over 10% in 2002. It is in fact a blend of two programs, one that anticipates trends by watching investment flows from large institutions that can move the markets, and the other which follows trends to be long in a bull market and short in a bear market. The system translates the data it monitors into long and short mechanical trading decisions.

The Shipman Systematic Program, which is also 100% mechanical, has only run since March 2003 and had returned 16% by the end of the year. This program invests in any one, or combination of all the major benchmark stock indices. It also pursues two distinct strategies: firstly, it follows long-term trends buying strength and selling weakness based on price action, momentum and volume. It also has a short-term counter trend strategy which is sensitive to market volatility and initiates trades around the long-term holding.

The program has been designed to take account of the way markets initiate and end trends. The hardest part for any trend trader, human or machine, is to recognise when a trend has properly started and when it is about to finish. Cunningham's trader who designed the system, Mark Shipman, found that there is currently a lot of volatility at the start and finish which has the potential to damage performance. The short-term trades are meant to exploit the volatility while the long-term strategy continues to benefit from the trend.

Cunningham's enthusiasm for the systematic programs comes from having spent a decade on the London futures exchange. He has watched traders repeatedly break discipline and change their selling targets when they became emotionally tied to a trade. Neither of the mechanical systems he runs is ever overridden by a human trader. His cardinal rules on any trade are: know the downside risk; know the exit points before opening the trade; and stick to both rules. 'Any money manager or trader who enters a position without predetermined exit points goes in to get his throat cut.' His advice for novice traders is to predefine the level of monetary risk before embarking on a series of transactions. For instance, if the level is 25% of cash being invested, walk away and don't trade when the market has taken that money. 'This is the best way to avoid trading risk, just stay out of the market for a while and have a think about the system you are using. When you have changed the trading method and given it several dry runs, then think about trying it with money.' If there is any doubt at all in the mind about the value of the trading system, it is better not to trade at all.

Cunningham also has some advice for investors ready to hand over their money to someone else to trade; poor discipline shows up in a lack of consistency in returns. As a trader, and CEO that has had to hire traders, he spends a lot of time looking at past performance. He suggests that at least a good three-year track record to demonstrate the results are the product of more than an unusually lucky streak. And don't just look at the returns, spend some time on the level of risk taken on in the portfolio to achieve the performance. 'A good trader with a discretionary style can adjust to market conditions, he can understand the risk and adjust his methods. Markets may trend in bigger or smaller amounts, so you better hope your manager is going to adapt to those conditions.'

TRADING OUTLOOK

Successful investing is an amalgam of two skill sets: being able to correctly predict the direction for prices, and then understanding how to trade that knowledge. Accurate forecasting of long-term pricing anomalies is essential for fund managers operating in a six-month to two-year holding period. Cunningham doesn't go in for too much long-term crystal ball gazing. His trading time-frame is short, and the window of opportunity from which he is trying to make money is often equally short. When the pattern of trading is on intra-day moves, the long-term trend is of academic interest. It may be comforting to trade short in a long-term bear market, but that doesn't guarantee success. Cunningham's style is more focused on minute by minute technical chart moves. 'In our opinion it is a fruitless task to attempt to forecast the level of markets too far into the future as there are too many variables and unknowns. It is far better to monitor the price action and react to what it is telling you.'

He does take note of the fundamental arguments. We talked about how the macro-economic data from Western economies can create a persuasive argument for a difficult environment for equities. Concerns about GDP growth in Europe, employment growth in the US, weak consumer confidence and modest corporate spending do not lend much encouragement to higher equity prices. But, says Cunningham, 'the point is however that the data can change quite rapidly and macro issues may conspire to make equities in general look more attractive relative to say bonds or cash. So, once again, rather than getting preoccupied with "what if scenarios" we believe it is best to watch what the market is telling us – and this is best illustrated by the technicals.'

The long-term charts can provide some guidance about the current and expected market tone. While the value of the analysis decays over time from the moment the

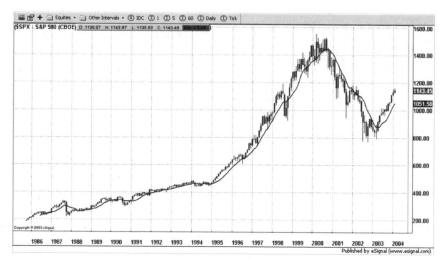

Figure 6.2   S&P 500, 1986–2004.
Source: eSignal. www.esignal.com

assessment is made, the approach is insightful and bears repeating. The chart of the
S&P 500 shows the market from 1986 to the start of 2004 (Figure 6.2). Each bar in
the chart represents one month of price action. The continuous line is a nine-month
Simple Moving Average (SMA).

Cunningham says that, based on the absolute price line, the chart indicates a market
in an up trend. The SMA can be used as a low-volatility directional indicator, and in
the chart it is trending higher so the market appears to be in at least a medium term
up trend which could continue for months or years to come.

> 'From our experience it would be impossible to look at this chart and decide
> that the longer-term picture is decidedly bearish based on empirical data. It
> is also not necessary to assume or predict that the market will go on trending
> higher – just to acknowledge that it is prudent to follow the prevailing trend
> but to be vigilant at all times of signs of an impending reversal.'

A shift to a bearish outlook based on Figure 6.2, says Cunningham, would require
a monthly close below the longer-term SMA's illustrated in the charts. A further
confirmation would come in the following month or week by the index posting a
close equal to or weaker than the previous close. He says that sustained price action
below the slower SMA would serve as a warning to lighten/liquidate long positions.
This is not the only signal he looks for to suggest a change to a more bearish trend.
Other warning signs are dynamic spikes (upthrusts) or bearish engulfing patterns
on the weekly or monthly charts. This is a graphical representation on a chart of
an explosive climax in bullish sentiment (or bearish sentiment) which effectively
represents the near-term end to a major trend.

Cunningham says that he, like most technicians, spends a lot of timing watching for the price to hit key retracement levels. The major retracement levels are 38.2%, 50 % and 61.8%. The expectation is that the markets generally find support or resistance at these levels. On that basis, the S&P could expect to see resistance at 1161 (50%) and 1254 (61.8%) on the S&P on the chart shown in this example.

IMAGINE THE MARKET

Cunningham suggests that investors who want to better understand the markets should try to visit an exchange with open outcry trading pits before they are all replaced with computers. It is the purest notion of how a market operates: a physical example of the thousands of traders seated in front of bid/offer screens around the world competing against each other. He says that traders trying to understand the way the market responds to news and trades on it should think of a how any trading pit operates. 'Watching the T-bond pit before a key US jobs report is an education in how markets react to news.'

Cunningham says that getting smarter with entry positions, and placing protective stops, comes with getting closer to the market. Recreating a mental image of the pits is a good starting point. As a former LIFFE trader Cunningham uses the image of the open outcry pits to visualise the opposition. 'On LIFFE there were three and half thousand people screaming their heads off in the pits, all trying to take the money.' He says a moment or two considering that image should make all investors or speculators focus on what they need to do to beat the market.

Cunningham also uses the image to help him to understand where other traders are positioned. Years of experience have given him an advantage over novice traders. Even without calling a bank he can make an accurate guess as to where the stop-loss positions on the trades are placed. He says the hardest parts of any trade are leaving the position when the trade is losing money, and restraining the desire to sit in a profitable trade too long. If the trader has a system they believe in, determining exit points and stop-loss positions gets a little easier with a good mental picture of what the rest of the market is doing. He makes the point that all trading is about strength of mind, and any tool that helps to sharpen the process is useful.

Part III
FUND OF FUNDS AND
THE HISTORIAN

7
Peter Toogood:
Picking the Best of the Best

'It is too easy to say the markets have bounced fifty percent let's sell them. My view is based on what I hear today and I can't agree that the future looks like a 17-year bear market. Some people may talk about that, but I don't believe it. I will get bearish on the stock market the day the greed ends.'

Peter Toogood's company is a microcosm of the revolution under way in the financial community – the migration of cash away from the traditional long-only fund management industry. His business, Forsyth Partners, has run long fund of funds since the late 1990s. They're benchmarked to an underlying index and buy the funds of the brightest and best managers in the money management world. But, like the industry at large, the model is changing, hedge funds with a total return mandate are becoming a bigger part of the business. Recent product launches have concentrated on offering a hedge fund of funds. The movement towards hedge fund products is a trend that all investors in pooled managed funds need to recognise.

The fund of funds concept has been around since the 1960s. The idea is simple enough, Toogood buys neither stocks nor bonds directly but invests in the funds of managers who do. Attitudes to fund of fund services among investors are deeply divided. Opinions vary from those who can't see the value in paying another set of fees, to those who like the idea of getting their asset allocation, fund-picking, and constant oversight of their investments all in one bundle. It is a facility that wealth managers and high-net-worth individuals would pay someone else to do anyway, if they weren't willing to devote the time to the job themselves.

What makes Toogood's fund of funds model unusual is the addition of a fund ratings product. His company provides assessments of how well managers perform, and how likely their funds are to do well in the future. It is this service that gets him through the front doors of the biggest and best asset management companies in the world, and it also means that he's on first-name terms with hundreds of the industry's smartest managers. That gives him a tremendous knowledge advantage when it comes to sorting the best fund managers from the also-rans.

The fund-rating service is the bedrock of Toogood's business and first came into existence in the UK in 1991. The start-up concentrated on assessing the strengths of funds registered offshore for UK investors. These have a slightly different legal structure to onshore UK unit trusts, but in most respects are similar. Their benefit for foreign residents in the UK and expatriate Brits is that money invested in them stays outside of the UK for tax purposes. Onshore ratings were subsequently added, but it wasn't until 1999 that the company began its own asset management business.

Among Toogood's strongest performing fund of funds are three core offshore managed funds, Forsyth Global Thematic (Euro), Forsyth Global Emerging Markets (Euro) and Forsyth Bond (US$). Annualised numbers since their inception show a healthy return against their benchmarks. Thematic has a remit to buy funds that invest in equities all around the world. Unlike a traditional geographically driven global fund, it is sector focused and has a bias towards industries and companies that are in an upswing in their business cycle. As its name implies, it may hold funds invested anywhere in the world. From opening in June 1999, the fund had annualised growth of 4% to the end of 2003 – that against its benchmark, the Morgan Stanley (MSCI) World Index, which had annualised returns of minus 5.1%. In 2003 the fund returned 14.6%.

The Forsyth Global Emerging Markets fund reflects the strong showing by Asian stock markets in 2003 and turned in 31.4% for the full year. Annualised returns since its inception in 1999 come in at 6% a year, against a flat performance for the MSCI Markets Free Index. Since it opened for business it has measured sixth of 86 funds in the same class.

The Forsyth Bond fund made 22.5% in 2003, placing it second out of 145 offshore funds invested in bond markets. Taking its annualised performance since its creation in 2001, the fund has returned 17% against 14.8% for its benchmark, the Lehman Global Aggregate Index.

Any investor should have been happy to hold these fund of funds through the last bear market. They beat their relative benchmarks and they made money. Toogood readily admits, however, that some of the company's other funds have had a more difficult time.

Across all the funds they manage, Toogood says the aggregate performance puts them around the 30th percentile, or better than 70% of all offshore funds. It is a respectable number, but he shares the frustration of investors who don't want to lose *any* money from their holdings. The difficulty is in finding a manager that can

Table 7.1 Offshore funds that lost more than the index

Index	24/3/2000–4/10/02 (bear market)	% funds worse than the index
S&P 500	−45.79%	67%
MSCI Europe (US$)	−44.10%	81%
MSCI Emerg. (US$)	−42.46%	64%
Japan TSE 1st Section	−52.22%	53%
Nikkei 225	−60.64%	13%
MSCI Japan (US$)	−50.26%	68%

Source: Micropal Offshore.

out-manouvre the bears when he is required to stay fully invested in the market. Clients pay for money to be managed, not left in deposit accounts. Unfortunately, when that means leaving it with managers that stay invested in the downturn, losses in absolute terms are the likely outcome. 'Through our research we employ the best manager ideas. The portfolios, though, are always invested – it is at the end of the day a relative and not an absolute product.'

The raw data demonstrates the problem against a range of different markets. Table 7.1 shows the percentage of offshore fund managers that lost more than the index in the bear market. Table 7.2 shows the percentage of all offshore funds that gained less than the index when the market rallied.

The numbers alone tell a powerful but depressing story. In nearly all markets over both bull and bear time-frames less than half the funds were able to beat their index. This weakness of long-funds in bull and bear market environments is stimulating a reassessment within the industry. The question the professionals are grappling with is: How does the performance gap get closed?

The market demand and the desire for performance in all markets has driven Toogood's group to add to its hedge fund of fund products. The latest offering called the Forsyth Leveraged Diversity fund is targeting 20% returns per annum. It holds a mix of hedge fund managers with the strategy of generating positive returns in both rising or falling markets. Like the industry at large, Toogood sees the trend towards

Table 7.2 Offshore funds that gained less than the index

Index	4/10/2002–30/1/04 (bear to bull)	% funds worse than the index
S&P 500	44.68%	82%
MSCI Europe (US$)	55.76%	75%
MSCI Emerg. (US$)	75.71%	65%
Japan TSE 1st Section	33.84%	51%
Nikkei 225	38.91%	74%
MSCI Japan (US$)	36.72%	66%

Source: Micropal Offshore.

the versatility that hedge funds can offer as only growing. Hedge funds are certainly no panacea but the performance of managers is drawing money into the industry. Toogood's hedge fund of funds are already gaining traction. His company currently manages about a billion US dollars across all products and he says new cash is coming in equally for the long fund of funds and the new hedge fund of funds.

While hedge funds come in many different forms, the basic idea is that they can adapt to market conditions by trading both the long and the short side of the markets. They operate on a total return basis and are able to make money regardless of market direction. Typically the more exotic the markets they invest in, the more volatile the performance. Toogood's hedge fund of funds invests in between 60 and 160 hedge funds. The diversity spreads risk and can smooth out the returns. 'It comes down to getting the best performance in an environment where stocks may not generate the best capital appreciation. We created the hedge fund products recognising that could be the best way of managing a market that could trade sideways for some time to come.'

Does this mean traditional long-only funds will wither on the vine and die as more money is attracted to hedge funds? It won't happen, says Toogood. They may have a larger role to play in the range of investment options, but will remain limited in size. He argues that their value comes from their uniqueness: they are small funds with a smart manager and a nimble investment technique. He believes that trying to scale-up those advantages destroys their value. Managers put in charge of too much money have trouble investing it. 'Hedge fund managers can operate effectively with $300 million, but when it's five or six billion the managers find it harder to pursue strategies that are focused on small cap growth stocks or global emerging markets.'

Toogood says hedge funds will also remain largely the preserve of the semi-professional investor, rather than being opened up to the general investing public. The problem is one of education. Hedge funds are able to operate with few external controls over the risk they assume or the markets in which they invest. Until the retail investor is able to understand the complicated strategies they use, they will remain off limits. Again, he says, any process that involves standardising or more tightly regulating hedge funds is in danger of destroying their inherent advantages.

Toogood believes that the long-only fund management industry is not as good at managing the markets through downturns as it should be. But, according to him, it will remain the mainstay of the business because the alternatives are weaker. He doesn't see who is going to advise the retail public about which hedge funds to buy because the financial advisers who act as the middlemen between investors and the financial industry don't have sufficiently detailed knowledge to make the decisions. Hedge funds have grabbed headlines, but the sector is also beset by fund failures and underperformers. A study by researchers at Capco in 2003 found that half of the hedge funds it studied over a 20-year period folded because of operational problems. 'I think the long world is here to stay. Hedge funds will offer more choice but will always stay marginal. Quite frankly there just isn't the talent out there to run them.'

BUY THE INDEX?

The alternative to trusting a fund manager is to buy the index of a stock market. Index tracking funds and the emergence of Exchange Traded Funds are designed for just that task. If the majority of fund managers are unable to capture the full benefit of rising markets, and don't protect portfolios when markets are falling, the index may offer an alternative. Fans of indexing point to years of evidence that the index beats most managers over the long haul, but the results benefit from careful selection of time-frames. Knowing that the index may win over 50 years is of little use to an investor with a 10- or 20-year time-frame.

Looking back, Toogood says 1998 will be seen as the peak for the long-only mutual fund industry. That year marks the topping out of a golden period for institutions where every new fund benefited from the inexorable rise in stock prices. Relatively youthful managers who had no experience of equity bear markets looked clever by buying and holding stocks, and in many cases passively tracking their benchmark index. The dilemma today for the industry, Toogood says, is that 'a generation of investors have grown up believing the way to make money is to own the small number of blue chip stocks that make up market indices like the FTSE 100, the CAC 40, or the DJIA. Indexation worked through what was an abnormal period for markets historically.'

He believes that investors and the investment community have to recognise that the index isn't always going to be the winner. While he doesn't foresee a bear market on the horizon, he believes that the market indices could see a period of sideways trade. For investors that means finding fund managers who are capable stock pickers or clever asset allocators, and this is where the best performance will be found. For the long-only fund management industry, that probably means developing new products that look like hedge funds and have an absolute return remit.

Toogood says there is a concentration of money under management taking place among the most able managers which will ultimately leave some investors out in the cold. The 2000–2003 bear market exposed how poorly most fund managers were equipped to deal with a concerted drop in stock prices. Bloodied by the experience of watching savings decimated by managers who in reality had done little but benchmark to the index, retail investors will be more discerning in the funds they buy. The process will be mirrored by institutional money-seeking absolute return mandates. His conclusion is that more money will ultimately seek out the best of breed, and a smaller number of managers will manage more money. As a result, some fund management companies that can't adapt will go out of business.

Toogood says that unless we get another long-term bull market the trend in the industry is polarisation:

> 'There will be fewer and fewer funds that will outperform the market. The good long-only funds will get bigger and that will make it harder for managers to perform, in the end they will be forced to close to new business. More star fund managers will go to the boutiques and hedge funds which only want long-term commitments from investors.'

The traditional fund management model operates like a distribution mechanism. Fees on client's funds are filtered into marketing and salaries, the managers manage the money and get well compensated for doing so. The companies require new investors to hand over their money to support the costs of marketing and to meet rising salary expectations. Toogood says investors were willing to accept this while the bull market lifted the value of everybody's funds, but the bear market has made investors more selective.

He sees a mixed outlook for the mutual fund industry. Much depends on the way it manages the challenges it now faces. Investors may find it increasingly difficult to get access to the best managers, and fund management companies will be under pressure to produce the same kind of returns as the best hedge funds and boutique asset management businesses. Currently hedge funds offer an alternative for the sophisticated investor, but lack of transparency, inconsistent performance and poor access will continue to keep most hedge funds off limits for the small investor. If Toogood's view on markets plays out then low cost index tracker funds may not offer much of an alternative either.

THE BASICS

Toogood is by instinct a value investor. If he were a stock picker he would prefer to buy on 12 times rather than 24 times earnings. But in his position he needs to wear both growth and value hats. He needs to appreciate both the absolute value of a stock and what the market is willing to pay. He hopes that is what the fund managers to whom he gives money are capable of doing. 'What we are doing is outsourcing that decision to the fund manager. He or she should be buying growth at the right price. We are dependent on them doing that, otherwise we might as well put the money in an index.'

There are three basic assumptions that underpin Toogood's ratings and fund of funds businesses.

1.   *Active managers add value.* Toogood believes some managers can consistently do better than the market. If you don't agree, Toogood says, you might as well dump money into index trackers and forget about trying to outperform the market.
2.   *Most managers do well some of the time; a few do well nearly all of the time.* It should be obvious that a fund that only invests in large-cap European stocks will struggle in a European bear market. Toogood believes that he adds value for investors by selecting the best of the best. Good managers will beat bad managers; the fund of funds advantage is in being consistently better than the average. It may not perform better than the best, but there are very few managers that have been able to perform well in both bull and bear markets
3.   *Fund of funds carry less risk than single manager funds.* Toogood says the job of a fund of funds is to diversify risk and average out returns. 'In reality they are aggregators of fund specific risk and will average-down returns. Many

clients are happy to avoid the 4th quartile box and a well constructed portfolio of funds can offset some of the single manager's risk.' The extra cost of another set of fees to a multi-manager structure should be offset by the better performance from using the best managers in each class. At least that should keep the clients out of the bottom 25% of the worst performing funds.

SELECTING FUNDS

The fund of funds manager requires different techniques to conventional fund managers. Their skill is in finding the best managers and monitoring their performance. But Toogood is also required to take a view on which assets are likely to outperform, and consequently which funds are best suited to current market conditions.

Toogood's investment process starts with a top-down analysis of the macro-economic picture. What assets does that favour? How is the market trading? For instance, does the market prefer small-cap growth companies, or large cap value. Once there is agreement on that it is a matter of using quantative tools to select the best make-up of funds. Toogood says they use a clever piece of software with an optimiser that calculates market beta, size exposure and style exposure to give the best returns for the lowest risk. It is the value investor's equivalent of bottom-up analysis to select the right funds. The aim is to buy the managers that can deliver in the current market environment.

He is basically agnostic about what asset class he puts money into. He is more concerned to pick the right asset class and the right manager for that asset class. Unlike a single fund manager who will concentrate on his own area of expertise, Toogood must have a view on cash, stocks, fixed-income products and commodities. 'I don't care whether the US market goes up, or Europe goes down. Whether the dollar or euro is higher, I just care about getting it right.'

The fund selection process is based on the research provided by the fund rating service and the interviews with managers. Toogood has his own list of factors that funds must satisfy:

1. Strength of investment process and the length of time it has been in place.
2. Continuity of investment personnel.
3. Investment style that has a proven durability over time.
4. Clearly defined investment objectives.
5. Strong and consistent risk-adjusted past performance record.

In the long managed funds Toogood operates a core and satellite model. In a portfolio of typically 20–25 funds, the core funds make up 60% of the total. The other 40% of funds are traded more frequently and are used to hunt for shorter-term opportunities. Even these funds will have had the ratings treatment before they make it into the Forsyth funds. Toogood relies on the intensive research involved in the ratings to remove the chance of any unwelcome performance surprises after the fund has been bought.

FINDING A NICHE

Toogood got into the fund rating business in 1994 when he joined up with the former Head of Fidelity Offshore, Paul Forsyth. Before that he worked as a financial adviser at UK wealth management company Holden Meehan where he experienced first hand the dilemma the new fund rating service hoped to address. Financial Advisers in the UK work with a client to find the best investments given the clients risk/reward tolerance and their short/mid/long-term goals. But the rapidly growing number of funds on offer and the paucity of good impartial screening made selecting the right funds more of a lottery than it ought to have been. Toogood recalls agonising over what products to recommend to clients and which to avoid. 'There was this universe of thousands of Unit Trusts, and you pretty much had to select them on the basis of past performance. There wasn't enough attention on changes to the mandate or the funds structure.'

Paul Forsyth spotted the opportunity when dealing with offshore investors and brokers. They knew about their own local markets but did not have the knowledge to prepare them to invest in emerging Asia or Japanese stocks. That knowledge gap made fund selection a hit-and-miss process. They wanted access to funds invested in these markets but knew little about the fund managers stock-picking style or track record. Forsyth's original concept was to help the offshore financial community to identify the best of breed among these funds, and create a working investment manual that carried updated information on their performance.

The new service set out to take an aggressive approach to weeding out funds that were poorly managed. It differentiated itself from existing fund-rating companies like Morningstar by screening out all funds not considered worthy of investor attention. For instance, when Toogood used the rating process on onshore UK funds, 2400 products were whittled down to around 250 that were considered suitable for further attention. 'That core 10% or so means that investors can ignore the other 90%. We wanted to remove the guesswork for the financial advisers, and act as the first line of due diligence.' With something like 80 000 investment funds around the world onshore and offshore, the goal is to focus on the elite selecting the best 10 or 20 managers in their particular sector.

The starting point for the new service was to identify the fund managers with the best track record in each market, then, through a process of screening and interviews, produce a qualitative measure. The idea at the time, says Toogood, was to slice up the world geographically and classify managers according to their basic approach to the task of picking stocks. 'At that point there was little concept about defining style or market cap. The plan was to go and see the fund manager every three months and find out if they were still using the same top-down or bottom-up approach they were following in the previous quarter.'

Today the scope of the fund screen has been extended to give a more detailed description of the manager's style, and the business is jointly run with Old Broad Street Research (OBSR). The manager is recognised as the lynchpin to any fund where stock selection is at their discretion. Every new manager goes through an interview to discover any style bias and the questions cut to the heart of his approach.

- Has he a natural inclination to buy small, medium or large cap stocks?
- Is he a growth or value investor?
- Does he take a top-down or bottom-up approach?
- In terms of the funds performance, has it beaten both its peers and the benchmark?
- In assessing for risk or how the fund will perform in volatile markets, how correlated to the market is the fund?

Toogood's process follows the managers through market cycles daily, weekly and monthly. They are measured for performance and the market conditions to which they are sensitive, or the changes in conditions to which they respond.

The interviews are still updated every 90 days to confirm that there has been no change in the manager's approach.

> 'We don't want anybody to be surprised by any fund they buy that has been given the Forsyth treatment. If it is described as a mid-cap growth fund and they have bought a fund that is not performing in a market that favours mid-cap growth then we have not done our job properly.'

The ratings given to the funds are designed to have a predictive quality, giving some comfort about future expected returns. The companies' own materials describe the top-rated triple AAA funds as being able to 'demonstrate very powerful investment processes and disciplines which Forsyth believes will translate into exceptional long-term performance'. There are in excess of 10 000 offshore funds, only 39 are triple AAA rated.

The ratings system, a blend of portfolio analysis and manager interviews, doesn't pull any punches. When Toogood or his researches discover changes they are unhappy about, they are not afraid to register their dissatisfaction. Below are a couple of updates taken from the January 2004 review. The customers of the service get a very clear message:

> '**Franklin Templeton Biotechnology** has been downgraded to a Forsyth–OBSR A Rating from an AA Rating. This is primarily as a result of disappointing relative performance against its peer group over a number of months and in varying market conditions. Whilst we remain confident in the team, we now feel that a Forsyth–OBSR A Rating is more appropriate.'

> '**Merrill Lynch Global Titans** has had its Forsyth–OBSR A Rating withdrawn and the fund has been removed from the Service. Performance has been disappointing for some time and, whilst we understand the reasons for this underperformance, the fund has nevertheless failed to keep up with its immediate peer group. We no longer believe the fund justifies inclusion in the Service.'

THE INTERVIEWS

The interviews give Toogood the kind of access to managers that is usually reserved for the institution's biggest clients. They can run from 30 minutes to an hour and the managers are willing to participate because they know the resulting rating can attract new money. The ratings are subsequently used by subscribers to the service to decide where they should allocate their own or their client's cash. More money for the fund means more fee revenue and ultimately, as long as returns are respectable, a bigger bonus for the fund manager.

In a typical week of appointments, Toogood can see up to 30 managers, taking their views on the state of market, their current portfolio structure, and any new ideas they may have for the coming quarter.

This is Toogood's diary for the week starting Monday, 23 February 2004. It shows the funds he will be discussing with their managers:

Monday, 23 February 2004
Gartmore CS Continental European Smaller Companies
Gartmore CS UK Fund
Henderson

Tuesday, 24 February 2004
MFS US Emerging Growth Fund
MFS American US Strategic Growth Fund
Sogelux US Large Cap Growth Equity Fund

Wednesday, 25 February 2004
Schroder European Alpha Fund
Schroder ISF European Equity AF Fund
Schroder Euro Equity Fund
Schroder WMF US Equity Fund
JP Morgan Fleming American Equity Fund
Merrill Lynch European Dynamic Growth Fund
Merrill Lynch OST European
Merrill Lynch IIF Euro Markets

Thursday, 26 February 2004
Investec European Fund
Investec GSF Continental European Equity Fund
Investec SF PAN European Fund
Investec GSF American Fund

Friday, 27 February 2004
Old Mutual UK Select Smaller Companies Trust
ISIS European and European Prime Funds
Merrill Lynch UK Blue Chip Fund

Every quarter around 1500 fund managers are questioned by Toogood or another researcher at Forsyth, asking their views on markets, stocks, interest rates, economic growth, personal plans, company and industry gossip, in fact anything that may change the way their fund is run or affect its performance. Many of the interviews are face to face if the manager is in London. Toogood also uses the telephone or video-conferencing to talk to those who are based elsewhere in the world.

The content of these interviews is incredibly valuable, says Toogood. Individual managers are usually frank about the stock ideas that haven't worked, and are honest about the prospects for their fund style, or geographic focus. At the end of the process Toogood updates a 300-word profile that describes the manager's current thinking, and his own view of the fund's performance.

CHALLENGING THE CONSENSUS

All wise asset managers are alert to the danger of the consensus view. The contrarian investor makes a point of trading against the market consensus, arguing that it has a poor record of predicting the future. In particular the history of bubbles. Whether in technology or way back to the Tulip mania of the seventeenth century, markets are littered with examples in which running with the crowd worked for a short time but the smartest money sold before the bubble burst.

The danger for Toogood in interviewing hundreds of long-only managers every week is that he only hears one view. We have already seen how badly the industry was able to forecast and capitalise on the last bull and bear markets. His inclination is to challenge a manager's opinions and take the other side of the argument. Toogood says that stress-testing a manager's views is part of constructing a rating. If the researcher is able to pick holes in the arguments for buying certain stocks or themes all the better. The process also has its benefits for the manager, who can find out whether his view is widely held or is an original piece of thinking.

BUYING EUROPE

Investing in Europe causes some difficulties for Toogood. The value added from being in a fund of funds product comes from the blending of manager styles. Some are better growth managers, some operate on lower risk, and some pursue a value strategy. There are many differences based on market cap, style of manager and trading ability. The variety allows Toogood to optimise performance and lower risk by mixing the styles. Changing market conditions may also require add him to more of one fund and reduce holdings in another. In the US markets he can find plenty of managers with different styles.

Europe, he says, doesn't give him the same opportunities. Screening the European funds proved to be a frustrating business. On beta to the market, or correlation to the index, they were all roughly the same. On cap bias, and measures of value or growth styles, they again proved similar. The results revealed that nearly all managers are all-cap and have a growth bias. Toogood puts that down to European equity markets' developing scale during a bull market, where much of the new money invested was unsophisticated and momentum driven. For him that means that buying exposure to European stocks comes down to picking the best manager in a fairly similar group. The one significant exception in the European long world, says Toogood, is Anthony Bolton at Fidelity who has focused successfully on the small and mid-cap segment of the European markets.

WHEN GOOD FUNDS DISAPPOINT

The Forsyth fund-rating process is meant to remove any elements of surprise for investors planning to put money to work in a particular fund. It recognises that most managers have an individual style better suited to some market conditions than others. Forsyth is trying to provide a consistent set of guidelines for every fund they rate to take uncertainty out of the buying process.

Toogood says that investors must be on the alert for signs that a fund or manager is starting to lose its way. The two most common reasons for funds to start under-performing are (a) the current fund manager leaves or (b) the institution moves the goalposts. 'The way funds fail is when the institution changes the ground rules. They either put more money into the fund than the manager can comfortably invest and control, or they move the mandate under which the fund operates.' The mandate is the set of principles that guide the manager's stock or bond selection. It might give the manager a relatively free hand or bind him to only investing in stocks of a certain size or type. It is the basis on which the fund is marketed and sold. Toogood says that the change in mandate can often have the most damaging impact on performance. It may be imposed at a time when a fund is underperforming in a particular market, but the mandate change may prevent any period of catch-up when the manager's original style comes back into fashion.

The technology bubble created an environment in which some institutions felt compelled to enforce mandate changes on funds they thought were not performing sufficiently strongly. The Fleming America fund managed by Jonathon Simon in the 1990s was an example of this phenomenon, but by no means the only one. Simon had demonstrated that he was a good picker of stocks and had built a reputation since the late 1980s for solid, steady performance. Toogood describes it as 'a mid-cap bias fund with strong valuation disciplines'. He says that, by valuation discipline, Simon had avoided buying into the technology story. 'It had a nominal 4% in Tech vs the index of 36%. Having been sold as a core US fund and disappointing on performance through 1999, a sector deviation was imposed on the fund and a weighting in excess of 35% was introduced in December 1999.' The fund was thus forced to raise its holdings of technology stocks.

The valuation discipline would have made the fund look like a star performer in the bear years of 2000–2003 as tech stocks imploded. But the imposed increased weighting in technology, says Toogood, changed the character of the fund and created a situation where its performance would inevitably suffer when the market became bearish on tech.

Most diligent small investors do work hard when they initially pick funds to make sure they're going to get the performance they're paying for. The problems will come later when a manager may move, or changes to the fund result in a dip in performance. Unless the investors are paying close attention, and are able to get the information they require, the decision to sell the fund may be too late. Toogood says that investors satisfied with a track record may sit back and assume that the fund will continue to wrack up the same returns year on year. That assumption can be costly.

WHEN MOST FUNDS DISAPPOINT

The rationale for paying managers to manage money is that they will do better than the index during bull markets and protect investors' cash during bear markets. Managers have the choice of selling holdings and raising cash levels when there is little available worth buying, or when the value of positions appears likely to fall. Unlike index tracking products which must, by definition, fall in line with the index, the hope is that an active manager will be proactive in avoiding risks to the portfolio. The prolonged bear market from spring 2000 to early 2003 demonstrated that very few active managers were able to beat the market.

Toogood claims that many funds are basically inactive and are the equivalent of index tracking products with the higher charges associated with actively managed funds. He saw plenty of managers who tried to chase the technology rally, but came too late to the story. Their funds had lagged the super-charged returns of the technology bubble and they broke discipline to participate in the last wave of gains. Unfortunately for many, the timing proved poor as they bought stocks at the top of historic valuations. 'Most had very strong active bets in technology very late and were hurt both by what they owned and, as importantly, what they did not own.' What they did not own were the small and mid-cap companies that had not risen during the tech rally, but that had good solid business models, were cash generators, and appeared to be undervalued by the market.

The managers that have the best record through the bear market, says Toogood, 'were not seduced into technology, and were left unhindered by their management to trade in their own styles. The true heroes maintained a valuation discipline to their process. They may have cut early in the hot sectors, but by God it paid across the whole of 2002.'

STAR MANAGERS

In Toogood's opinion, the best managers have something beyond a good stock se-lection process. It is the factor X that differentiates the stars from the body of fund managers who view beating their index as the prime concern. The stars are skilled at recognising markets, and have the best instincts of traders, sensing when to let a stock run or cut it short on small losses. As Toogood describes it: 'The best managers can price assets, assign it a target stock price and then know what the market will pay. It is a limited list!'

I asked him to select five from the thousands he has interviewed over the years as the masters of their universe. These are the managers he chose with his own brief explanation of their strengths. They have all demonstrated a long and consistent period of outperformance for their given funds.

Bill Miller – 'Combines understanding of the importance of generating free cash flow with an unnerving ability to identify the best franchises like ebay and Amazon.' [*Miller runs the Legg Mason Value Trust. He has notched up a 13-year record of beating the S&P 500. Miller runs a concentrated portfolio and likes to buy stocks that are out of favour with the market.*]

Tim Russell – 'The arch exponent of managing stocks through the business cycle and repositioning the fund accordingly.' [*Russell is at Cazenove. He runs the UK Growth and Income fund. Before that he ran a similar find at HSBC.*]

Roger Guy – 'Acknowledged by his peers as probably the best trader in the long world. Acutely market aware.' [*Guy is involved in running a range of European funds at Gartmore. He also runs the Alphagen Capella Hedge Fund.*]

Crispin Odey – 'Truly inspired asset allocator and stock picker respected by his peers. Also admired for his business building credentials.' [*Odey runs his own hedge fund company. He is mentioned elsewhere in the book as hiring Hugh Hendry, one of the Mavericks profiled.*]

Anthony Bolton – 'Acknowledged as probably the best bottom-up stock picker globally. Attention to detail a constant focus upon company management and a belief in a buck for 50 cents is the key to his success.' [*Bolton is a veteran at Fidelity and took up responsibility for the Special Situations fund from its launch in 1979.*]

A WORD ON PAST PERFORMANCE

The small print on all funds sold now carries the caveat that past performance is no guarantee of future returns. The phrase has the well-worn feel of a piece of wisdom that deserves to be taken for granted. Not necessarily so, says Toogood. He acknowledges that his own fund-rating service is about finding funds that are going to perform in the future and is not about picking yesterday's winners. But, he says, stop and think about the consistent success of the best in their field; Bill Miller may not beat the S&P for a 14th year, but with 13 already under his belt who would bet against it.

'The notion that past returns don't have any bearing on future performance is an odd one. If your manager has shown he can adapt to market conditions and perform he is probably the best bet for tomorrow. Anthony Bolton will still be Anthony Bolton, nothing has changed.'

'I'M A BUSINESSMAN FIRST'

Toogood's days tend to follow one of two patterns. During busy periods updating fund profiles and checking the validity of ratings, he will be in the city of London, pounding the pavement between fund management buildings. His diary is carefully arranged to allow as many manager interviews as possible in the time available. He has trained up enough researchers to allow him to ease back on the number of interviews he personally conducts, but I get the impression he would rather maintain this very direct source of market intelligence.

When not on the road conducting interviews he is in the firm's Croydon headquarters. Croydon is a satellite town of London and sits to the south of the British capital. It has several benefits: rents are significantly below central London prices and it is just a quick train ride into the city. It also happens to be close to the London Borough of Bromley where Toogood grew up and has spent most of his life.

As Chief Investment Officer, and a Partner, he combines the research and asset allocation roles with management responsibilities. An accountant by background, Toogood describes himself as more businessman than professional money manager. He is conservative in his attitudes to risk and credit. He is credit averse and has made a point of owning his own home outright, preferring not to pay interest on a mortgage. He also thinks that being in business comes with enough risks, and that worrying about how to pay a mortgage in a downturn is one less thing to occupy his time. The conservative money management principles came from his father, a former Director with the drinks group Bass. He instilled in Toogood a basic business acumen that drives the development of the company and the approach to fund selection.

Toogood believes that the discipline of running and owning a business gives him an edge in his discussions with fund managers. It is an insight that gives the conversations a two-way nature that might not otherwise be the case. When they talk about reasons for buying companies, and the benefits of operational gearing or leverage in the business models, Toogood can relate to the examples. He is required to apply the same tools in managing his own business.

'What most fund managers actually don't have is any experience of running a business for themselves. They're buying equity in companies, and they know the principles, but they have never made the business decisions. I actually own a company, so I know what good companies look like.'

He has been involved in running or setting up companies since leaving Exeter University with an Accounting degree in 1988. Before joining the UK financial advisers Holden Meehan in 1991, Toogood spent several years working on family business ventures in Eastern Europe. The collapse of the Berlin Wall was the catalyst for looking for new privatisation opportunities in Hungary. He was 22 years old and shuttling between Vienna and Budapest trying to put together deals in the wine and spirits market. By his own admission he had a lot of fun, but the wild west nature of some of the business being done in that part of Europe at the time was one of the reasons for returning to the UK.

Toogood is in his late thirties. Of medium height and build, he has a fleshy oval face. The cheeks are reddened from windburn, the result of days spent on the golf course. He is a keen golfer and plays off a low single-digit handicap. Golf is his main relief from the pressure of work and he plays every weekend and often several days during the week. Fund managers with whom he has a good personal relationship are likely to find themselves invited down for a game on his local course. It is a good place to swap industry gossip and share views on the broader market picture. Toogood talks quickly and often. There are few silences in his conversations, years of conducting interviews with fund managers have engendered in him a natural manner of filling gaps with questions or more of his own thoughts.

By nature he has a rather pragmatic outlook on life. His inclination is to expect disappointment, rather than positive surprises. In an off-the-cuff remark he suggested that at least that way the disappointments are gentle and the good things all the more pleasurable when they happen. Perhaps that is a reflection of years working in the fund-rating business where few managers are able to sustain outstanding performance in all market conditions. Inevitably when they do have a row of several good years, the only place to go next is down. The fund manager interviews I have been fortunate to listen-in on have the feeling of a confessional when the performance has disappointed. The manager is contrite and Toogood softens his tone and nods sympathetically. Offering a few words of comfort he places a metaphorical hand on the manager's shoulder encouraging him to do better over the next quarter.

TAKING A VIEW

Toogood buys economic research from several different independent providers. He lays out tens of thousands of pounds on the reports but believes they add another perspective to the fund manager views he gathers daily. He does get a lot of research from investment banks, but is still happy to pay non-affiliated research companies for their macro-economic reports. 'We need to be able to form our own opinions. We have to be able to show clients we have an independent view so that we can demonstrate we are managing their money with confidence.'

He also buys in independent technical analysis on the major markets. Again Toogood takes several sources, although he is sceptical about its value for much more than calling market turns.

'Beyond that, I don't believe it works in isolation of other types of analysis. We often ignore our advisers when we don't agree with their ideas. Last year was a perfect example, our technical analysts were looking for a breakdown in equity markets in the second half of 2003. I couldn't see it, so we decided not to act on their advice. Where it did work was the US equity market low in October 2002, and we were happy to follow their timing.'

Toogood calls TA an inexact science. He is more confident about the ability of the technical analysts to call the time-frame of a turn, than to call the price to which the market will rise or fall. It is one more input that he blends with the economic research and the fund manager interviews to get a market view.

THE BIG PICTURE

A note to the reader: what follows are Toogood's views expressed in January 2004. Investing is a dynamic process and inevitably some of the opinions will alter as market conditions change and the true direction of the US economy reveals itself.

On the question of whether equity markets face a further significant bear phase connected to the technology boom and bust, Toogood is sanguine. He is convinced that the world is witnessing a deflationary boom similar to the period from 1880 to 1920. Global interest rates remain low and the consequent cheap money continues to fuel a series of asset price bubbles. Emerging markets and commodities will be the main beneficiaries of the bubble money. He is a big believer in the China growth story, and thinks the timing is right for consumer demand in that country to grow. That will provide a natural market for Western cash and technology. India will also participate to a lesser extent. This is how Toogood describes the situation to his own December fund report:

'The Western world is fat and happy and the East needs capital to grow. The West will fund this growth and find itself the beneficiary of their appreciating wealth. Investment strategies must turn perceived wisdom on its head. The threat to stability in the brave new world will be Western intransigence.'

Toogood's advice at the time is to maintain a real economy focus, staying with emerging markets, commodities, selectively Japan and some Europe. He says it is a market environment where the question for investors is the risk profile they choose not the return. When I asked what funds he could recommend for a passive investor for 2004, Toogood had four recommendations:

1.   Llegg Mason US Small Cap
2.   Jo Hambro European Equity
3.   JF Eastern Smaller Companies
4.   Gartmore Latin America.

There are two risks to the story of moderate positive returns for equity markets over the next decade. In Toogood's opinion, if interest rates are hiked aggressively to combat inflation, the markets will struggle to make headway. The other threat still remains trade protectionism. The West needs to recognise that some industries may flourish and others fade in the face of new low-cost competition. The wrong response would be to impose protectionist measures to defend jobs. Beyond these threats Toogood is not pessimistic and dismisses the gloominess of the bears, saying that the deep-rooted desire of people to get rich will support the equity story over the long term.

8
David Schwartz:
Stock Market Historian

'Whichever country or index you look at, whichever century, the market always returns to its long-term trend-line. We are way above that long-term trend-line now.'

David Schwartz falls into a small coterie of investors who have developed their own completely unique system for analysing markets. A late arrival into the world of investing, he was into his early 50s before he began predicting market direction and share price movements using his homespun methods. Investors with no formal training in the financial industry have a choice: start reading and learning about decades of collected market wisdom or take a blank piece of paper and figure out for themselves why markets go up or down on any given day. Schwartz chose to see his inexperience as an advantage rather than a drawback, and with his head free of notions about stock valuations, earnings flow or balance sheet leverage, sat down and crafted a system that made sense to him.

He eschews fundamental analysis and is only moderately interested in the chart patterns that dominate the work of technical analysts. Although he describes himself as a stock market historian – a term that partially explains his methods – it is a convenience and he would be more appropriately labelled a 'market statistician'. Through the complex manipulation of decades of price data he sets out to discover which stocks, sectors or markets rise or fall in a given month or set of market conditions.

New Yorker Schwartz might have remained unknown to the world, an eccentric statistician beavering over stock tables at his home in the British Cotswolds but for some notable success with directional calls in the last few years. His 'sell' antenna forecast a sharp decline in technology shares in December 2000. As the already falling NASDAQ sat around 4000 he put on the record his view that the index would retrace to below 1500. In the event, of course, subsequent developments backed up his historical numbers which suggested that the technology market's high valuations could only be an anomaly. But what marked the call out from other analysts concerned about stretched technology stocks was the accuracy of the points decline. He clearly stated to a level that would have to be breached before the market stabilised.

In 2001, he used his statistical analysis of the behaviour of American stocks after Pearl Harbor and the outbreak of the Korean War to forecast the likely impact on the markets of the World Trade Center attack. His expectation, again correct, was that the US market would fall by about 15% and then rally. To get the number Schwartz ran through the history of daily market closes around other periods when the United States has been involved in military campaigns, or has experienced a military-related market shock. He was able to build-up a pattern of market behaviour that was again repeated after the US military invaded Iraq in 2003.

FINDING PATTERNS

He may have come late to the business of stock-picking, but it was in his first career in market research that he developed and honed the tools he uses today. In the market research field the process of cross-tabulating data is used to sift and assess preferences about products or politicians: What kind of breakfast cereal do people eat? What sex are the shoppers who choose cornflakes? How old are they? Who do they vote for? The aim is to build up enough data to show a pattern of behaviour that can be used to predict future buying decisions.

> 'I figured I could apply a standard market research analytical approach to a field where it had not been applied before – the markets. Instead of trying to find out who was voting for whom, I wanted to know whether a stock rose in a particular month and about it's relation to inflation or interest rates.'

Schwartz's first difficulty was getting hold of enough data for the UK market to make his analysis meaningful. In the US, information on the DJIA is readily available right back to its creation in 1897, but in the UK his quest for similar price data came up empty handed. After further fruitless searching he finally persuaded the FT group, which compiles the benchmark indices for the UK, to sell him data for the FT30 running back to 1935, when closing prices for the market were first systematically recorded. The arrival of the raw numbers heralded the start of months spent manipulating and squashing the figures into tables. He calls it basic mind-numbing cross-tabulation, something to do in the morning before you go into the garden for a little light pruning later in the day.

He presumed that if his theory was correct and price data from the markets could be manipulated in the same way as voting decisions, he ought to discover some statistically meaningful forecasts about future prices. He crunched bull and bear markets through daily, weekly and monthly computations, each time determining where the market sat relevant to the 5-, 10- and 30-day moving averages. He looked at whether it rose each January; if it did, on which days did it show the greatest gains or losses? Did it rise or fall in previous months? Was the primary trend for markets bullish or bearish? Were interest rates going up or coming down? The painstaking process involved analysing one variable by others over and over again for each month of the year for every year data was available. Through cross-referencing tens of thousands of small pieces of information he aimed to uncover trends or patterns that could be exploited.

Schwartz went into the process expecting to find some evidence of seasonality as it seemed to be common sense that some times of the year would be better for buying stocks than others. As a former businessman he understood the importance of economic cycles and knew that companies make more sales in certain months of the year. Did markets, he wondered, also operate in cycles, and if there was a discernible seasonal trend, would it be significant enough to base an investment decision on? The data obliged, suggesting that on an annual basis the summer months are the poorest for stock investors. It also produced the best and worst dates for market returns; according to Schwartz's numbers there is a 77% likelihood of the UK market rising on 6 June, but only a 28% chance of seeing gains on 26 September.

He describes the information as like suddenly finding a code to unlock the markets. He had come to the data with an open mind and no background in analysing stocks. Now he was building up historical records on which days and months over decades had given the best and the worst results. Schwartz's bull and bear market work had already convinced him of the merits of investing with the market trend; he could see even poor companies get swept upwards on days when the markets rise, and good companies often fall when the markets go down. Where in the past he had made the common mistake of buying at the top of the market and selling at the bottom, he could now invest with statistical conviction of getting the trend right.

Table 8.1 is an example of the data he began to build. It reflects as a percentage the likelihood that the market will rise on any of the first 10 days in January.

He felt he had created a basic investment tool. The analysis revealed the probability of the market rising or falling on any given day. If he did nothing else with the data it could at least help him to decide the days on which to invest, and how much he should put at risk. Schwartz doesn't know why certain days should be better than others; he presumes there are psychological or economic forces at work that have yet to be explained. Some periods suggest environmental answers – for example, the summer months could be poor because of the length of the days or the high average

Table 8.1   January: Profit odds summary for the month

2nd	68%	5th	58%	8th	54%
3rd	56%	6th	53%	9th	53%
4th	69%	7th	46%	10th	44%

Note: Pattern of returns for the first trading days of the year.
Source: Daily Stock Market Trends, David Schwartz.

temperatures suppressing trading interest. He is not particularly interested in spending time looking for answers, it is enough that he has discovered the *what*, rather than the *why*, of the market's behaviour.

I suggest to him that in some quarters, especially among fundamental analysts, his work would be regarded as statistical voodoo. Critics of any historical-based analysis think there is little predictive information content in past prices. Schwartz is untroubled because he feels that the data is too conclusive to be ignored.

APPLYING THE DATA

Pointing out that UK share prices decline in May, June and September about 50% of the time over the long term is, on its own, an interesting snippet about the market. But when it comes to putting cash into stocks it suggests that there may be good reason to look at other months where there is a likelihood of better odds. On its own, it's a fairly crude piece of trading information, but he felt it was of marginal value in the action of buying or selling an individual stock rather than the whole market which is why he decided that the data needed further contorting to reveal more secrets. Armed with the odds of a market rising on a specific date he thought he knew the best days to buy stocks, so now he needed to know which stocks to buy. The next stage required a system that could isolate a handful of stocks from the thousands that trade on the London Stock Exchange.

When the markets are open he takes a morning walk to clear his head and then likes to be in front of his trading screens a little after 6 am. He works from a snug L-shaped study on the second floor of his country house near Stroud, and most days he will sit at the terminals for a 12-hour stretch watching price movements with only the briefest breaks for coffee or lunch. The walls of the study are hung with shelves full of books and paperwork, and there are several old posters advertising US government Liberty bonds. When I visit, he apologises several times for the untidy state of the study. It is fair to say that there are few flat surfaces in the room that aren't covered with reading material on the markets.

Two desks arranged at right-angles are the nerve centre of his trading operation. Schwartz, positioned in the middle, swivels between the two in a modern high-backed black office chair. On the left-hand desk sits a computer with two large monitors and at any one time there are dozens of windows open across the screens showing the shares he owns, the four sectors he is concentrating on, and some of the 75 sectors or subsectors he follows. All of the windows have live real-time prices that are continually updated while the market is open. There is also a laptop computer on the desk which serves a dual function: it is the source of level 2 information on stocks showing what bids and offers are available and how wide the spread is; it also gives him access to his broker, which is a well-known discount service.

On the right-hand desk there is a further computer which holds a database of all the statistical work he has painstakingly built up over the years. Using trading software, he is able put the data into visual form and pull-up thousands of graphs. The system also allows him to draw in his own support lines or moving averages. Typically, if Schwartz becomes interested in a stock or sector he takes the live price information from the left-hand monitors and cross-checks it with his historical data on the right-hand computer. If he is convinced of the viability of the trade, the order gets fired across to the broker through the laptop.

Once comfortably seated behind his computer monitors he begins most mornings downloading, from DataStream, the closing prices for the 36 sectors listed on the London Stock Exchange. In addition to data running back to 1935 for the London market daily closing price, he has a database on every sector in the UK going back to 1965. With the newly downloaded daily closing prices he updates his charts and checks on the sectors he is following.

He will trade a whole sector if his data suggests that there is money to be made. In November 2003, Schwartz shorted the house-builders, suspecting that their strong performance from the beginning of the year was losing its momentum. He says he took good profit as the FTSE Construction and Building Materials sector fell from its October peak for the year.

He decided very early on in his analysis that taking a sectoral approach made the most sense, as stocks in a sector tend to react together to the economic cycle and often collectively to news stories that may impact only one company in that industry. But, it quickly became apparent in his models that a whole sector is still too large for accurately predicting how an event for one company will affect others. General Retailing presented one of the biggest early challenges with grocers at one end and companies selling luxury clothing at the other – Schwartz recognised the different businesses operated on different models; from the stack 'em high, sell'em cheap philosophy of the Supermarkets, to the sell few but sell expensive approach that works with Boutique clothing retailers.

It seemed logical to subdivide industries into subsectors; where there are four Grocers in the retailing segment he pulled those Grocers out and created a mini-sector. He then created an index for each of these subsectors, multiplying the market value or capitalisation of the company against its share price, adding those values together and dividing by the market value of all the companies included. That number, repeatedly calculated using daily closing prices, was then plotted to create an index that could be turned into a graph. Schwartz says the stocks in his subsector indices are more correlated than the broader sector and he can use that sensitivity to confirm that a stock is moving on company-specific information rather than news for the sector as a whole.

These sector charts are the starting point for his daily fishing trips. Through a process of screening he continually searches out sectors that have demonstrated a three-month period of outperformance over the FTSE All Share Index. He begins by overlaying the 50-, 100- and 200-day moving averages on long-term charts to sniff out the sector's relative performance. Schwartz says that different sectors give clearer signals using different trend-lines; for the IT Hardware industry, for example, he has found that a 75-day moving average gives the best results while the Construction sector works on a 125-day trend-line.

The next stage takes the handful of sectors with the brightest prospects on to short-term charts where he uses seasonality analysis to discover which months matter. Again using the IT Hardware example he found that his data from 1989 to 2001 suggested that November was a better month to be in IT Hardware stocks than March. In November the sector rose 11 times in 13 years; in March it managed to rise only 5 times. He checks the performance of the sector for three months before a significant gain or fall. He is looking for relative strength. The sector may not be rising at the time of the analysis, but if it does well in the market environment as he is anticipating, it could be the right place to put cash.

The sectors are broken down into constituent stocks, and tested for their performance against the sector average and the FTSE All Share. Schwartz focuses on companies that have outperformed their peers and the market in bull, bear and range-bound trading conditions. He is looking for a track-record of returns to invest in; ideally there should be a consistent upward trend on a three-year view.

When he is satisfied with the stock's prospects he tracks it minute by minute, watching how it's traded by other market participants. He has two absolute trading rules: cut losses immediately, and don't buy a stock without a clear support line. Ideally, he wants a stock with a clear trading channel that is repeatedly bouncing off the same support price and he will trade in and out of the stock taking small profits. If the stock breaches the support line he sells it immediately.

PICKING STOCKS

VISLINK is a good example of the stocks Schwartz is looking for. The microwave radio and satellite transmission business bounced off a long-term low in March 2003. Detecting a channel he thought he could trade he first bought the stock in late-May at £14 and sold out at £17. He bought again in late-August at £17 and sold at £23. In November the price had fallen to £18.50. He went back in at that price and at the time of writing was talking about selling the position. The stock was trading at £25. He traded in and out of VISLINK three times over an eight-month period, comfortable that his resistance and support lines (drawn on Figure 8.1) would hold.

Schwartz prefers to hunt out stocks in the small-cap segment of the market because he feels there is a more level playing field in this area for the retail investor trading against the professionals. 'My reason is that I have nothing special to offer when I trade big caps because I am going head-to-head against some of the smartest City traders – with inside information, big spending power that can move the markets, and big research departments to boot.'

A few more examples illustrate the kind of companies that Schwartz is looking at, and the trends he is seeking to uncover. At the time of our interview, at the end of 2003, he was optimistic about a position taken in a UK company called Patientline (Figure 8.2) which supplies hospital beds with digital TV and the internet. The stock

Figure 8.1   Trading over an eight-month period.

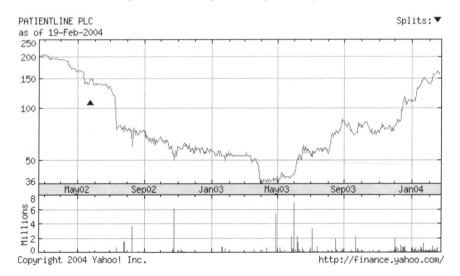

Figure 8.2   The position taken in Patientline plc.
Source: Yahoo! Reproduced with permission of Yahoo! Inc. © 2004 by Yahoo! Inc. YAHOO! and the YAHOO! logo are trademarks of Yahoo! Inc.

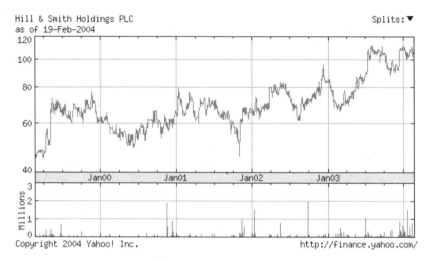

Figure 8.3   Investment with Hill & Smith.
Source: Yahoo! Reproduced with permission of Yahoo! Inc. © 2004 by Yahoo! Inc. YAHOO!
and the YAHOO! logo are trademarks of Yahoo! Inc.

had bounced off a long-term low in March of that year and he was enthusiastic about
the likelihood of its price doubling from his entry level.

Hill & Smith is another of his small company investments (Figure 8.3). It supplies
materials to the construction industry and has shown a similar bounce off the long-
term low it reached in 1998. Schwartz says he likes the sector and this company had
a promising chart formation. Again, the stock demonstrated a good upward price
channel over a period well in excess of his three-year guideline.

If he likes the general tone of the market and his historical data suggests that the
conditions are likely to reward investors, he will occasionally take opportunistic short-
term bets on beaten-up stocks. This satisfies his day trading instincts and the positions
are rarely held for long. A lot, he says, depends on whether he feels comfortable with
the market on any given day or if he is in the mood to trade. On these days he'll
open a window of 3000 shares from the London market, hunting among the biggest
percentage losers for pricing anomalies – companies that have been oversold on bad
news or maybe taken a hit from a profits warning. He pays little attention to the gravity
of the news or company fundamentals and uses his experience of price patterns to
identify stocks he thinks have been oversold on a short-term basis.

BACKGROUND

Born in the Bronx when it was considered a nice middle-class neighbourhood,
Schwartz's accent still betrays his New York roots. He is a tall man with a spare
frame, now in his early 60s; age, if anything, appears to have increased his vitality.

He speaks quickly, but softly, his voice rising with excitement at the punch-line of a good story, or hesitating with brief self-reflection when he is questioning one of his own conclusions.

The son of a fireman, he left the army in 1961, armed with a degree in statistics and a desire to get a job. He had already done some casual market research work while at University in New York City. It had been enjoyable, and it seemed to suite his statistical background. His timing was excellent. The world was waking up to the power of television and advertising on consumer behaviour, and America was enjoying a consumer goods boom. The market research companies became extremely powerful because their data, a compilation of consumer responses, could decide whether a particular advertising campaign ran nationwide or sank without trace.

Schwartz saw the writing on the wall and started his own company in New York, the Consumer Response Corporation, which took on work for Saatchi & Saatchi, Kellogg and other Fortune 500 companies. It was that work – cross-tabulating data to determine trends and consumer attitudes – that led him to take on the advertising research for the Reagan Presidential campaign in 1979. The job involved market research to measure public attitudes to the campaign.

He is discrete about whether it was that experience that gave him a healthy cynicism about government and the wisdom of officials in general, but his suspicion about the actions of politicians and their agents came out several times in our discussions, whether he talked about Alan Greenspan's 'short-term fiddling with interest rates', or the need of the incumbent President to stimulate the economy ahead of elections. He brings that same outlook to the markets and he steadfastly ignores tips and is doubtful about the motivation of most investment bank research. He is very much a product of his background. If he can't prove the veracity of a statement through his own knowledge or research, he is unlikely to give it too much credence.

He demonstrated that single-mindedness with his own business. At a time in his career when most would find it impossible to step aside at the height of their success, he decided to sell-up and retire. As he describes it, he no longer wanted to be in a service business where all of your assets go down in the elevator every night. In 1986, aged just 46, Schwartz sold the company on for a 7-figure sum and set about working out what to do with the rest of his life. His English wife had her own ideas and a planned trip to France was postponed in favour of a flight to Britain. His current home is about three miles west of London near Stroud in the Cotswolds and came to his attention during a chance visit to the hairdressers. He says it is typical Schwartz; most things in his life seem to have happened by accident. Waiting for his turn in the chair he picked up a copy of *Country Life* magazine and found among the properties for sale a very pretty but slightly run down country hotel. He says the drive up to Stroud turned out to be one of the most expensive car rides in history.

His interest in financial markets evolved from a determination to invest his payoff wisely. He decided he needed an investment process he could understand, and that led to the crunching of decades worth of historical data. In terms of his total portfolio, the money he uses for his stock purchases and the occasional foray into spread-bets is marginal to his total net worth. Most of his cash is stashed in fixed interest investments, like bonds and guaranteed interest accounts. As he happily points out, his trading is for entertainment, he ran a business and sold it, he doesn't have to make his livelihood from the markets, which is not to say he doesn't take it seriously. He views the market as a battleground where it delights him to think he could be taking money from the pockets of professionals like the Market-Makers.

Even though his stock market of choice is the London market, nestled in front of his computers in the Cotswold Hills he is physically a long way from the brokers and investment banks that do much of the business. He couldn't like it any better. He is indifferent about his physical distance from other market participants and since he decided a long time ago not to act on investment advice or tips, he doesn't spend much time discussing his own holdings with other investors. He likes the geography of the London market, opening as it does as Asian bourses are winding down for the day and New York is just starting to wake-up. The US market open can bring volatility into the afternoon session in the UK, which suites his opportunistic trend trading.

A QUESTION OF TIMING

Schwartz doesn't read financial books for insights or guidance on sharpening his data-focused methods. When it comes to stock market forecasting he prefers to go his own way, believing there are few other useful precedents for the unique approach he has created. That sounds cocky, but he doesn't mean it to. He just hasn't found that the techniques of other 'experts' work with his own.

He is convinced that his historical analysis works, but there have been noteworthy occasions when it has failed to give accurate timing of market weakness. In 1997 he began to feel that the market was overextended. From the historical data he predicted that the markets were vulnerable to a sharp drop and had even started calculating the size of the bear market to come. The signals reminded him of his earlier work crunching data when one of the first tasks he set himself was to count the duration and frequency of bull and bear markets over a 60-year period for the London Stock Exchange. His data suggested in September 1997 that the UK market was overdue a correction, and the coming months would see a pullback. In fact the call turned out to be premature, the FTSE 100 would go on to make another 25% in the next six months.

Schwartz says the call wasn't unrealistic at that time, he just couldn't have foreseen that Alan Greenspan would come to the market's rescue. His statistical analysis couldn't account for the intervention of the head of the US Federal Reserve cutting interest rate cuts. He believes that the injection of easy money in the face of the triple whammy of the Asian currency crisis, the Russian debt débâcle, and the collapse of Long Term Capital Management threw out his numbers.

He argues that his timing of the approaching bear market may have proved right if Greenspan hadn't cut the Fed Funds rate three times in 1998. He was convinced that the economic cycle and overvaluation in 1998 would bring about a sharp correction in stock prices. 'I thought Greenspan could not change things that were due, only the shape of how it happens. Stocks were overextended.'

Greenspan slowly raised interest rates through 1999 and 2000, but, says Schwartz, he had already set in place a share-price bubble and delayed the impending bear market. A more aggressive tightening might have prevented some of the excesses of the technology rally, but the timing with the turn of the millennium discouraged that course of action. As Schwartz puts it, 'when logical people start to wonder whether airplanes will fall out of the sky, or the banking system will crash because of mis-dated software, it's not a good time to cause a drop in equity prices by raising interest rates.'

Because of his bearish outlook from 1997, he sat out the big run up in technology stocks, but rationally he couldn't understand the valuations. From the spring of 1998 he began paring back his exposure to equities and made further cuts in the late-summer of 1999. 'I felt like a jerk in the next few months. Fortunately, events finally went my way. But the bigger point is not my eventual success, but my willingness to stick to a point of view that I believed in.'

He is in no hurry to increase the amount of cash he invests in stocks. Despite being tempted to double the size of his average investment between March and June of 2003 he resisted the urge because of his long-term negative view. He believes that momentum trading with the short-term trend can be extremely profitable, but few investors have the skill or gut feel and lose money by following the pack late in the day. He advocates a disciplined stock selection process based on good analysis with a strong approach to cash management.

> 'Most small investors assume the name of the game is picking winners and selling at the right time. To my way of thinking, a more important element is controlling your capital – committing more capital when prospects are rosiest and cutting back (sometimes by a great deal) when prospects are less rosy.'

OUTLOOK

At the beginning of 2004 Schwartz put on record his expectation for the UK market to rise about 12% or to around 5000 points for the year. He believes that the positive trend in Western equity markets that started in March 2003 will last between 12 and 24 months – which could see it run into 2005. Schwartz is convinced the broader trend is still for lower stock markets, but he concedes that history is not conclusive on the subject of bull rallies in secular bear markets. The major downturn in the UK market that lasted from 1928 until 1940 contained a super rally from mid-1932 to the end of 1936. There is the possibility that the bull run could be extended even if the broad trend turns out to be a disaster.

Analysing historical data going back to 1700, he has found 17 very steep bear market downturns when UK shares fell by at least one-third. Of those 17, 16 bull market rebounds occurred afterwards and stocks rose for at least 24 months. The one exception proved to be in 1825. Although Henry Ford famously declared 'history is bunk', Schwartz says history is pretty useful for signposting what *could* happen, 'this tendency for big drops to be followed by healthy bounce-back rallies has been occurring with monotonous regularity for more than 300 years.'

How will the US election and its impact on the American economy affect the British stock market? Schwartz's data shows that bear markets were underway in the UK during 12 of the last 21 American election years. Although his forecast is for a positive 2004, political uncertainty often holds back significant price gains in the middle of the typical election year. The plateaus often run for five or six months.

Schwartz is critical of pre-election spending, suggesting it will only add to the US stock market's woes when prices correct. He expects price swings to be erratic as President Bush tries to create a 'feel good' factor.

> 'We have never ever seen such reckless pump priming in the run-up to an election. Johnson tried it to a limited scale in 1967, a combination of Vietnam and domestic pump priming. They called it the guns and butter strategy. It contributed to a 1000 Dow in 1969 and an inability to break above this level for many years. It also contributed to the high inflation of the early and mid '70s.'

If the market sell-off through 2000–2003 appeared brutal, so is Schwartz's forecast that the Dow will halve to below 5000 points in the next major correction. He insists the Dow is still at levels after the three-year bear market where historically it is overvalued. He thinks that on the bigger picture the gains achieved in the 1980s and 1990s were exceptional, and some give-back is inevitable.

How will the market sell-off take place? Schwartz tends to favour the Japan scenario. In the last bear market the NASDAQ dropped pretty much unchecked for 18 months, whereas the Nikkei unwound initially quickly but then more slowly over the next 14 years. History, he says, shows that downturns of the magnitude the markets are due tend to last at least a decade. In Japan the Nikkei peaked at 39000 and started to fall after 31 December 1989. It then declined gradually for more than a decade, only bottoming and changing the trend at the beginning of 2003.

Schwartz says there will still be opportunities to make money on the long side of the market. There have been periods during the past 14 years on the Nikkei when it was possible to buy into short-term uptrends. Success requires good timing and smart stock selection. It is not a period for buy and hold and he says investors should forget the idea that buying the index will save them from losing money. If his call on the rest of the decade comes right, indices will struggle and good active fund managers will be in great demand.

ADVICE

Schwartz's bleakest message is that buying shares over the next 10 years may not be the wisest investment. He doesn't expect attractive returns, and argues that capital growth from the UK stock market has barely beaten inflation for long periods over two centuries. His view is controversial and sits at odds with studies that suggest that stocks are a better long term investment than fixed income products like bonds as long as dividends are reinvested. He rejects the argument, saying that few small investors reinvest dividends and thinks that, for many prospective investors, keeping their cash in a savings account would best serve their financial interests.

Where they are committed to investing in stocks he believes that too few small investors make good use of the edge they have over professionals. Schwartz says the only significant advantage they have is their opportunity to control the amount of capital at risk. That is the amount of money invested at a given time. He thinks retail investors should be more active in taking money 'off the table' when the market turns sour. While financial institutions may have to be fully invested because they have mandates from their clients to do so, private investors are under no such pressure.

His message to the retail investor is sit down and calmly work out where you have a lead over the market, whether that comes from being the boss of your own company where you are directly involved in the fortunes and management of a listed business, or in the expertise you may have as an accountant, plumber or software developer to understand the broader trend in your industry. Schwartz's advice is stick with what you can understand and if that means missing out on a stock that is going up, so be it. It's better to miss the gains than sit in a stock that could turn sharply against you if you don't know why it's moving.

If this sounds like Buffett-style folk wisdom it isn't meant to; unlike Warren Buffett, Schwartz has no interest in fundamental analysis. He never looks at a company's accounts and has only a passing interest in a basic valuation number like a p/e. Asked whether he thinks fundamental analysis works for finding stocks, he shrugs his shoulders, it may do but its not what he knows so it has no place in his investment tool-box. He may have run and sold a successful business before turning his attention to financial markets, but he takes little notice of the business models of the companies he buys.

Schwartz sees little reason to leave money in a falling market; he believes that buy and hold is a strategy for fools. The historical data has shown that market conditions are constantly changing, which means that investment styles have to change. Buy and hold is akin to locking in one trading technique, and is doomed to failure.

A trader of trends and themes, he questions the validity of every movement however long it has worked. He feels that investor horizons have shortened and opportunities are on the table for less time. The increased participation of Hedge Funds and the greater leverage in the market through Contracts for Difference and other derivative products makes tracking and understanding short-term moves much harder. He is convinced that that makes the bigger trends even more important. The 'gunslingers', as he describes them, may create a wilder ride but ultimately the primary trends will be revealed in the data.

He is agnostic about why a stock appears to be moving or the trend changing. Schwartz will buy a stock on a dead cat bounce, he'll buy it as a takeover story, or even as a restructuring play. The themes are less important than the price movement. The overarching question is that it should be an environment, as determined by the history of the month and the market tone that favours that style of investing. When he recognises the style that is working he will repeatedly try to search out other examples through his analysis. If that makes his investment style difficult to emulate, he is unsympathetic. He thinks being straitjacketed by one investment approach is what loses money for amateurs and professionals alike. Why buy a long fund that invests only in technology shares? Or limit equity market holdings to large cap blue chip stocks? For him both methods represent a denial of history which repeatedly demonstrates that winning styles last only as long as it takes for the least sophisticated small investor to read about it in the Sunday papers.

If history provides the system for Schwartz's investment process, its spirit lies in the idea that every trend, fundamental or technical, is temporary. Just understanding that basic principle and acting accordingly he believes will stop investors losing a lot of cash. Market recognition of successful themes or styles ultimately renders them ineffective. He has his own example to illustrate that fact. Back in the late eighties he started to write a column in the *Financial Times* about the work he was doing – and to illustrate a point about seasonality he picked out April as the best performing month from 50 years of data. The numbers revealed there was a clear advantage in putting money to work in stocks in late March to exploit the April rise. Does the rule still apply? Well, no – the historical trend still stands because of the weight of data, but of the last eight Aprils up to 2003; four have seen the market rise, four the market fall.

Despite spending very little time on macro-economics or news flow, Schwartz does subscribe to a wire service called Updata. He accepts that the institutions probably get their news slightly faster but doesn't see that as a handicap. He doesn't trade solely on data in anticipation of a trend change, but first waits for confirmation in the price. If he has already identified a stock as worthy of further attention, his level II trading screen will reveal any significant pick-up in interest from buyers or sellers. He is convinced that most news is only market-moving over the short-term, very quickly becoming factored into the stock price. He feels his edge comes in understanding the pattern based on a longer term reading.

Schwartz's trading technique can be simplified into several observations. When the market plateaus, he will look for shares or sectors that are very volatile to play short-term bounces. When the market is making a steady move up he looks for sectors bouncing off support lines or busting through resistance. If the market is moving down he hunts for shorting opportunities in stocks breaking through support lines or unable to breach resistance.

A STORY ABOUT RISK

Schwartz has an extremely low threshold for risk by his own admission; he will not buy a stock unless he can see a clear support line. In common with technical analysts, he regards support and resistance lines as giving useful information about where the weight of the market is willing to buy or sell. If a stock he holds falls through its support, he sells. If his entry point is somewhat higher he may sell before the support line is breached. His goal is to avoid all losses. He doesn't have a specific stop-loss target, but will run for the exits well before the stock is off 10%. He admits to many times agonising over a stock that has tipped him out on a down move before – absent his stake – rallying sharply beyond his entry price.

That's nothing to the agonising he would do if he failed to bail-out after a stock plunged through his support line. He decided after early painful losses that good portfolios are built by focusing on not losing money – as opposed to making it. Emotionally he reacts much more badly to losses, feeling like a 'schmuck' if he doesn't exit a down trade quickly enough. As a rule, he is less concerned with winning trades and suspects he sells his winners far too quickly.

A 'bad' experience early in his working life has left a deeply ingrained lesson about putting too much money into one trade, however good the reasons for loading up appear to be. In 1967 when insider trading rules were less strict, his first wife called him up at the office to urge him to buy shares in the company she was working for. It's a cert, she said; the company is set to announce it will be taken-over on the coming Friday. So Schwartz took a large lump of their hard-earned savings and bought the stock. Sure enough the announcement came and the stock rose rapidly all through that Friday. They were overjoyed, dining lavishly that night on the prospects of the boost to their savings when they had sold the shares and got back the 500 dollars or so they had used to pay for them.

But Schwartz couldn't feel comfortable holding the stock over the weekend, partly it was the thought that the money came too easily, partly that the stake represented such a large part of their net wealth. Finally, after arguing his case they decided first thing Monday morning he would call the broker and sell the stock.

In the middle of that Monday morning his wife rang the office in a panic. Schwartz was in a meeting, but his wife told the secretary it was an emergency and that he must be pulled out of the meeting to take the call. When Schwartz picked up the receiver he says his wife was 'wild with fear'. She asked with some trepidation whether they still owned the stock. The company she said had announced the take-over was off and the share price had started to plunge. Fortunately, he was able to calm her down and had managed to sell the shares as soon as the broker's office opened, but the experience of that weekend left a profound impression on his trading.

At any one time he spreads his trades across 5–12 positions, any more and he feels he can't give the minute by minute attention they require. He ran more stocks in the past, but again his caution about the market environment means that he is uncomfortable with anything over 12. He describes his stakes as modest; each position is no more than £4000, and represents just a few percent of the money he has allocated for stock trading.

A WORD ON TECHNICALS

Schwartz has created a process for analysing markets based on statistics. His trading, however, appears to draw heavily on the tools familiar to a technical analyst. He overlays his charts with moving averages to throw-up buy or sell signals and draws in support and resistance lines to identify stock price channels and momentum. When Schwartz first set out his ideas, he was initially intrigued with Technical Analysis and felt he had found some fellow travellers. After all, TA is also the hunt for predictable patterns in stock prices and is apparently not so different from crunching historical price information to find the odds of a stock rising or falling. Both approaches, through different means, are intended to reveal patterns that can be exploited for profit.

He has cherry picked some of the tools from the technicians armoury, but is not only uncomfortable being viewed as a practitioner, but is also critical of a great deal of technical work, insisting that analysts are good at showing where the market is but not where it is going. Piqued by the abundance of what he considers the poor chart analysis reported in the media, Schwartz spent a summer working through 200 so-called Head and Shoulder tops.

Put simply, a head and shoulders price movement sketches out the image of a head with surrounding shoulders. It is one of the most commonly used tools of the technical analysts and falls into the category of a reversal pattern. It is typically looked for at the end of a long rise in the price of a stock. The left shoulder, head and right shoulder represent successive rallies in the stock price, but technicians believe that the pattern as whole indicates that a fall in prices is coming. If the right-hand shoulder is punctured – known as piercing the neckline – technical analysts think the stock price will drop sharply.

In typically systematic fashion Schwartz measured the height of the left shoulder in each occasion, the duration of the move, and the market conditions when the move started. In all he tested the pattern with hundreds of different variables to ascertain how often reported head and shoulders movements led to a fall in the share price. The result, Schwartz says, showed that a head and shoulders pattern predicted a sharp fall in the share price only half the time. Statistically, of course, that suggests that the pattern is irrelevant. He does feel, however, that careful measurement of the height of the left shoulder, the length of the peak and the percentage change from the start of the initial rally to the neckline can improve the pattern as an indicator of a future price movement.

He has dismissed them from his own investment research because of the length of time they take to interpret properly. He suggests that too many technicians waste time hunting for a head and shoulders top during a bull market because the downside tends to be too limited to exploit profitably.

SUBJECTIVE SYSTEM

Schwartz describes his own approach as undisciplined, inconsistent and constantly changing, which he thinks are its strengths. He calls the technical analysis he uses pretty unscientific, involving lots of subjective judgement. His system is rooted in the analysis of historical prices, but his trend-trading methods are thoroughly modern. The countless hours spent trawling through sector after sector have given him a useful intimacy with the UK market which more than compensates for his lack of formal financial training.

Beyond the Schwartz system his greatest asset is the relentless energy he brings to investing. He is never satisfied with his own analysis and is on a constant quest to test and improve his methods. I suspect there aren't too many new investors faced with their first foray into the markets that would sit down, reject the conventional wisdom, and methodically design their own system. Schwartz's insight has been to take a lifetime of knowledge in one field and apply it in another.

Conclusion

'When it comes to the future, there are three kinds of people: those who let it happen, those who make it happen, and those who wonder what happened.'

Anonymous

There is no consensus in this book about the medium-term outlook for Western financial markets. On a one-to-three year view opinions range from the extremely bearish Philip Manduca and Hugh Hendry to the more upbeat deflationary boom scenarios expressed by Michael Browne and Peter Toogood. At the extremes it is a difference between the reassertion of a primary bear trend, and equity markets that settle into a steady but unspectacular decade of modest year-on-year gains.

There is more agreement on the size of returns investors must be prepared to accept. A realistic target for the next few years might be at best a steady 3–6% per annum. Ultimately financial markets reflect the bigger story of what is happening in economies. Investors should forget the exceptional period of the double-digit returns equity markets witnessed in the 1980s and 1990s.

At the heart of the bears case is the unsustainability of a US-led model where low interest rates, low inflation and rising debt create long-term prosperity. If the bears are right, there is little point in talking investment, the goal will be financial survival. Cash and gold are king until the dust settles – at that point valuations will be an incentive to buy. Assuming, as Hendry warns, the world hasn't got depression.

The broad message from the optimists appears to be that certain stocks may make strong gains, but whole markets may not. History attests to long periods of sideways or directionless trade, the Dow took 16 years to re-test the peak of the 1966 bull market. By 1982 a generation of investors had sat out the equity story. Will the new investors in technology stocks in the 1990s ever return to the market? I asked Hendry what financial writers he is reading currently for insight, and his answer was 'very old, grey haired guys'. It sums up the dilemma for anyone seeking a good money manager; there just aren't too many professionals left in the markets who remember how a sideways market feels.

Slow and steady has profound implications for the way portfolios are built and managed. The wider public may not see them but there are changes underway in the asset management business that reveal an industry slowly casting off its old skin. Relative return or benchmarking to a market index *is* giving way to absolute return or benchmarking to cash or inflation. The drivers are twofold: concern to avoid a repeat of the losses in the last bear market; and recognition of a passing peak for the traditional long-only industry. Typically, some time after the professional money has made the switch attention will turn to providing a similar service to the retail investor.

PRESERVATION OF CAPITAL

The baseline for all of the Mavericks is preservation of capital. This was the one theme that cut through all investing styles or techniques during our interviews. The retail investor dreams of the 10% or greater annual return on investments the markets have promised for the last two decades. In contrast, the starting point for the money managers in this book is not how to make money, but how not to lose it. They all, where possible, refuse to hold losing positions. Protective stop-loss levels are almost universally deployed, and trailed to lock in gains. There is an equally disciplined approach to profits. A common practice is to state an exit price before entering the trade and constantly reassess the progress towards that target.

There is an active approach to money management and, for some, that evolved from losing a lot of money in the past. Portfolios are diversified, stakes are small as a percentage of the portfolio size and, where possible, money is spread over asset classes. A point continually stressed by those who lost money in Russia in 1998 is that investors and most professional fund managers are never sufficiently prepared. Market events of the magnitude of the Russian market collapse may be infrequent but they must always be guarded against. Even in a rising market, a bearish Hendry buys protection in the form of puts, or index futures that make money if the markets fall.

Retail investors relying on their fund manager to protect their money need to think again. The investment industry proved a poor seller of stocks when the 2000–2003 bear market started. The financial community also felt the pain, shedding tens of thousands of jobs and, as has been mentioned, it is slowly embracing an absolute return philosophy. It is also spending more time on quantifying risk. But, traditional measures of potential portfolio loss like Value at Risk (VaR) are only as good as the inputs. VaR is set up to provide a worst case scenario for the investor on a portfolio over a given time-frame and level of market confidence. The more bearish Mavericks say that events like Russia, the Asian currency crisis and the last bear market show that more of the unthinkable market shock scenarios should be run through the models.

NEW MARKETS OR OLD MARKETS RETURNED

The year 2003 established solid up-trends for several markets that have spent years out of favour. There is a wide measure of agreement that the best medium-term markets are just at the beginning of new growth cycles:

1. *Gold.* The precious metal has already covered a lot of ground from its lows of less than $300 an ounce. A longer-term prediction of $800 an ounce came up several times in interviews.

2. *Commodities.* The rise in commodity prices has surprised none more than the producers that have been scrabbling to meet rising demand. Rising prices are geared into China's growth, which may have its hiccups as capacity supply and demand even out. The advice is still to take advantage of the inelasticity of supply. New supplies of base metals have to be dug up, new soft commodities like soybeans have to be grown.

3. *Japan.* There are still sceptics who think that the country has yet to recover from a decade of falling prices. The Mavericks that look at Japan see a bullish story. It is suggested that the best buys may be in the small and mid-cap domestic economy rather than the big exporters. The stock valuations are encouraging investors to investigate opportunities.

4. *Emerging Asia.* These markets are seen as beneficiaries of recovery in Japan and growth in China. Again, prices are an incentive to buy after valuations plummeted in the wake of the 1997 currency crisis.

As a general rule, the Mavericks consider the overall tone of the market more important than the ability to select individual stocks. On the basis that a rising tide floats all boats, there is a greater emphasis on the correct asset allocation strategy than there would have been five years ago. The answer then was always to focus on holding stocks because they had consistently risen in value. Whether bullish or bearish on the US economy, the new (old) markets are perceived as offering the best overall investment environment.

TIME HORIZONS

Investor time horizons are short. The current growth areas are in products that operate over days and weeks like CFDs, spread betting and derivatives. That trend is reflected in the interest in hedge funds as such funds cover a multitude of styles and techniques. They do, however, share a basic investing philosophy that is geared to an absolute return mentality and reflects a focus on managers that actively monitor and trade portfolios.

Like any growth industry there are tensions. The flow of funds seeking new managers will create periods of overcapacity and contraction. Also, as Toogood remarks, the hedge fund sector will share the same talent constraints as the traditional long-only industry. Institutional money will push developments in the absolute investing world, but without changes to regulation and the evolution of a tier of knowledgeable advisers the trickle of retail money into hedge funds will be slow. That is unlikely to trouble the hedge fund managers who in any case view retail money as fickle. They prefer larger single dollops of cash from institutions that buy into the managers' investment process and stay loyal through the good days and the bad. It is also more economical to attract.

MAKING IT HAPPEN

All of the Mavericks use charts for timing investments. For some, that may be the extent of their use of technical analysis, but it demonstrates a belief that there is information in the price of a stock. Committed Elliott Wave practitioners like Murrin and Locke go further, using patterns to determine timing as well as the entry and exit prices. For them, fundamental analysis has a junior role and the pattern transmits all necessary dealing information. The goal in most cases is to catch a change in the trend and ride it until it starts to fade.

A stock is sold quickly if the trade turns negative. It may also be sold if it has exceeded the predicted target price, and the novice investor may find this the most difficult discipline to understand. Where a price target is specified at the time the position is opened, the holding is sold when it is reached. Browne, Cunningham and Murrin all pursue this philosophy rigorously. There is continual analysis to check that the reasons for the target price are still valid, but all would prefer to take a small profit than risk a bigger loss. If the idea is still valid there will be time for another go at the same trade. A new position can be established with a new target price and new stops.

Universally, the Mavericks believe in either changing styles or sitting out the market if conditions don't suit their investment methods. Toogood blends his fund of fund holdings according to his view of how the market is evolving. Hendry insists that listening to the market is the best lesson learned but rarely practised. Self-awareness and an ability to read the levels of fear and greed are cited as skills that will both protect capital and produce profit. Recreating the image of a snarling trading pit, or thousands of smart traders waiting to pounce on your money, is a good way to focus the mind on the opposition each time a trade is made.

INVESTING IN THE FUTURE

I wrote this book because some questions were praying on my mind. My aim was to raise awareness of a debate that is underway about the current and future direction for the, primarily, Western equity markets. In the 1990s few would have challenged the idea that buy and hold could be wrong. Relative return worked extremely well as an investment philosophy when markets only rose, and did so at a historically brisk pace. Back then, we rarely discussed the subjects that dominate investment decisions today. Suddenly, the business media is talking about disinflation, deflation, overcapacity, pension crisis, demographic crisis, budget deficits, tax give-backs higher commodity prices and emergency interest rate levels. These have become the topics of the moment. Unfortunately many of them appear to be the sharp end of a long cycle that will be here to stay for some time. For instance, no Western government has so far offered a satisfactory solution to how more pension money gets paid out by a declining workforce.

The investment styles of these Mavericks range from straightforward valuation-based stock-picking, through distressed valuation opportunities to nuclear proliferation and astral numerology. I don't begin to guess at which method is most effective. The answer is probably all of them, depending on the person using it. It is interesting to me that all of the Mavericks enjoy a loyal public following for their insights, either with me at CNBC, or in other media. At times of uncertainty, unusual investment styles get greater prominence as investors search for new truths about the markets. What surprised me most after writing the book was how eight professional investors with such different approaches to the markets, could find common ground on so much of the future.

APPENDICES

1
Hugh Hendry: The Odey Eclectica Reports

HENDRY'S SUGGESTED READING

Reminiscences of a Stock Operator, Edwin Lefevre (New York: John Wiley & Sons, 1994)
The Money Game, Adam Smith (Random House, USA Inc., 1976)
www.dowtheoryletters.com, Richard Russell
www.prudentbear.com, *Credit Bubble Bulletin*, Doug Noland

ODEY ASSET MANAGEMENT: ECLECTICA FUND MANAGER REPORTS

January 2003

Investment Manager's Report

How is one to explain our simultaneous ownership of gold shares, commodity futures and government bonds? Eclectic certainly. Sensible? Well ... our investment thesis is that the monetary expansion by depressed central bankers could ultimately result in paper currencies returning to their intrinsic value (i.e. not a lot); obviously good for our gold and commodities. But like the virtue of St Augustine, we don't see inflation becoming worrisome just yet. Just ask the Bank of England, which unexpectedly cut interest rates by a quarter point and had to contend with shares falling by 2% – so much for Pavlovian responses. The bond market, in contrast, rose. Investors simply have too much equity and not enough income. Elvis is not the only person who should be leaving the building. I hope you are too.

Stock Insight Gold Stocks

While January has been kind to our asset allocation, the early days of February remind me that the hardest things for a fund manager to do is load up at the beginning of a bull market and hang on all the way up until the market becomes wildly speculative and toppy. Now is therefore the time to review our flagging gold stocks. The price of bullion is up 20% since December and yet the shares have now lost their immediate gains. Explanation? Investors are prepared to pay high premia to intrinsic value to hold an option on companies' gold reserves. When the gold price is expected to increase (increased volatility in option parlance), the value of this option grows. Remember the great breakout early last year. However, in November, the shares were discounting $370 gold despite a $320 spot price. We were paying up for the option value inherent in the companies. Today the option is much cheaper. Equities are (virtually) discounting spot prices. Optionality has returned. We believe the gold price will go higher; the next move should take the equities with it. First the shares, then the bullion, then the shares . . . just like the '70s.

Top Holdings

Longs (gross 169.19%)

1. Euro-Bund Future 28.3%
2. Reuters CRB Index Future 23.7%
3. Soybean Future 8.6%
4. Ashanti Goldfields 6.6%
5. Durban Deep 5.9%

Shorts (gross −34.57%)

1. France Telecom −7.7%
2. eBay Inc. −2.2%
3. Intel Corp −1.9%
4. Citigroup Inc. −1.5%
5. NASDAQ Tracking ETF −1.5%

February 2003

Investment Manager's Report: Bad things happen in bear markets . . .

The former husband of Hollywood starlet, J-Lo, has just won the American edition of 'I'm a celebrity, get me out of here'. Apparently his tearful admission that he still wasn't over his former belle won over the audience. Well, 'I'm a fund manager, get me out of here!' February was shocking. We paid the sin of being too aggressive in our position size. If we are right, and a bull market for gold and tangible real assets is emerging from the bust in financial assets, smaller positions are called for. Why? Because no one is allowed to make money. Bull markets use volatility to exclude the majority. Volatility with stop losses ensures one is constantly buying high and selling low. Our results reflect this. Accordingly, in March we have scaled back to a modest 20% gross equity position. The figures below refer to positions held as of 24 February.

Devro Stock Insight (Long)

This Scottish-based sausage skin manufacturer typifies the point. It represents one of our few long positions. The price has fallen over 90% from its peak recorded over five years ago. This was the result of a series of biblical like plagues, a collapse in emerging markets, a disastrous acquisition and general management incompetence. It has had its bear market. And yet the business has withstood it all. It retains a 76% global market share, generates prodigious cash and the shares yield 10%. Better still, we have switched off our computer screens, i.e. the charts are no longer the appropriate discipline for such optionality.

Top Equity Holdings

Longs	Shorts
1. Ashanti Goldfields 9.6%	1. SPDR Trust Series −3.5%
2. Durban Deep 4.7%	2. Capital One Financial −1.2%
3. Anglogold Ltd 4.5%	3. Citigroup −0.7%
4. Gold Fields Ltd 3.9%	4. Barclays plc −0.6%
5. Freeport-McMoran 3.5%	5. CDW Computer Centres −0.6%

March 2003

Investment Manager's Report: A bear market for bears?

This market has made fools of optimists. But as the evidence of recession in the UK and US grows daily, we may be set to experience the first serious rally in this bear market. Are we encountering a bear market for bears? First, companies are priced, if they are cyclical, on the basis that they won't last the winter, and in the case of growth companies, as if they will never grow sales and earnings again. Both are untrue. Second, having fretted about the absence of panic days, Lowry's now report 4 such days - investors are at long last appreciating the potential risks. Third, selling pressure has dissipated; investors have simply become bored of selling stocks. Accordingly, we believe that there are numerous attractive opportunities for the adventurous investor and, at the time of writing, our long positions have risen considerably from the month-end position below. We have no active currency positions and no bunds.

Stock Insight (Long): UK Coal

The relatively peaceful years following WW2 allowed international trade to rise from 5% to 20% of global GDP. But with current relations fractious with our French, Russian and German partners, not forgetting disharmony in the Middle East, international trade could suffer from the Iraqi fallout. This could herald a political move in favour of national champions. Surely we require domestic sources of coal and steel?

Accordingly we have turned our eye to some fallen angels. UK Coal has a market cap of £110m and no debt; it sells for just 15% of sales. Its present value is captured by its interest in Australia and its UK properties, not counting British coal. The business makes losses but with no investment in mine renewal, underlying free cash flow of £50m covers a 12% dividend yield 3.4× times. Corus (we prefer British Steel) is a similar case, as it trades with no expectation of future profits. Indeed, it can be purchased today for just 8p when the working capital could be liquidated for 24p. Roll on the bankruptcy.

Top Equity Holdings

Longs
1. Newmont Mining 1.9%
2. Devro plc 1.1%
3. Autostrada Torino-Milan 0.9%
4. Anglogold Ltd 0.9%
5. Anglo-Eastern Plantation 0.9%

Shorts
1. Interbrew −0.4%
2. Ericsson −0.3%
3. Sogecable −0.3%
4. Aviva −0.2%

April 2003

Investment Manager's Report: Angels Dancing... German Bunds

They say you learn more about your investments when they fall in price. Rising prices are quite boring. After all, shares are supposed to rise. But when the price unexpectedly declines you gain wisdom. At what (lower) price level will speculators be prepared to buy? The German 10-year bund future is a case in point. Having spent three years failing to rise beyond 113, they broke higher in January, rising to 117. However, in March they promptly collapsed, falling to 112.5. That is to say, they fell back to their breakout level. However, this has acted as support and today they trade just below their all-time high. Bonds are in a bull market. We will see new highs, of that I am certain. But what an odd time. For equities have also stormed back from the dead prompting the question: Is this bear market set to become truly historic in proportion? What do I mean? Well, the great bear markets from the past have all been characterised by epic counter trend rallies. Not the limp impostors of the 4th Quarter 2001 and 2002. But many bull markets in which the principle indices rally 50% from their previous lows. Fanciful, perhaps? However, we continue to be impressed by the shear quantity and variety of shares, to be found in all sectors of the market trading above their 1-, 3- and 12-month moving averages. These stocks are in bull markets. Furthermore, if the Dow is to rise 50% then surely the Dax and Nasdaq could double. With selling pressure continuing to abate, this summer promises to be a scorcher.

Stock Insight: Royal Gold – Beware the gold diggers

Any fool could make money in gold stocks? (Remember February, anyone?) A rising gold price and fixed cost base combine to create glittering earnings. Easy? Well, not quite. As the past few months have painfully demonstrated, gold miners take advantage of rising bullion to mine lower grade, higher cost, previously uneconomic gold and their South African cousins have to contend with Rand fuelled domestic cost inflation. Accordingly, in the short term, while the price goes up, margins don't. Instead, we like Royal Gold. Rather than operating mines, they take a percentage royalty on the dollar value of the gold produced from the mine. Even more attractively, this percentage ratchets up as the gold price increases. The cost base is genuinely unchanged: this extra royalty stream is 100% profit. Like all gold stocks this looks expensive at current gold prices; unlike the others, however, Royal Gold has genuine optionality on the gold price. Newmont also shares many of these positive characteristics.

Top Equity Holdings

Longs	Shorts
1. Newmont Mining 9.8%	1. N/A
2. Nokia 4.9%	2. N/A
3. Aventis 4.8%	3. N/A
4. France Telecom 4.8%	4. N/A
5. SAP 4.6%	5. N/A

May 2003

Investment Manager's Report: Marshallian 'k' is back

So what is it? It is the surplus liquidity in the economy, over and above that necessary to fund physical growth in nominal terms. Tatha Ghose of Kleinwort describes it as 'the growth rate of free liquidity after accounting for the demand for money'. It is interesting because it is a state of disequilibrium. Since March we have seen central banks monetising freely, beginning in the US. Japan, in its need to stop the Yen from rising, has if anything monetised harder than the USA, and Europe slightly less. The effect is to be seen on risk premia in all asset classes. It has felt like a bull market. It may have a little further to run, but unless it also leads to a substantial pick-up in economic activity in the second half of 2003 and beyond, it will be remembered for what it was: a moment to savour – a touch of Marshallian 'k'. Japan, however, feels different. There is much to suggest that we are close to the bottom. Prices are trading at their 50-year moving average. Investors have now made nothing out of Japan for 50 years! More importantly, speculators are being offered very generous valuations (see below) and this is being met with investor apathy.

Stock Insight: Yurusho Japanese Banks

Bear market bottoms are all about forgiveness. Resona is the latest wrongdoer to be absolved by the clement authorities. Following the injection of $17bn of taxpayers'

money, Resona now sports a capital adequacy ratio of 12%, making it the best capitalised of all the city banks in Japan. We are now left with a bank with net loans
outstanding of $240bn, on which it earns net interest income of $5.1bn (a margin
of 2.1%), before the charge for bad loans. For this, we pay $4bn, or just 18% of
new book value. Where could it trade should more prosperous times return to Japan?
Well, Barclays has net loans of $338bn and net interest income of $10.4bn (or 3.1%
of loans). And is capitalised at $50bn, or 2 times book. Could we make 4× or 5×
times our money? You bet.

Stock Insight: Celtic

May was a wonderful month for the fund but a disaster for my football club, Celtic,
who were defeated in the UEFA cup final. Nevertheless triumph may result from such
adversity. Football is in financial crises. Clubs are valued as if they have no financial
future. It is a situation reminiscent of the nursing home sector two years ago when
we invested in NHP. There is much optionality: the club is capitalised at just £15m
and trades on 4× profits. And yet Celtic sell 56k season tickets for c£400, generating
+£20m of annual revenues. Assuming perpetuity, this stable revenue stream is worth
£200m. And then we have TV rights and merchandising. If commercial logic can
succeed then prices could rise 5-fold. But why invest now? Football has some merit
within the context of subdued economic growth. The product has a similar addictive
property to tobacco; 80k fans travelled to Seville for the cup final, consuming 1% of
global air traffic and lots more sangria. But what about players' wages? Well, with so
many clubs close to insolvency the bubble in star wages has been pricked. They may
be a perpetuity after all.

Top Equity Holdings

Longs	Shorts
1. Newmont Mining 17.5%	1. Ericsson −2.7%
2. Royal Gold 11.9%	2. BMW −2.6%
3. Barrick Gold 5.0%	3. Aegon −0.9%
4. International Power 4.4%	4. Fannie Mae −0.4%
5. United Utilities 4.3%	5. N/A

Asset Allocation: The portfolio retains a large, multi-asset class balance sheet, as
    shown below.

Equities: Long 194%, Short 7%	Govt Bonds: Long 52%
Corporate Bonds: Long 2%	Commodity Futures: Long 10%
Active Ccy: Long 37% EUR/USD,	
Long 4% EUR/ZAR	
Long 4% EUR/JPY	

June 2003

Investment Manager's Report

Putting $350 billion of tax cuts to work, with the Fed lowering interest rates seriatim, is as gentle as throwing Mont Blanc into Lake Geneva. It will start the world economy in the third quarter, but will it create the conditions for an enduring economic recovery? The jury may be out, but not me. No. The longer this orchestra plays, the fewer new tunes they show themselves to know. Evidence. This rally has been led by the technology sector. A bear market is only over when the rally is led by the financials. Directors are selling on a 6/1 ratio. Volatility has fallen to all time lows, showing not only that 'optionality' is now non-existent, but that more capital needs to be employed to generate the same returns. At the same time, liquidity continues to shrink, telling investors that the chances of getting out if there is a change of sentiment are falling. Everybody lost money in 1929 in the US; the clever money lost it in 1932. The man in the street could not imagine being so stupid. Remember stock markets rise when profits rise. Yes profits are depressed because investment is weak (Capex is capitalised, revenues equal profits after costs), but look at tax rates. Profits are still associated with fat cats. The breeze that turns the pages of the markets today will be far from gentle by winter's edge. Today who cares? Only the idle turnover tells the story.

Stock Insight: Surgutneftegaz

Western oil companies have a growth problem. New assets in traditional fields are increasingly difficult and expensive to develop. With Russia starting to open up, the majors are drawn in, looking to the massive reserves in the Caspian Sea for their future. BP has led the way with the TNK deal. But look at the local players: Surgutneftegaz is growing volumes by 8% each year, and the stock trades on 6× P/E; BP on 12× is twice as expensive for less than half the growth. Meanwhile the CEO is pondering over what to do with a $5bn cash pile, equivalent to a third of the market cap. Can anyone suggest the next takeover candidate? Our investment in Surgut will be *sehr gut* for us.

Stock Insight: Kanaden

Bear markets throw up exceptional valuations. In an inflationary world we might look for dividend yields of 7% or 8%. Such opportunities sadly don't present themselves after a long deflation; there are no profits. Instead, in Japan, we calibrate value according to sales multiples, treading in the footsteps laid down by Keynes in the 1931–32 market crash. Sales provide a commonality across time and industry. In so doing, we stumbled across Kanaden, a company with sales of $1bn but an enterprise value of just $30m; a price to sales ratio of just 3%. We have our doubts over the quality of this business, an affiliate of Mitsubishi Electric, selling electronic components, industrial machines and computers, but we are prepared to buy even lousy companies on valuations such as these when we should make 5× our money. If only we could find such opportunities in Europe.

Top Equity Holdings

Longs
1. Newmont Mining 13.8%
2. United Utilities 5.6%
3. Agnico-Eagle Mines 2.6%
4. Devro plc 2.2%
5. Severn Trent plc 1.9%

Shorts
1. Lloyds TSB Group −1.5%
2. JP Morgan Chase −0.9%
3. Unilever plc −0.5%
4. Glaxosmithkline plc −0.5%
5. Delta Air Lines plc −0.5%

Asset Allocation: The portfolio retains a large, multi-asset class balance sheet, as shown below.

Equities: Long 135.4%, Short −4.5%   Govt Bonds: Long 18.2%
Corporate Bonds: Long 2.0%   Commodity Futures: Long 4.9%
Index Options: Long 2.7%
Active Ccy: Long 13.7% USD/CAD, Long 3.4% NZD/USD
            Long 4.4% USD/CHF, Long 12.7% CHF/NOK
            Long 5.6% EUR/GBP, Long 7.8% EUR/HUF
            Long 3.5% USD/HUF, Long 3.5% EUR/USD

July 2003

Investment Manager's Report

Expectations are now high that, thanks to the US government, the world economy can get back to work. Iraq was a takeover bid, where to spend $40 billion to take over $16 billion of revenues looked a good deal, given the chronic underinvestment by previous management. The cost has soared to over $60 billion and now it looks like the numbers can only be achieved if this acquisition is merged with another one. The talk of recovery and the size of the spending has scared the bond market and the speed of the fall (15% at the long end) has testified to how leveraged the bond investors were. Stockmarkets have held up well in the face of the bond fall, primarily because they can take comfort from any growth in economies or inflation. However, since 8 June even they could not advance, merely consolidate. Whither from here? For my money we are nearer the top of the inflation cycle – government spending and the oil price have pushed things up already – so much so that inflation will be falling next year. Economists are confused in the developed world because, in the face of a steepening yield curve, individuals appear to have borrowed against the house at 5½% to invest in cash yielding 1–2%. This apparent irrationality is explained by the fact that with these levels of interest rates the elderly are having to dip into their capital (by remortgaging) to support their lifestyle. Now more and more, in the face of rising costs (education, healthcare, petrol, etc.), individuals are looking to borrow rather than looking to their wage packet to solve the problem. It took seven years in Japan before the Japanese banks started to underperform, and while that delay was due partly to the fact that the borrowing was done by corporates there, it remains true that, as in the USA and Europe today, banks carried on lending aggressively, encouraged by the low incidence of non-performing loans, that followed on from falling interest rates. If I am right banks will give up lending, not when interest rates start rising, but when the collateral against which they are lending is falling. With first-time buyers now no longer biting, that day may be nearly upon us. Only when banks are no longer lending can the final leg in the bond bull market take place. To stop it will be exceptionally difficult. The change-over of the governership of the Bank of England provided a glimpse into their thinking. Mervyn King's interview in the FT made clear that the lessons for this decade were that individuals must assume the risks of life, not expect the state to bail them out, and they should not expect the life of plenty to continue – faltering economic growth and the need for taxes to rise will put pay to that. Knowing that the man who brings hope, brings everything, does not allow me to bring you hope. Happy Holidays!

Stock Insight: London Clubs

Betting on red would have been the correct course for playing London Clubs in recent years. Beginner's luck at the expansion game encouraged management to play on, but as the market turned they lost heavily; houses were sold; vultures hovered over the remaining assets. Now it looks like the black is back in play. A strategy of folding Aladdin in the US and sticking with the strong UK hand has regained the lenders' sympathy, and the underlying business is once again raking in the cash. Despite the debt burden we are only paying $1.3 \times$ EV/Sales for a business that used to make 20% operating margins; on $4 \times$ earnings the odds are stacked in our favour.

Top Equity Holdings

Longs	Shorts
1. Newmont Mining 13.6%	1. Lehman Brothers Holds −0.8%
2. Clariant 2.6%	2. Freddie Mac −0.7%
3. Ashanti Goldfields 2.4%	3. Washington Mutual −0.5%
4. Devro plc 2.2%	4. Scottish & Newcastle −0.3%
5. Pan American Silver 2.0%	5. Alcatel −0.3%

Asset Allocation: The portfolio retains a large, multi-asset class balance sheet, as shown below.

Equities: Long 103.0%, Short −11.8%	Govt Bonds: Long 16.0%
Corporate Bonds: Long 1.9%	Commodity Futures: Long 13.9%
Index Options: Long 2.8%	

Active Ccy: Long 33% EUR/USD, Long 12% EUR/JPY
           Long 3% EUR/GBP, Long 3% USD/BRL

August 2003

Investment Manager's Report

Mr Market has never been well received in the boardrooms of major investment houses. Remember 1999 when Mr Market barged in through the green baize door, wearing tech boots and piping the song of rising revenues. Buffett's refrain of only buying simple businesses was initially cited to preclude respectable houses from investing in tech shares. But castles in the sky compelled respectable investment houses to 'crave-in' long before his passing. Today Mr Market is wearing his commodity 'hard hat' and this time his tune is all about the monetisation going on and the unwillingness of central bankers to raise interest rates. As this global monetary accommodation meets the inelastic supply curves of real or tangible assets, prices rise, witness energy prices, gold, commodities and US property. Until interest rates get raised, fear of inflation quickly replaces the deflationary worries. Investment policy committees may well not like what they see but commodities have hijacked the train of events. Superior growth cyclicals such as Havas and Accor will not do. Mr Market requires a basket of unpronounceably grubby businesses from Outokumpu to Rautaruukki (see below).

Stock Insight

This market environment requires that we rummage around the knacker's yard of the economy. It certainly has not been 'hot-to-trot' in the zinc market. Prices are at a 70-year low in today's money, with half of world production loss-making. Arcon is a case in point. An Irish zinc mine that has been robbing Tony O'Reilly of his great fortune. Zinc is presently priced at 35c/lb. The range in real terms since 1950 reads 34c to 195c. At 50c Arcon is on 4 times earnings, at 100c it's just optionality. New prospecting has been curtailed and higher cost mines mothballed. With the supply-side under control, Asian demand growth could outstrip mine capacity and drive metal prices higher. The smelting side is still burdened with overcapacity. Falling prices and stretched balance sheets have discouraged rationalisation. However, change is afoot. Some Scandinavian horse-trading has transferred Outokumpu's mining and smelting assets to Boliden, with downstream fabrication assets going the other way. As metal prices rise and the smelting market looks to consolidate, the going looks a trifle firmer for Nord Deutsche Affinerie, Toho Zinc and Umicore.

Top Equity Holdings

Longs	Shorts
1. Newmont Mining 10.7%	1. Fannie Mae −0.9%
2. Royal Gold 4.9%	2. Nokia −0.9%
3. Durban Deep 4.5%	3. Countrywide Financial −0.6%
4. Ishares MSCI Emerging 3.5%	4. Washington Mutual −0.5%
5. Barrick Gold 3.0%	5. Tesco −0.4%

Asset Allocation: The portfolio retains a large, multi-asset class balance sheet, as
    shown below.

Equities: Long 173.8%, Short −20.3%   Govt Bonds: Long 38.9%
Corporate Bonds: Long 0.8%   Commodity Futures: Long 21.6%

Options (delta'd) Index: Puts on S&P 500, FTSE, EuroStoxx 36%, Commodities:
    Puts on Gold, Silver 25%, FX: Call on EUR/$ 3%
Active Ccy: Long: EUR 27%, GBP 23%, CHF 3%, USD 13%
              Short: AUD 15%, BRL 7%, CAD 15%, HUF 9%, IDR 3%, JPY 23%,
              PHP 3%, RUB 9%, ZAR 9%, SEK 3%

September 2003

Investment Manager's Report

Stock markets always let me down at this time of year. They go up. There is something
about the shortening of the days. This year is no exception.

Low volatility.	Growing trade friction.
Ridiculous earnings multiples.	Politicisation of markets
Falling bond markets.	Record buying on margin.
A rising oil price.	Record insider selling by Directors.
Current Account imbalances.	

The answer is that none of these reasons need be the causa causans for a stock market
fall but equally these straws mean that the market is certainly not eating but probably
smoking grass. What no one is worrying about is liquidity. The property bubble
is predicated upon how easily it is to borrow from the bank against your house. Try
selling it. Smaller companies are now 20% more highly valued than larger companies,
while they should be selling at a discount to reflect the lack of liquidity. When the
ability to change your mind is not priced into markets take care, because it is never
safe when it feels so safe. Changing one's mind is easier than changing one's spots.

Stock Insight

Geology can be an inexact science, and the mining industry has had more than its
fair share of Ukridges. Nickel is found in two forms: sulphides and laterites. Sulphide
deposits are the industry standard (costing $2/lb to produce), whereas laterites are
lower grade, more expensive to treat and usually uneconomic. Back in the late 1990s,
rumours of a new technology abounded. Overly enthusiastic miners looked at laterite
deposits in Australia and forecasted a doubling in world supply at half the existing cost
base. The world stepped back. No one in their right mind would invest in a sulphide
mine. But Stanley was in charge. In 2000 he finally admitted that the new procedure
didn't work. Shareholders in Anaconda Nickel lost 95% of their money. The history

lesson is relevant today: look at the fallout. Nickel demand grows at 5% compound. World consumption is 25% higher than it was in 1997. However, with no successful investment, mine capacity has remained flat. Chinese demand is tipping a tight market over the edge. The sky's the limit for the nickel price. The warming irony is that we are now buying the Ukridge's company, Anaconda Nickel, for 8% of the previous high. New management have patched up the balance sheet and are focused on the mining. Even at $3.50 nickel, Anaconda was only on 10× earnings, leveraged three times to moves in the commodity. In other words, it had tremendous optionality on nickel price appreciation. Forget new technologies: with Anaconda joining Norilsk, Lionore and Pacific Metals in the portfolio, we're finding love among the nickel miners.

Top Equity Holdings

Longs
1. Ishares MSCI Emerging 7.4%
2. Anglogold Ltd 4.7%
3. Durban Deep 4.1%
4. Gold Fields Ltd 2.6%
5. Royal Gold Inc. 2.5%

Shorts
1. JP Morgan Chase −4.8%
2. Citigroup Inc. −3.2%
3. Nokia Corp. −1.9%
4. Freddie Mac −1.2%
5. Banco Santander −1.2%

Asset Allocation: The portfolio retains a large, multi-asset class balance sheet, as shown below.

Equities: Long 134.7%, Short −16.9%   Govt Bonds: Long 116.7%
Corporate Bonds: Long 1.4%   Commodity Futures: Long 24.4%

Interest Rate Futures: Long 17.7% 3 Month EURIBOR (10-yr equivalent)
Options (delta'd) Index: Puts on S&P 500, FTSE 100, DJ EuroStx 50
60.1%, Commodities: Calls on Gold, Silver 5.9%
Currency Exposure: Long: 85.8% EUR, 2.8% HKD
                  Short: −82.2% USD, −5.7% ZAR

October 2003

Investment Manager's Report

There is nothing better than a good funeral but this market has refused to lie down and die. Last month was the market's best gain since long rates started to rise in June. Economically, Europe remains the bystander. We have watched the US government push Mont Blanc into Lake Geneva but will the lake be like a millpond two weeks later? How long will this recovery last? All of the indicators give little answer. The waves are still lashing the shore. Employment is growing in the US at +120 000 per month, which keeps the wolf from the door. Optimism is high in the stock market and record profit margins in the 3rd quarter are encouraging capex. The weakness to the bull's argument comes from the rising bond yields and the negative effect on mortgage refinancings in the US. My bet is that the 1st quarter of next year in the US will be weak, but I am becoming part of a shrinking minority. Mr Market is not only discounting the profits recovery for this year, but also another similar rise in profits for next year. How lonely it feels to be a bear.

Stock Insight: Graftech A razor sharp consumable?

The joy is threefold. Its electrodes are consumed in electric arc steel mills leading to repeat business. Its customers are witnessing something of a renaissance off the back of the China syndrome. And the business is an oligopoly with only two overseas competitors, SGL Carbon and a Japanese consortium. Previous management were too brazen with their market power and the competition authorities brought them to book. Resulting fines and depressed margins pushed the highly leveraged companies to the brink. However, Chinese growth has returned pricing power to the industry. With the players positioned evenly in Europe, the US and Japan respectively, this is now a currency game. As the dollar weakens, the Europeans and Japanese struggle. SGL and Mitsubishi must increase their $ prices by 20% just to stay profitable in the US, allowing Graftech to bank easy profits. We therefore have that rare thing, a company with pricing power. And on 1.5× sales, making 16% margins, the stock is inexpensive. Furthermore, we hold a free option on further currency-induced price increases.

Stock Insight: Barrick

Our macro-economic view on gold is well documented. However, stock selection within the sector is a thornier issue. Barrick, for instance, is hated by the stock market. Why? The company's notorious hedge book is meant to protect profits from any gold price weakness. In today's environment, that's the equivalent of admitting you like the Bay City Rollers. However, look at the recent results. Cash costs actually declined, unlike most of the industry that has laboured under a combination of strengthening producer currencies and low grading. Furthermore, Barrick have sold all their gold at spot prices, rolling over the hedged ounces for a rainy day. While Barrick continue to do this, they deserve to trade at a closer multiple to the peer group: they trade on a mere 4.5× sales whereas Newmont has reached the lofty heights of 6× 2004 sales; outliers such as the formidable Goldcorp trade on 11× and Glamis, 20×.

Top Equity Holdings

Longs	Shorts
1. Newmont Mining 10.1%	1. AXA −1.2%
2. Ishares MSCI Emerg. Mkts 3.2%	2. Bank of Ireland −1.1%
3. Ashanti Goldfields 2.3%	3. Citigroup −0.8%
4. United Utilities 2.1%	4. Tesco plc −0.7%
5. UK Coal 2.0%	5. Lastminute.com −0.6%

Asset Allocation: The portfolio retains a large, multi-asset class balance sheet, as
   shown below.

Equities: Long 127.6%, Short 6.6%   Govt Bonds: Long 78.8%
Corporate Bonds: Long 0.7%   Commodity Futures: Long 31.9%

Interest Rate Futures: Long 2.8% 3 month EURIBOR (10-yr equivalent)
Options (delta'd) Index: Puts on S&P 500, FTSE 100, DJ EuroStx 50 138%,
   Commodities: Calls on Gold, Silver 5%
Currency Exposure: Long: 3% GBP, 11% HUF, 2% IDR, 3% KRW, 2% RUB,
   16% USD
                        Short: 26% EUR, 2% JPY, 9% ZAR

November 2003

Investment Manager's Report: The devil is in the detail

This has been a year of biblical proportion. I am reminded of Jesus, fasting in the desert
for 40 days and nights, seeking clarity for the difficult road ahead. Then, as now, such
fastidious abstention brought much temptation. Look at the bear market rally. Both
the German and Nasdaq markets are up almost 80% from their lows. Such wonderful
gains could be ours if we would only renounce our blessed risk control. Indeed, there
have been days when even pious managers have been enticed. But such temptations
seem laced with the symmetry of disappointment. In 1929, the Dow lost 48% into the
October low. It then rallied 48% into the following June. The economy had not yet
succumbed to the weakness of the equity market. Everyone became bullish; everyone
lost. And there are parallels today with the US' 3Q GDP growth of 8.3%. As the good
doctor (Richebacher) points out, economic growth in nominal terms (i.e. in actual
dollars spent) and expressed as a YoY growth rate, comes to just 2.5%. Is the devil's
work complete? The economic news is good but expectations are high, and the bulls
are fully invested. Perhaps the devil is in the detail after all.

Stock Insight: Usec

It is 14 years since the Berlin Wall came down, but this dramatic event is still throwing
up unusual investment opportunities. Then, behind a shield of secrecy, the superpow-
ers battled for a technological edge. Now uranium, used in nuclear power plants
instead of bombs, is a force for good rather than evil. The US and Russia are cooper-
ating through the Megatons to Megawatts programme to turn weapons-grade uranium
back into power plant feedstock. As governments in the US and Europe privatised the
assets, the victors in that 1950s technology race emerged. The US kit, operated by
Usec, is 20 years behind the rest, and correspondingly the highest cost. The Europeans
launched into the US market. Enrichment fees collapsed, and Usec, already investing
heavily to catch up technologically, were the losers. Fortunately Bush doesn't seem to
like seeing his national industries being blown up, and has built a new wall, blocking

out the French with 50% import tariffs. Unsurprisingly, spot prices have recovered; Usec's margins will mushroom from 3% to well above 10% even without their new centrifuge machine. Valued on 0.75× sales and yielding 7%, this one could go nuclear.

Top Equity Holdings

Longs	Shorts
1. Newmont Mining 9.3%	1. Lloyds TSB −1.3%
2. Placer Dome 3.1%	2. HBOS −1.1%
3. Sumitomo Metal Mining 3.0%	3. Sony −1.0%
4. UK Coal 2.8%	4. Securitas −0.7%
5. Cameco 2.6%	5. Freddie Mac −0.6%

December 2003

Investment Manager's Report

Someone once said that there are certain things that cannot be adequately explained to a virgin, either by words or pictures. It is therefore with some trepidation that I will attempt to outline our present investment policy. The portfolio today was devised three years ago when we had concluded that the onset of a powerful bear market was imminent. We calculated that this would be bad news for the economy as much capital had been invested unwisely. Spending would have to moderate and the economy would decelerate. The coincidence of historically high debt levels, we reckoned, would galvanise monetary authorities and their printing presses. This monetary inflation would have consequences for different sectors: we alighted upon the much-maligned 'old economy'. Starved of investor affection, denied investment, we speculated that bottlenecks would soon transfer pricing power into the hands of yesterday's dogs. What we missed was China and India. The magnitude of the emerging market boom has sent shipping rates higher, so much so that the world has become a smaller place. Freight costs, in some instances, exceed the cargo value. Global cheap competition has vanished in some previously unattractive areas such as steel and coal, propelling a fantastic boom. Who would have thought that Antofagasta, a copper mine in Chile, would become the 100th largest company in the UK? Welcome to the world of economic mean reversion, flares in your trousers and coal and gold shares in your portfolio.

Stock Insight: PetroKazakhstan: non sufficit orbis

Hedge fund managers find it difficult to switch off. Imagine my discomfort then, when settling down on Christmas day, I was confronted by the James Bond thriller, 'The World is Not Enough'. My thoughts drifted back to our oil shares. Finding oil in the former Soviet Union is not difficult. But as James Bond discovered, much of the value consists in getting it from a quasi-landlocked Central Asian country to its end market. PetroKazakhstan, despite one of the lowest lifting costs in the world, has had to battle with state-run refineries and pipelines in an effort to export their oil economically. The solution has been to build their own pipeline, bypassing the state-controlled bottlenecks and saving the company $2.40 per barrel. Now Kazakhstan still retains more than a vestige of the old Soviet customs. The government has recently tightened controls on the media and banned foreign aircraft. This stock should be at a discount to its Western counterparts. However, at these oil prices, PetroKazakhstan is on 4× earnings. This is half the rating of the Russian peer group and a fraction of BP's. Christmas cheer after all.

Top Equity Holdings

Longs	Shorts
1. Harmony Gold Mining 6.1%	1. Ishres MSCI Taiwn Ind Fnd −0.5%
2. Diamonds Trust Series 5.2%	2. Freddie Mac −0.
3. UFJ Holdings 2.9%	3. JP Morgan Chase & Co. −0.3%
4. Burlington Resources Inc. 2.8%	4. Infineon Technologies −0.2%
5. Sumitomo Mtal Mnng Co. Ltd. 2.7%	5. Eurotunnel plc −0.1%

Asset Allocation: The portfolio retains a large, multi-asset class balance sheet, as shown below.

Equities: Long 186.2%, Short −59.1% including Index Puts

Bonds (10-yr adj): Long 61.3%   Commodity Derivatives: Long 24.7%

Currency Exposure: Long: 3% AUD, 100% EUR, 7% GBP, 2% RUB, 3% SEK
                          Short: 5% JPY, 3% NOK, 7% USD, 7% ZAR and EUR
                          Calls 105%

II
Michael Browne: Sofaer Fund Reports

SOFAER CAPITAL: EUROPEAN HEDGE FUND MANAGER'S REPORT

January 2003

After the sharp falls in December a relief rally was to be expected. However, although markets started the year by moving forward sharply and at one point were up over 4%, fundamentals soon re-asserted themselves with a plethora of profit warnings led by the UK retailer Dixons and markets reversed their gains just as sharply.

The 2003 IBES estimates are for a rise in corporate profits in Europe of 30%. We are very sceptical. A combination of economic weakness and the strength of the euro may well leave earnings flat at best. This leaves the European equities on a P/E multiple of 17.5× which is not cheap. A market with negative earnings and no better than fair value is not attractive in our view.

The fund has focused on the quality of balance sheets and cash flow generation as the key to both longs and shorts. In a negative month it was pleasing to see that our long position in Wanadoo was the largest profit contributor, although closely followed by our shorts in German financials. Unfortunately this was offset by our longs in the Swiss financials. However, the majority of our positions were profitable and more than compensated for the losses on our short in Safeway.

The outlook for the markets is poor. Negative liquidity, a poor profit outlook, a strengthening euro and deflation would be enough without the threat of war in Iraq. While the war may be resolved quickly, there is no quick fix for corporate profits.

February 2003

February was volatile, starting at market highs and ending on its lows. The outlook remains poor. Economic activity continues to disappoint and the euro continues to rise, putting more pressure on earnings. To this we may have to add a higher oil price and possible terrorist activity stemming from military action in Iraq.

Perhaps the most important issue is the brewing financial crisis in Europe. The insurance industry has seen its solvency destroyed by falling equities and bad loans. It now has to cope with redemptions and a consumer boycott of its savings products. At the same time, bad debts in Germany now look as if they will swallow at least one of the quoted banks.

The fund performed well in February on the back of its shorts. Alstom, Clariant and Rolls Royce were key performers, while Standard Chartered, Ciba and Airliquide were all money-making longs. Although our long position in Wanadoo was our largest loss-maker, we remain confident about the fundamentals.

In our view, markets have yet to capitulate although we expect that they will, despite lower interest rates. Valuations are no better than fair and analysts' forecasts remain far too high in our opinion. Given the significant downside risks we see ahead, the portfolio remains defensively positioned with a net short exposure.

March 2003

Selling pressure continued until the middle of the month, concluding in three days of capitulation. We had anticipated looking for this and took action to prevent the fund being negatively impacted from a rally, as it had been in October. At this point the fund was up 1.9% and we took profits in a number of shorts that had reached our price targets. But the lesson of October was that the beta of our shorts rises sharply in a rally. To counteract this we invested 0.3% of the NAV to purchase insurance in the form of a heavily out of the money call option.

This strategy was successful and the fund rose another 1.8% of which 1% was from the call option. We will continue to monitor the market conditions and may take similar action in future should similar conditions occur.

The fund is now neutrally positioned. Our stock selection has led to the addition of France Telecom as a long and TUI as a short. We continue to focus on balance sheets as our principle criteria for longs/shorts and the performance in March reflected this: Alstom and Corus were key successful short positions.

Looking forward, whatever happens in Iraq, economic conditions continue to deteriorate. We do not expect that business or consumer confidence will recover significantly. As a result, earnings and economic forecasts remain too high for 2003. Against this backdrop the markets will not be able to make positive headway, even though there may be occasional, sharp rallies.

April 2003

Despite a lack of positive economic data, the equity market rally continued with a vengeance. The European and US corporates earnings season has delivered more positive than negative surprises. Although sales growth is unimpressive, cost-cutting is helping margins and hence earnings.

Equity funding has improved markedly, as shown by the ease of which the large rights issues by France Telecom and Allianz were digested. Corporate bonds are trading at yields not seen since the last recessions and the 1998 Asian crisis. Easier access to funding, coupled with potentially less downside risk to earnings could lead to equity risk premiums declining still further from very high levels. This would be positive for markets. However risks still remain to European corporate earnings. The euro continues to rise sharply against the US dollar, thereby hurting the translation of dollar profits. The European economy sees little sign of recovery, particularly Germany.

Liquidity may well find its way to the equity markets eventually as investors switch from government bonds and corporate bonds, which have seen strong returns in the last 12 months.

The strength of this rally has caught us by surprise. Our shorts, which have been focused on those companies exhibiting poor fundamentals and funding problems, have rallied the hardest. Having reduced these, we have taken further action to cover any exposure that is heavily shorted, as well as selling assets to reduce debt and raise fresh capital. Our financial longs, notably Swiss Re and Deutsche Borse, performed well.

Perhaps the outlook is improving; however, as the picture is still very unclear we believe that taking a more bullish stance is premature and prefer to wait for better entry levels to raise exposure.

May 2003

The European markets were flat during May despite the euro appreciating 5.3% against the US dollar. This resilience comes from the expectation that the ECB will cut rates by 50 bps. The euro strength caused particular weakness in sectors such as chemicals and autos, where European corporates' competitive position relative to other parts of the world has been harmed. Where the effect is primarily translation (i.e. overseas earnings translate into fewer euros) there has been less pressure.

The yield on corporate debt has continued to collapse, as we highlighted last month. This has had a dramatic effect on the equity prices of highly leveraged companies, most notably Alstom, which rose 88% during the month. We closed this short position out during the month, but it alone cost the fund 1.7%, or nearly two-thirds of the total drawdown for the month. Other shorts, most notably Richemont and Karstadt, were responsible for the rest of the negative performance.

We mentioned in our intra-month comment that we are finding more potential opportunities on the long side, in contrast to our experience of much of the past three years. This has continued to be the case, most notably in the telco stocks. Another theme we are focusing on as bond yields continue to come down is companies offering a high yield, especially when combined with restructuring. In consequence, at the time of writing, the fund is now 22% net long (beta-adjusted basis), and has gross exposure of 54%. We have hedged most of our market exposure by purchasing a put option.

Over the last 15 years, when the yield on corporate bonds has fallen below 7%, economic recovery has followed. We anticipate that this relationship will continue, and we therefore remain optimistic that the outlook for earnings and market confidence is sunnier than it has been for some time.

June 2003

European markets rallied in June and have now risen for three consecutive months for the first time since end 2001. The ECB rate cut, coupled with the continued strength on Wall Street, were factors but short covering has remained the dominant feature. We mentioned last month the weakness of the auto sector which this month proved to be one of the strongest.

Although the markets rose, the fund did not participate. As in May, the longs we hold on fundamental grounds did not move and some of our larger positions such as BSkyB, Wanadoo and Air Liquide even fell slightly. The telco sector as a whole also failed to rise. On the other hand, compared to May we were more successful in controlling the drawdown from shorts in a rising market. The largest single drawdown from a short position was 23 bps. Following a review of our stop-loss process, and in the light of statistical analysis to prove that our stop-loss process adds value on the short side we will now cut unsuccessful shorts more aggressively than we have in the past. There were a number of successes: Debenhams, a long-standing investment, received a bid approach. We believe that the unlocking of value by venture capital companies will continue and will be a consistent source of positive momentum in the markets. The index put option in the portfolio cost us 20 bps. In exceptional circumstances, it has been a cheap way of hedging our long positions without putting excessive capital at risk. The total portfolio capital invested in options at month-end was approximately 1%.

We continue to believe that there is good value and positive momentum in the long positions mentioned above. The lack of stock selection success during the last two months has been disappointing but our experience of 10 years as fundamental managers has taught us that at times it pays to be patient and wait for catalysts to materialise. We expect fundamentals to come to the fore again over the forthcoming first half reporting season. We continue to build the gross exposure towards a normal 80% as fresh ideas emerge.

July 2003

European markets rose steadily over the month and have now risen for four consecutive months for the first time in four years. This performance is even more impressive as July saw the bulk of the first half earnings reports. There were very few disappointments and those that did disappoint were met with buying. Most importantly for us, those stocks that beat expectations were rewarded.

Four of our top five performers in July reflect this: Friends Provident, Amadeus, EADS and Atlas. The shorts lost money overall despite positive returns from L'Oreal,

Aventis and five others. Nine shorts were closed and two partially closed as they breached stop-losses.

The first half of the year has been driven by liquidity; July may well be the beginning of the market differentiating between stocks and sectors, rather than imposing blanket market moves. We continue to find excellent cash generation and value in the mid-cap stocks across a range of sectors and, as a result, we remain comfortable with our net long portfolio. With bids for two of our stocks still outstanding (Debenhams and Pechiney), it seems that others are also seeing value.

August 2003

European markets continued to make steady progress rising 2% during August. The markets have now risen for four consecutive months reflecting the improving corporate news and economic statistics. One consequence has been sharp falls in bond prices.

In this environment, cyclical and technology stocks performed well, while more defensive sectors such as pharma and telcos underperformed. Financials came under pressure from the bond market weakness. The fund's performance came from its long positions, where we were pleased to see sectoral breadth: the top five performers are all from different sectors. The majority of the shorts lost money but in the main these losses were small. The performance supports the view we articulated in our July summary that alpha is returning to the market.

During the month we have continued to increase our long positions. The French auto sector is a good example of value, good management and improving fundamentals. We are also finding value elsewhere, and this has led to a rise in the gross exposure of the fund.

With valuations attractive, earnings momentum improving and liquidity escaping from the bond market, the outlook continues to be positive for European markets in general.

September 2003

September was a difficult month for the fund. The trends evident in August continued for the first week before being halted in an eight-day collapse, the second longest sequential fall in European market history. Market weakness was prompted by fears around 9/11 and exacerbated by the strength of the euro. This downward lurch was broadly based and the fund, with its net long bias, suffered as a consequence. Many companies entered pre-announcement purdah, with the result that corporate news was almost entirely absent and there were no new positives for our stocks. The market move took a particularly heavy toll on two sectors where we have significant holdings, consumer discretionary (Renault and Valeo) and insurance stocks.

During this difficult period, the economic news from Europe has been improving: broad money supply is now growing at the fastest rate for 10 years and bank lending is accelerating. Current expectations in the IFO survey continue to rise and PMI surveys now indicate growth. As importantly from our bottom-up perspective, sell-side estimates in aggregate suggest strongly that in 2003 corporate free cash flow generation as a percentage of GDP will be at record highs.

With the fundamentals improving and free cash flow valuations attractive we have not altered our long stance. We continue to review the portfolio and see greater opportunities in longs than in shorts. We are confident that by focusing on undervalued corporate cash flows, as we have for the past 15 years, we will continue over time to create profits for the fund. We are disappointed by September's performance, but do not believe that chasing market movements will lead to consistent added value.

October 2003

Global economic news continues to improve and conviction is growing that even Europe has turned the corner. Recent German IFO data showed that current conditions are improving and expectations are close to all-time peak levels. In the UK the interest rate cycle has now moved to a tightening bias and investors are beginning to ask how fast and how high rates will increase. Our best guess is that they will only rise slowly and that rate increases in Europe remain some way off, but we accept that capital markets may well enter a period of reflection as they assess the implications.

European markets recovered all of September's currency-induced fall in October. The strength of the currency continued but a rising US market and further liquidity flows into equities contributed to a strong upward move in equity markets.

At the end of September we were 57% net long, as our bottom-up valuation of companies continued to throw up significantly more long than short opportunities. We maintained this profile until the final week of October, when we hedged the long positions with index futures. Against a background of markets close to peak levels and continuing uncertainty over the direction of the euro, we aimed to protect performance.

We continue to believe that the background for European equity markets is favourable. Economies are recovering, valuations are generally towards historic lows, earnings momentum is now upwards and there are net inflows into the markets. The main risks to this view remain further appreciation in the euro and the reaction of US equities to the likelihood of interest rate increases in 2004. If company valuations come down as a result of these factors we would look for a lower risk entry point.

November 2003

Global economic news continues to improve with Europe starting at last to make a material contribution. Sentiment indicators started to rise six months ago but indicators of current business conditions have only just started to move upwards. We are encouraged by the strength of export-driven growth, despite the impact of the stronger euro.

The Bank of England increased interest rates by 0.25% as expected. This seems to be having an effect on consumer sentiment, as retail sales and house price growth have both slowed. Unemployment in the UK remains at a low of 3.0% primarily due to the Blair government continuing to create jobs within the public sector. Elsewhere in

Europe, high unemployment rates continue to dampen consumer sentiment, although even here there is some evidence of improvement.

The European equity market was up slightly in November. Significant divergence was seen between large and mid-cap indices. The FTSE 100 was +1.3% while the FTSE 250 was down −0.2%. The experience in Germany was similar: the large-cap Dax index rose 2.4%, while the mid-cap index was only +0.6%. Corporate earnings results have been mixed. Yield plays and value stocks performed poorly, while high P/E stocks with a poor earnings track record continued to do well. The fund's exposure to mid-caps was not helpful to November performance in this environment, nor was the insurance we took out against a fall in the market in the form of short index futures and long put options. These accounted for approximately half of the month's negative return.

We feel confident that on a 12-month view European equity markets have the potential to rise by 15% or so. Earnings revisions continue to improve and valuations, currently below historic average levels, should revert towards the mean. Interest rates are likely to remain low. Corporate balance sheets are strong, share buy-backs are increasing and margins are stable or rising. Companies are now positioned to invest for growth by increasing capital spending, employment and acquisitions. We are particularly encouraged by the efforts in Germany to free up capital within the financial sector and increase the flexibility of the labour market. The market appears to be entering an earnings-driven phase, a period which should be one of lower risk for equity investors and also suit our own investment process.

December 2003

The index rose over 3% in December but the gains were all posted in the quiet Christmas period at the end of the month. Oils and telecom stocks, underperformers during the second half of the year, led the market, while financials, which have registered strong gains since March, underperformed. Against a background of continuing euro strength, which would normally be negative for the market, we suspect an element of window dressing towards the year end.

The fund rose 0.2% during the month. Our long positions in German financials and our short futures hedges, which we removed during the month, were the main negative contributors. The long position in Anglo Irish, which has now risen 80% since we first bought it, and the short in Inditex, which fell sharply in response to yet another profit warning, added most value. Other long holdings such as Renault, Thomson, Hays and Friends Provident were a little disappointing but we believe that the release of earnings results in the first quarter should be the catalyst for a further move.

There are good reasons why European equities should make further progress in 2004, such as forthcoming tax cuts and sharply improving confidence in the service sector. Even with an average EUR/USD rate of 1:30 for the year we estimate corporate earnings could rise by 13% or so and faster growth is not impossible given that, in a recovery year, earnings growth in excess of 20% is more normal. On this front, both the IFO survey and the experience of the US in 2003 are encouraging.

2003 was characterised by unusual market leadership. Those stocks with the least attractive valuation and negative earnings momentum led the rally from the second quarter onwards. The last time this phenomenon was seen was in the early 1990s when it lasted around six months before giving up leadership to good value, strong earnings momentum names. In 2003 technology stocks were the major beneficiaries of this effect and, at the time of writing, are now at relative market valuation levels only exceeded in the 2000 bubble.

III
David Murrin: Emergent Fund Strategy

EMERGENT ASSET MANAGEMENT: ALTERNATIVE AND BALLISTIC FUND REPORTS

Month	Return	Strategy	Tactics/Comments
January 2003	+1.34	*Alternative* • Long Russia sovereign and corporate bonds • Long Bosnia sovereign bonds • Short Mexico, Brazil and FX	The fund's performance in January benefited from all areas of the portfolio. Bosnia and Russia bonds appreciated considerably, with Russian sovereign bond prices reaching all time highs. The US dollar weakness caused further difficulties to the Mexican and Brazilian currencies.
	−10.1	*Ballistic* • Short Russia and Poland • Short Korea and Taiwan	Started the year conservatively short and were stopped out, which inclined us to go long, which, in turn, was also stopped out.
February 2003	+1.65	*Alternative* • Long Russia sovereign and corporate bonds • Long Bosnia sovereign bonds • Short Mexico, Brazil and FX	Uncertainty in the Iraq conflict began to create rifts between the major economies of the world. Russia again managed to reach new highs, baked on its new significance in the world order.

(Continued)

Month	Return	Strategy	Tactics/Comments
	+3.1	*Ballistic* • Long Russia and Turkey	Still relatively unclear on market direction, so traded lightly and short-term. Russia and Turkey looked both technically and fundamentally good risk/rewards and they provided uncorrelated strategies to the global markets.
March 2003	−0.35	*Alternative* • Long Turkey • Long Bosnia sovereign bonds • Long Korea, Thailand and FX	We took profit in our currency positions in Korea and Thailand but were slightly caught out by Turkey's decision not to let US forces use their bases, resulting, in prices being pushed sharply lower.
	−3.5	*Ballistic* • Long Thailand, Taiwan, Korea and Singapore • Long Russia and Turkey	Were a little early in adding to our long positions, as we were beginning to call a near-term bottom to the market. Strategies were loss-making on a mark-to-market basis, but were carried forward into April.
April 2003	−5.72	*Alternative* • Long Turkey and Brazil • Short Russia and Korea • Long Indonesia corporates	Continued negotiations with the US caused major gyrations in Turkey's bond prices, together with a few short positions in tighter credits like Korea and Russia, which stopped us out.
	+4.3	*Ballistic* • Long Thailand, Taiwan, Korea and Singapore • Long Russia and Turkey	Long strategy from March started to perform well in April, and we added positions as the momentum upward gained speed.
May 2003	+3.16	*Alternative* • Long Turkey, Russia and Brazil • Long Indonesia and Russia corporates	The fund sat long and benefited across all assets as spreads continued to tighten.

Month	Return	Strategy	Tactics/Comments
	+5.09	*Ballistic* • Long Indonesia, Thailand, Taiwan, Korea and Singapore • Long Russia and Turkey	Emerging markets continued to rally along with the global markets, and we were now looking for completion of the move to late summer.
June 2003	+2.14	*Alternative* • Long Turkey and Brazil • Long Russian, Indonesian, Bulgarian and Argentine corporates • Short strategies in Russia and Brazil	We continued to benefit from credit spread contraction and added to the gains at the end of the month with tactical shorts in Brazil and Russia
	+9.5	*Ballistic* • Long Indonesia, Thailand, Taiwan, Korea and Singapore • Long Russia, Poland, Hungary, and Turkey	Acceleration in the equity markets occurred, and we started to take profits as initial targets were met. Waiting for better risk/reward trades in Asia and Russia.
July 2003	+2.36	*Alternative* • Short Brazil and Russia	We went into the month looking for the US Treasury market to remain under pressure and consequently emerging markets bonds to struggle. This was correct in July, allowing the fund to take profits from tactically shorting Brazil and Russia.
	+3.65	*Ballistic* • Long Thailand, Hong Kong and Taiwan • Long Turkey	Equity markets continued to grind higher, so we continued to buy dips and raise stops higher as markets rose.
August 2003	+4.14	*Alternative* • Long Brazil, Mexico and Russia • Short Indonesia Rupiah • Long Thai Baht vs Korean Won	After the US Treasury market began to bounce, we turned our tactical shorts into longs and benefited from a general fall in global markets. We continue to view the corporate bond markets in Asia and Argentina as the best areas of opportunity, as risk appetite increases on the back of equity strength.

(*Continued*)

Month	Return	Strategy	Tactics/Comments
	+4.81	*Ballistic* • Long Thailand, Hong Kong and Taiwan • Long Turkey and Russia	Looking for completion in many of the up moves in Emerging Markets, but still chose to remain long until solid evidence that the markets are finished. Possibly in September.
September 2003	−2.44	*Alternative* • Long corporates in Indonesia, Russia and Argentina • Long Turkey and Venezuela • Long Thai Baht vs Korean Won	Due to short-term Treasury weakness at the beginning of the month, we were stopped out of a few of our sovereign positions. We cautiously expected bond markets to drop further, when we added a few short positions in Russia and Brazil, both of which were stopped out near month-end.
	+4.09	*Ballistic* • Long Thailand and Hong Kong • Long Turkey • Short Tech	Started to hit project targets on our long Asian positions which, according to our longer term road-map, gave us indications to start putting on higher beta short positions.
October 2003	+0.59	*Alternative* • Short Russia • Long Turkey and Mexico • Long Thai Baht vs Korean Won	We anticipated Russian weakness mid-month when local bond markets went through a minor panic following the arrest of Yukos' CEO Mikhail Khodorokovsy. Only to bounce back and be relatively unchanged on the month.
	+2.59	*Ballistic* • Long gold, Turkey • Short Brazil, Russia and Tech (Taiwan and Korea)	Our gold and short positions were stopped out early in the month. Short Russia and long Turkey attributed solid returns.

Month	Return	Strategy	Tactics/Comments
November 2003	+0.80	*Alternative* • Long corporate and sovereign bonds • Long South African Rand	In a benign US dollar environment, we looked to sell short the local rates though currency forwards, especially in Thailand and Korea. Both worked well and we started taking profits.
	−0.62	*Ballistic* • Long Turkey • Short Russia and Tech (Korea, Taiwan and Hong Kong)	Turkey traded marginally lower for the balance of the month, but was hit hard by the bombings. The market quickly rebounded but cost the funs slightly on the month. Our short tech strategy worked well during the month but cost the fund on a mark-to-market basis in the last few days of the month.
December 2003	+0.11	*Alternative* • Long corporate and sovereign bonds • Long South African Rand	The Rand position was stopped out due to a strong Central Bank intervention, which triggered a sharp decline over a two day period. Our bond positions worked well during the month, but a strong year end sell off in the US treasury market, impacted our mark-to-market.
	+1.40	*Ballistic* • Long Gold and Russian Oil Companies • Short Tech (Korea, Taiwan and Hong	All of our strategies contributed to December's gains.

IV
Philip Manduca: Titanium Fund Reports

TITANIUM EUROPEAN EQUITY: EDITED FUND MANAGER REPORTS

July 2003

A falling EUR/USD exchange rate and surprisingly strong second quarter GDP growth in the US certainly provides a more encouraging backdrop for the export sector in Europe, while domestic demand could be boosted by progress on structural reforms in Germany and France. Generally, the second quarter results season has been reasonable, with companies showing clear evidence of accelerating restructuring measures. The recovery in equity markets since March clearly anticipates that any acceleration in revenue growth will feed straight through to companies' bottom line. However, we remain concerned that pricing power remains absent and that any volume growth will be offset by price declines.

Although we could be positive on the direction of equity markets over the coming months amid encouraging signs that the corporate expenditure cycle may have finally bottomed, we find it increasingly difficult at an individual stock level to find compelling new long ideas. The recovery in equity markets since March has closed the majority of the valuation anomalies that we had invested in earlier in the year while our work suggests share prices are, in many cases, pricing in unrealistic recovery expectations in an environment where company results continue to highlight deflationary pricing in many end markets. Consequently, our net new idea flow remains to the short side.

Largest Positions:	*Long*	*Short*
	GFK AG	T-Online AG
	Centrica PLC	Orange SA
	KCI Konecranes	Sagem SA

August 2003

European equity markets continued their slow climb of the wall of worry in August, with the MSCI Europe index rising 1.5%, albeit on subdued volumes. Economic data releases continued to mostly support the bullish sentiment towards stocks with continuing evidence that the US especially is on a recovery path at last, even if most of the earnings improvements seem due to cost-cutting. Technology, autos and basic resources were the sector leaders in August, with financials falling back after July's strong performance as bond yields rose. The export sector gained more support as the EUR/USD exchange rate dropped, with some economic commentators forecasting a fall towards parity, a level last seen at the end of 2002. The weakening euro combined with a pick-up in US demand is certainly a more positive environment for European export businesses, but European domestic demand remains weak as unemployment continues to remain stubbornly high in the key European economies.

September is historically a poor month for equity markets but there is strong momentum and positive sentiment behind the rallying markets. A purely valuation-based investment approach can be deflected by periods when multiple expansion takes place and many valuation disciples have suffered before in these types of markets. While only ahead marginally in August, we are encouraged that our approach focusing on both valuation and catalysts is enabling us to negotiate these difficult times. New investment ideas are rigorously stress tested and we are being particularly strict on our expected catalysts as our ideas are predominantly short and we are wary of fighting the tape at this juncture.

Largest positions:	*Long*	*Short*
	KCI Konecranes	Sagem
	Centrica	T-Online
	GFK	Wanadoo

September 2003

Volatility in the equity markets had fallen since March, and low volatility can often signal a degree of complacency among investors, leaving the markets vulnerable to potential shocks. Currency moves and concerns over rising oil prices appeared to act as catalysts for the weaker performance and the equity market decline was broad based. Only three of the more defensive sectors posted gains, while recent strong performing cyclical areas such as Steel, Autos and IT Hardware led the decliners. Our bottom-up focused research continues to indicate that many of the stocks we follow have priced in a lot of hoped for good news and the upcoming quarterly results season will be especially important as investors look for evidence of a stronger economic environment feeding through into companies' top line.

Largest positions:	*Long*	*Short*
	KCI Konecranes	Sagem
	Centrica	mmO$_2$
	GFK	Mediaset

October 2003

The third quarter reporting season is now a few weeks old, and generally results have been mixed to somewhat positive. While in most cases earnings are improving considerably, this is generally due to cost-cutting which has been far more prevalent and advanced than would perhaps be expected from a region with such high labour market rigidities, and this has been a significant factor behind improving earnings. Top-line developments have however tended to be more mixed: either volumes are still sluggish (Media, Capital Goods) or pricing is weak in spite of strong volumes (Technology). While price inflation is clear in Basic Materials and Oils, there is a notable lack of pricing power in most other sectors that we follow. Even Services' sectors are finding pricing problematic at the moment, indicative of the fact that supply exceeds demand in most industries today. Emerging market sources of supply such as India (in Services) and China (in Manufacturing) are exacerbating pricing for European companies grappling with an appreciating currency.

Largest positions:	Long	Short
	KCI Konecranes	Sagem
	Centrica	T-Online
	GFK	mmO_2

November 2003

Analysing our current portfolio and research pipeline, our portfolio is positioned in those stocks that are at the most extreme ends of their valuation ranges on both the long and short side and we remain comfortable that highly positive returns will soon follow. Indeed, if every current holding were to hit our return targets, the portfolio would generate return above 15% from this point.

A pick-up in volatility among some of our pipeline stocks has enabled us to be more opportune in trading our positions and we continue to exploit opportunities as they arise. This may be accentuated in December as many long-only investors digest their first year of positive returns in three years and seek to adjust their portfolios leading into year-end.

Largest positions:	Long	Short
	KCI Konecranes	Sagem
	Centrica	mmO_2
	Euronext	Marconi

December 2003

At the end of December the portfolio was 103% invested, with a net long position of 32%. With the increase in volatility trading in the fund has increased, with the consequence that trading has been quite brisk in the opening days of 2004. Consensus appears to be of the opinion that 2004 will continue to build on what is becoming a globally correlated economic recovery, while at the same time expecting negative Bond returns and single-digit Equity returns. As always, we do not take market views but pick stocks that will generate returns to the portfolio of 15–20%. For 2003 as a whole, performance was largely negatively affected by shorts in so-called 'High Beta' names. By and large we still maintain positions in these stocks entering 2004, as we believe these stocks to be fundamentally misvalued and 2004 to be a year where Equity performance will be more reflective of underlying fundamentals, as opposed to sector rotation.

Largest positions:	*Long*	*Short*
	Euronext	Sagem
	KCI	mmO_2
	VNU	T-Online

V
Chris Locke: Oystercatcher Management

SIGNIFICANT SPIRAL CALENDAR DATES

2005	2006	2007	2008	2009	2010
05/02/2005	02/01/2006	25/03/2007	01/01/2008	15/02/2009	07/03/2010
10/03/2005	04/06/2006	21/04/2007	21/01/2008	17/03/2009	18/10/2010
16/03/2005	13/06/2006	26/04/2007	15/05/2008	03/06/2009	15/12/2010
06/04/2005	02/09/2006	15/10/2007	02/06/2008	13/07/2009	25/12/2010
24/04/2005	07/09/2006	14/11/2007	29/06/2008	05/09/2009	
01/05/2005	04/11/2006		26/08/2008	03/11/2009	
02/06/2005	19/11/2006			10/12/2009	
03/06/2005	13/12/2006				
24/09/2005					
02/10/2005					
05/10/2005					
16/10/2005					
31/10/2005					
23/11/2005					

Trading Technology used for Charting

Esignal Feed – Provides real time market data.
Tradestation 2000i – Software package for manipulating data.
Advanced GET – Technical charting package.

LOCKE'S RECOMMENDED READING

Elliott Wave Principle, Robert R. Prechter & Alfred J. Frost (New Classics Library, 1998)
Trading Chaos, Bill Williams (John Wiley & Sons, 1995)
New Trading Dimensions, Bill Williams (John Wiley & Sons, 1998)
Tunnel Thru the Air, W.D. Gann (Lambert Gann Publishing, 1987)
Four Dimensional Stock Market Structures and Cycles, Brad Cowan (www. cycletrader.com)

CHRIS LOCKE'S EDITED TV COMMENTARIES

22 September 2000. 'Dear Geoff, There will be no let up today with the selling. If we come in under 1450 december S&P (currently 1442.75) the risk will be a sell off towards 1390 possibly today . . . repercussions in the US. Investors have been all too greedy of late. . . . Buying shares at a P/E over 50 and in some cases over 100 and far more. This will change very quickly.'

25 September 2000, to Squawkbox. 'US Indices VERY BEARISH PATTERNS. Hourly from Friday's low is small wave 4. This rally WILL NOT TAKE US FAR.'

3 October 2000. 'No change in view. So far rallies have been very shallow. Good resistance building around recent rally highs. TIME IS RUNNING OUT FOR THIS MARKET TO RALLY MUCH. NEW OCT. LOWS EXPECTED VERY SOON. The Nasdaq at moment leading the way at the moment . . . A very bearish scenario . . . Again, the key for the S&P 500 Dec. contract is 1450 and then 1430. . . . Under 1430 I believe that the chance is that the bull market as we know it will be over.'

9 October 2000. 'Indices. . . . CHAOS . . . as forcasted here. . . . TECHS ARE ONLY IN WAVE 3 DAILIES . . . MORE BIG DOWNSIDE TO COME. . . . S&P . . . 1450 and 1430 Dec broken . . . may see small rally here from friday . . . but MORE BIG DOWNSIDE TO COME BEFORE LOWS. . . . You have heard it here this past month.'

12 October 2000. 'maybe nearing time for correction. . . . LongTerm still exceedingly bearish unless bulls can get S&P Dec back over 1430–1450. Intel for example nearing my projection for this mover 35–33. Short term charts setting in 5 wave downside . . . On some now make or break levels. JUST A WORD ABOUT WHAT COULD UNRAVEL ON LONGER TERM. This C Wave unfolding from rally highs 1550 SPOO should comprise 5 waves. WE ARE CURRENTLY IN WAVE 3. . . . There will be a 4 rally eventually . . . then a massive panic selloff for the 5th . . . I believe the Oct Low will mark end of 3rd . . . 26/27 Oct if you wish. Everyone will believe the bear has finished and will pile in the markets. . . . That's when an almighty collapse will occur once the buy is over that will take unprecedented chunks out the last 10 years. . . . Does that make sense . . . this C wave will take us to the beginning of 5 on way up weekly at 1070 11/98 back-adjusted S&P 500. . . . If this current wave 3 surpasses that level on this move now, i.e. 50% retracement that is from 87 lows . . . then expect the 5th to come in around 942 (0.618) or lower to top wave 1 at 840.'

17 October 2000. 'Dear Geoff, NO SIGNS YET THIS MARKET SELLOFF IS OVER. US STOCK MARGIN DEBT IS AT THE HIGHEST SINCE 1986. Credit Crunch is upon us. Even Xerox corporate credit is considered "junk." RISK IS STILL BIG FOR FURTHER DOWNSIDE MOVES AS FEAR NOW UNWINDS. US IN-DICES Having met some minimal downside targets, markets are in what appears to be only a corrective phase basis current elliott wave count. I would expect new lows very soon. I say again basis S&P 500 bulls must get this market above 1430 very quickly to stop this very negative looking weekly chart. My reading is that THE BEAR MARKET HAS BEGUN AND WILL BE A LONG DRAWN OUT BEAR MARKET > > > > NOT A FEW WEEKS.'

1 November 2000. 'Geoff, INDICES. Are we out of the woods yet? All this exuber-ance!! The Nasdaq after lows last week played catchup yesterday. HOWEVER, SO FAR FAILED TO TAKE OUT MAJOR RESISTANCE LAST WEEK. Nasdaq 100 and Composite breaking yesterday's highs would mean back to testing last week's high of 3500. S&P 500 dec broken 1430, 1450 next major resistance. Dow, still hold-ing above 10650–10700 . . . 5 waves concluded dailies as pointed out possible last week on most indices. DOES THAT NOW SIGNAL LOWS IN AND BULL MAR-KET RESUMES? . . . NO, NOT FOR ME YET. LONG TERM CHARTS WEEKLY STILL LOOK HEAVY. Yes, as I said there has been value out there on some of the stock . . . but some of these techs still look unfinished downside. . . . TREAT THIS RALLY WITH CAUTION AT MOMENT AND TAKE CARE IN THE PICKING OF STOCKS UNTIL WEEKLIES HAVE TAKEN OUT RESISTANCE. RISK IS STILL DOWNSIDE AT MOMENT IF FAILING HERE.'

9 November 2000. 'WE HAVE THE SETUP FOR THE BIG 3 DOWN I WARNED YESTERDAY MORNING BEFORE MARKET OPEN. $/STOCKS/BONDS ARE ALL VULNERABLE. $ WILL BE REPATRIATED DUE TO UNCERTAINTY US. IF BULLS CANNOT TAKE US IMMEDIATELY ON RALLY BACK ABOVE RE-CENT RALLY HIGHS RISK IS THIS MARKET WILL SLIDE. THE ODDS ARE NOW THAT THE OUTCOME OF THIS RECENT RALLY POINT TO DOWN-TREND RESUMING RATHER THAN BULL MARKET RESUMING > > > THE LIKES OF WHICH WE HAVE NEVER SEEN BEFORE. . . . THE RALLY ON S&P 500 WEEKLY CHART IS JUST INTO CROSSING MOVING AVER-AGES WHICH ARE TURNING THE MARKET BACK DOWN. INDICES . . . I gave the warnings on some heavyweight techs recently due for another major leg down elliott wave. . . . WE ARE NOW IN THIS. . . . CHECK OUT ALL INDICES CHARTS. 1430–1450 S&P 500 DEC as mentioned many times here as the key is turning into major resistance. Nasdaq 100 very weak action . . . cannot even regain 3500 . . . Dow . . . above support but 11000 resistance building up. . . . FOR ME RISK IS MAJOR DOWNMOVES HAVE BEGUN UNLESS WE TAKE OUT NOW THE RESISTANCE ABOVE. ORCL,BRCM,CSCO . . . ETC ETC. . . . I WARNED YOU.'

20 December 2000. 'Where do we go from here?...CYCLE LOWS 21ST–25TH DECEMBER...BUT THIS SHOULD BE BRIEF....IT MAY NOT BE STRONG ENOUGH TO KNOCK ME OUT OF SHORTS...BUT I SHALL SEE HOW WE UNFOLD....NASDAQ COMP AND 100 INDEX...LOWER STOPS ON ALL SHORT TERM SHORT POSITIONNS TO 2665 AND 2605 RESPECTIVELY....ABOVE THESE LEVELS WOULD CONFIRM SHORT TERM LOWS IN...TAKE NOTE THOUGH...LONG-TERM CYCLES DOWN THROUGH MARCH NEXT YEAR SO TAKE CARE IF RALLY...SHOULD BE SHORT-LIVED...RISK IS STILL MAJOR DOWN INTO LEVELS I MENTIONED LAST ON YOUR PROGRAMME...2200–2000 NASDAQ 100 WITH EXTENSION MAYBE TO 1500....ALSO TAKE NOTE S&P 500...THIS IS ONLY WAVE 3 SO STILL MAJOR DOWNSIDE RISK....WATCH THE 1300 LEVEL....THE NEXT KEY POINT...I DID WARN SELL INTO Alan Greenspan's (AG) COMMENTS AS WELL.'

3 January 2001. 'AS RECOMMENDED SELLING PAST WEEKS....REMAIN SHORT $ ALTHOUGH WE COULD BE HITTING SOME SHORT TERM SUPPORT...SELL RALLY...EURO BUY DIPS....STAY WELL LONG IN SHORT END ONLY EURO/SWISS DENOMINATED....NYMEX CRUDE ABOVE 2760 FEB FOR FURTHER RALLY...BUT SELL INTO DECENT RALLY...LOW 20 SOON....'

26 January 2001. 'IF BULLS THINK THEY WILL BE ABLE TO HIDE BEHIND THE DOW AND BROADER INDICES...THEY BETTER THINK AGAIN...LONG TERM 5 WAVE TOPPING...AND WITH THE P/E ON THESE DOW STOCKS ON SOME RUNNING ALREADY HIGH. MAKE SURE YOU ARE BACK SHORT ON THE $ BY NOW...BECAUSE THE FUN IS ONLY BEGINNING FOR THE PANIC SELL OFF THAT WILL TAKE EURO TO PAR....STAY IN SHORTEND...AVOID LONG END...EURO/SWISS DENOMINATED...AND CONTINUE TO BUY THIS DIP GOLD LONG TERM...I INCLUDE AGAIN 15 MINUTE NASDAQ AND SP00 FUTURES...THE SAME ONES AS YESTERDAY AND DAY BEFORE....YOU CAN SEE THE WAVES UNFOLDING. I suggest you take a look at the charts...very important...and no bears around except me...a typical bear market unfolding.'

22 February 2001. 'This is the panic and capitulation...(for this move daily timescale ... (not weekly)...I have been waiting for...and it's coinciding with my predictions last year for 1st quarter lows around March...where this capitulation ends I'm not too sure....There was a big difference between 1998 highs and 1998 lows...check these numbers out on SP00s and Nasdaq....I warned last November that we will have obliteration of wealth back to 1998....I make my money on the smaller time scales...but it's my belief that we are entering a good 3 years of hardship and possibly 10 years of hell!! To sum up....We shall see how it unfolds...but I for one am reducing NOT INCREASING my borrowings in this economic climate...DEBT WILL NOT BE GOOD...investors will believe that they will be able to borrow more to pay for other debt because it is cheap. . . . TAKE NOTE . . . this will NOT be the case . . . and if AG is giving you that impression . . . IT's ANOTHER CON.'

5 March 2001. 'No change in views . . . CSCO is added to my watch buy list . . . I recommended buying Nokia last Thursday. . . . Oracle Friday bought also on open at 16.50. . . . Buy Microsoft on dips. . . . REMEMBER . . . I am positioning for a countertrend rally larger and longer than January . . . but bear in mind . . . I am very bearish once this rally is over . . . YOU DO NOT SELL ONTO THIS AVERAGE . . . IT IS TOO HIGH RISK AFTER THE FALLS WE HAVE SEEN. . . . It's all a question of risk/reward . . . watch the Dow 10300 level . . . it's very important . . . I have said many times past weeks . . . I am encouraged by the action on SOX . . . it normally needs the Nasdaq . . . But remember what I said . . . I am not trading upside same volume as I have done downside from last summer . . . BECAUSE THIS WILL BE A "CON" RALLY.'

23 March 2001. 'We need some more evidence of lows but yesterday's action was encouraging. However you will still see bears selling into this rally so it will be choppy . . . but to enable to see a decent short covering rally to last we need those bears to fuel the short squeeze.'

22 May 2001. 'INDICES I keep saying this but it's VERY important. . . . KEEP THOSE LONG STOPS VERY TIGHT. . . . RAISE WHEN YOU CAN TO PROTECT PROFITS. . . . I am still very nervous of this market and will not risk much on this long move but continue to give benefit of doubt. Short term cycles should be going down to 23 May but are not . . . this market is over extended and when the likes of US Treasury Secretary, O'Neill says recession averted that gives me cause for concern.'

17 August 2001. 'Well, we tested S&P CASH July lows and held. . . . Option expiry today. . . . I mentioned past weeks that any move under July lows will confirm wave 3 down is upon us . . . we stopped ONE HALF handle from that break. . . . I will rejoin on a rally or SELL UNDER THE LOWS OF YESTERDAY I.E. UNDER 1165 S&P CASH . . . WE COULD BOUNCE FROM HERE . . . BUT AS I SAID > > > > VIX IMPLIES A SHALLOW BOUNCE. . . . LONG-TERM RALLIES ARE FOR SELLING HOLDINGS . . . NEVER FORGET. . . . I THINK THAT IF IT WAS NOT FOR OPTION EXPIRY WE WOULD HAVE HAD A ROUT YESTERDAY.'

11 September 2001. 'I HAVE COVERED ALL SHORTS FROM MAY HIGHS AND HAVE STARTED TO BUY SELECTED STUFF . . . THIS IS A DANGEROUS GAME TO DO . . . NOT FOR WIDOWS AND ORPHANS . . . 2 MORE TRICKY PERIODS . . . END SEPTEMBER AND IST WEEK OCTOBER FOR A POSSIBLE DOUBLE BOTTOM OR NEW LOWS.'

13 September 2001. 'Geoff, Death is nothing at all. I have only slipped away into the next room. . . . Cantor's poem sent out to it's employees . . . DO NOT PANIC . . . THIS IS CAPITULATION. IT'S ALMOST OVER THERE IS COMING A MASSIVE RALLY . . . PLEASE TELL YOUR VIEWERS OUT THERE. . . . THIS

MOVE FROM THE LAST YEAR AND FROM HIGHS MAY IS NEAR COM-
PLETION...DO NOT SELL HERE...I PREDICT WE WILL SOON BEGIN
TO RALLY SHARPLY FROM LOWS. INVESTORS WILL HAVE ANOTHER
CHANCE TO LIQUIDATE IN THE MONTHS AHEAD. SHORT SELLING WILL
BE VERY DIFFICULT FROM HERE ON...SHORTS WILL HAVE TO COVER
AS WORLD'S CENTRAL BANKS PUMP INTO THE SYSTEM AND STOCK
LENDING IS CURBED....CHECK OUT 1929–1932....THIS IS POSSIBLY THE
COMPLETION OF 5 WAVES 1929 BEFORE A STEEP RALLY B WAVE (MY SCE-
NARIO ONE I WAS GIVING)...IF IT'S MY SCENARIO 2 WE WILL HAVE
STILL A MAJOR RALLY. WE ARE NEAR TO A MARKET SOARING UP-
WARDS....'

21 November 2001. 'Geoff, Just look at this bear divergence price/oscillators from
26 September.... Something is clearly not right for this rally to be long-lasting. If i
am wrong... well we have to take out those long term averages and resistance which
I doubt we will... As Christopher Calendar says "... The clear cut denial in evidence
on Wall Street, where analysts and strategists construct bullish scenarios out of less
than whole cloth is exactly the delusional sentiment I have envisioned for this time
period when I first forecast a major peak in December 2001 two and a half years
ago"... think about it.'

7 January 2002. 'I will just say one thing today... all must take care here... HIGH
FRIDAY S&P = 0.382 (fibbo) ALL TIME HIGHS TO SEPT LOWS... AND 0.618
MAY HIGHS TO SEPT LOWS...THAT'S WHY MARKET TURNED BACK
DOWN SHARPLY FROM THAT LEVEL FRIDAY AT 1177 AND THAT'S WHY
I SAY THE 1170'S IS VERY IMPORTANT....IT IS A VERY CRITICAL LEVEL
I HAVE MENTIONED SINCE OCT/NOV... LONG-TERM AVERAGES JUST
ABOVE AS WELL....I DO NOT THINK WE WILL BREAK...I SUSPECT
WE WILL HEAD BACK DOWN NOW TOWARDS 1100...BUT WE SHALL
SEE...S&P P/E AT ALL TIME HIGHS....WSJ HEADLINE LAST FRIDAY US
ECONOMY APPROACHES THE THRESHOLD OF RECOVERY....IF ALL MY
LINES BREAK UPSIDE HERE...FINE...BUT WE ARE AT ALL TIME HIGHS
P/E'S....THIS IS EXTREME DANGEROUS STUFF....'

19 March 2002. 'Good Morning Geoff, I am looking for a large reversal here after
Greenie meeting to the downside... today will be volatile but actions into early April
should give some good signals in what to expect coming months. WE ARE STILL
NOT ABOVE MY LEVELS 1177 and MOVING AVERAGES.... It will be volatile
today.'

9 April 2002. 'ANY RALLIES FROM HERE SHOULD BE THE FINAL CHANCE
FOR INVESTORS TO LIQUIDATE STOCKS LONG-TERM... WE ARE IN THE
4 YEAR CYCLE TURN WINDOW...IT IS NOW ACTIVE AND OPEN UN-
TIL END APRIL...AND I EXPECT A HIGH AND THEN DOWN FOR 15
MONTHS...TIME IS RUNNING OUT...SELL IN MAY AND GO AWAY PSY-
CHOLOGY ADAGE WILL NOT HELP INVESTORS EITHER....'

7 May 2002. 'Like I said from last December perception of glass half full will turn to half empty as that saros 137 Solar Eclipse kicks in June pinpointing 36 year highs in emotions (p/e's) . . . I sure have talked enough about it and warned . . . hope everyone has his winter "overcoat" . . . I don't like calling for this . . . I hoped I would be wrong . . . but we have just been in a "mania" phase similar to the Dutch Tulip period . . . the South Sea bubble . . . etc etc . . . and almost NO-ONE saw it. . . . The signs are always the same . . . CUCKOO LAND VALUATIONS WAY ABOVE THE AVERAGE 15 . . . NO MATTER WHAT THE BROKER/BANKER TOLD US THAT ACCORDING TO THEIR MODELS VALUATIONS WERE NOT OVERVALUED . . . I REPEAT AGAIN . . . DESTRUCTION OF WEALTH BACK TO 1994–1995 LEVELS IN THIS NEXT STAGE.'

20 June 2002. 'WE HAVE ALL THE INGREDIENTS FOR A "CRASH". . . . It happens very rare . . . but you never know . . . 18 June–24 June.'

10 July 2002. 'Good Morning Geoff, INDICES I had a good look through everything yesterday trying to find technical reasons whether we have hit the lows the past week. . . . I am really trying to find reasons. . . . BUT CONCLUSION IS I HAVE FOUND NONE. . . . THE VOLATILITY INDICES SHOW THE PANIC HAS NOT STARTED YET BUT COULD VERY WELL IN THE COMING DAYS. . . . '

19 July 2002. 'DOWN into August 1 to August 8 . . . UP to August 22 . . . DOWN to SEPT 12 . . . UP TO SEPT 18 . . . DOWN TO OCTOBER 14.'

21 August 2002. 'Good Morning Geoff, The markets are setting themselves up for another fall . . . this period has seen another good correction within what I believe is a continuing BEAR market. The market has rallied thus far towards the lower head and shoulders neckline and last September lows basis S&P . . . this can be best counted as a small wave 4 before new lows . . . the second alternate count is that 5 waves down completed from the March highs which would mean a larger wave 1 complete in C of eventually larger 5 waves down . . . EITHER scenario is super bearish on the outcome . . . however the second count would mean we are further down the bear line . . . meaning we are about to retrace 50% of the rally we have just seen without seeing new lows before another consolidation period . . . the first and preferred count of mine is we see new lows first . . . so we shall see how it unwinds. . . . Either way Bear market is NOT over and has just begun. . . . I want to show the larger picture S&P to remind investors the big picture . . . then FTSE and DAX . . . I remain short indices.'

17 September 2002. 'If we have any rally it should be short-lived with lower highs over a couple days but I put this as a low probability . . . action Tuesday confirms to me market in big trouble. As I mentioned last week this has NOTHING to do with terrorist attacks . . . or even now Iraq . . . it's to do with companies TOO overvalued still and NOT bringing in the winnings. . . . Glass half full turning to half empty FAST. . . . Idea is still down into Mid/End October before any chance of a tradable low. . . . JPM warning just supports my JPM case I put forward a year plus ago. . . . THIS SHOULD BE UGLY.'

27 November 2002. 'The way I see it at the moment is another sell-off to come maybe two into a perceived low next June/Oct 2003 . . . when we have an extreme like in March 2001 and Sept 2001 then I will probably recommend a purchase . . . or the pattern has to change from here . . . this current swing upside should be almost complete by my reckoning. . . . If I am wrong and we are back into a bull market not much will be missed on the long run having not caught wrongly all the other short term lows that many did . . . to sum up bear market until otherwise.'

13 January 2003. 'If Market has inverted then 10 Jan. was the high and we head DOWN all the way into MARCH . . . so getting bullish here may be at just the wrong time.'

February 2003. 'Good Morning Geoff, Indices. . . . On FULL ALERT for tradeable low from here on. . . . Cycles into March lows . . . 10 March +/− for the 3-month cycle turn point . . . 17 March for the yearly cycle turn point . . . the point turn on the yearly cycle could extend a little more time through . . . what does this mean? . . . I expect to see a rally from this low (and I think that low is between now and 10% lower) up well into May . . . similar to March 2001. . . . Last year we saw a high in this period (1173). . . . We are near or at all levels I have mentioned as targets the past months for European Indices. . . . What bothers me however is we are not at the levels I have hoped for in the US for this move . . . THIS MAY BE A CURRENCY FACTOR . . . or we may still get to fulfilling those levels . . . if so we have to move fast from here (capitulation) because time is running out FOR THIS MOVE to lows . . . I will mention the levels for European Indices as well . . . chart to show is weekly S&P and daily DAX. . . . THESE ARE POSSIBLE TRADEABLE LOWS . . . NOT BEAR MARKET LOWS . . . TOO EARLY CALL FOR THAT. . . . No bear market lows will be confirmed until the longterm moving averages have turned. . . . Idea theoretically is Tradable low due now to −10% . . . rally into May down into August + . . . Look for the usual reversal patterns from here (key day reversal for example) to take the low from capitulation.'

June 2003. 'The date 29 July looms fast. This date I have mentioned since the beginning of the year. I am convinced it's a deep point in the market despite being asked whether it is an inversion. THIS DAY IS CONNECTING THE DEEPEST POINTS OF 1929 AND 1987 MATHEMATICALLY WITH THE NEXT DATE ON THE SPIRAL AT 29 JULY 1987. It is also connecting major events from 1945. The first spiral those 2 dates were lows. Therefore the probability is that 29 July will be a deep point. Gold. No change. Basically I remain out since beginning year 350–365, however I will be watching the 2nd seasonal/cycle low due beginning August (1st was April) as per expectations. Only above 398 confirms the bull.'

30 July 2003. 'Well, the 29 July timeframe hits obviously as a high. To recap. . . My idea early this year in January was down to March . . . up to May . . . down to July August. . . . We nailed the lows and got the rally to May . . . 790–900 basis S&P . . . Selling 900–950 was too early and wrong . . . but covered on the break 965 for move up to 1020 was good . . . OK . . . The next move down has just been postponed.

I believe we are finalizing the best of the bear rallies since the bear begun.Too many similarities with 1987 at the moment and bulls need to break that pattern here to succeed or we will see large pressure downside. Long End. Perfect . . . I want to show the 10-year US notes today. Bunds are similar. I suspected earlier 12 March was the highs this year . . . but we pushed just through that level on the next high and I just moved the counts over completing a 5 wave sequence from year 2000. This market is in trouble . . . despite oversold we can extend much further.'

13 August 2003. 'The largest cap index S&P will show eventually the way. I mentioned last week that bulls have to break the pattern of similarities between now and 1987. So far they are able to do by holding 962 S&P. I will show the 10-year notes today. I still believe long-term highs are in place basis price (low in rates) We are bouncing off the 200 week EXMA's which is allowing for a rally. Any prolonged break under that 200 week average could eventually lead to rates of 5.5%. $/Euro remains in a multiweek correction. I still look for accumulating euros in the 112–108 area. 119.50 needs to break upside to confirm the next move of strength. $/Yen still looks to be a good long-term play here on any break into new lows for the $. Gold. Continue to accumulate scale down 345–330 which upper level we have already seen . . . look for move to new highs on the year as long as 317.50 holds.'

17 September 2003. 'We are in wave 5 up from the March lows. So far pattern remains higher highs/higher lows. Last week we failed to see 2 consecutive closes back in the range basis S&P so short term trend remains up. $ . . . All I can say is WATCH the YEN . . . 1 year patiently waiting . . . the YEN break will confirm the next major depreciation for the $.'

22 October 2003. 'I remain concerned as you know that we have inverted the 4 year cycles. October should therefore be a high and we should move 1st DOWN into December. I have many cycles concluding between 17 June through October. I am CONVINCED this is a HIGH. On the large CAP S&P we remain barely above 17 June highs (2.75%) and barely moved above 1040. We have bumped into the 200 week EXMA's. THE S&P SMALL CAPS SHOW A LARGE EXPANDING TRIANGLE SINCE 2000 (NORMALLY A MAJOR TOP PATTERN).'

19 November 2003. 'SELL ANY RALLY IF ANY INTO 20–24 NOV . . . 10% BREAK ON MARKET EXPECTED INTO DECEMBER. INVESTORS JOINING THIS IN ONLY JUNE RISK LOSING ALL VERY FAST. Bulls need to take the momentum sharply up from here to negate the NEGATIVE momentum I said would arrive quickly and that would mean a sharp break above 1072 for 1120 to negate my calls. CRB . . . Intra-month breaking well through 250. I will show the chart back to 1970 . . . the beginning of the last Saturn cycle of 30 years. . . . INFLATION INFLATION. . . . ERRRRR . . . OR SHOULD I SAY STAGFLATION . . . 3 year BLIP?'

VI
Richard Cunningham: Asset Management

CAMPLC.COM EXAMPLES OF ANALYSIS

19 December 2003

EUR/USD Daily Chart (Figure VI.1)

Congratulations to those that followed our trading suggestion to buy euros @1.1910. The 1.2250 profit target has been attained today, realising a nice $3\frac{1}{2}$ big figures profit. We are happy to be square now as the rate of ascent appears steep to us, increasing the likelihood of a sharp snapback as more euro buyers join the party late only to be shaken out as the bigger, earlier players take profits on their long positions. Our averages are positively positioned, suggesting further gains but as the RSI pushes up into overbought territory we prefer to await a pullback before re-establishing a fresh long euro position with a view to the move extending to a target of around 1.2480.

GBP/USD Daily Chart (Figure VI.2)

As the pound makes 11 year highs versus the US$ our short-term chart suggests that, according to the level of the RSI, we are approaching levels where we should expect at least some degree of profit-taking which should serve to stem the tide in the short term. By studying the short-term chart Figure VI.2 it is clear that the price action has been contained within a rising trend channel therefore we would anticipate rising support around 1.7250. It is also evident that at these RSI extremes the price action has faltered/slowed. So although there is potential for the pound to push higher still (rising resistance currently at 1.7475–80) we prefer to await a pullback. A retracement into the 1.7250–75 area would tempt us back in but with a stop-loss below 1.7160.

Figure VI.1 EUR/USD Daily Chart
Source: eSignal. www.esignal.com

Figure VI.2 GDP/USD Daily Chart
Source: eSignal. www.esignal.com

23 September 2003

FTSE 100 Future (Figure VI.3)

At the time of writing the FTSE is challenging the annual high (4287.5) with a daily close above there, strengthening the case for a sustained advance in this medium-term

Figure VI.3   FTSE 100 Future
Source: eSignal. www.esignal.com

trend. Our intra-day charts show today's move as looking overextended so a pullback can be anticipated; nonetheless, this is viewed as an opportunity to establish a long position. A retracement to the 4240–50 region would appear to be a good level to enter the trade with a stop-loss beyond 4190. Our initial target is in the 4420–50 region, achievable within the next week or so, and a trade into this area would be our cue to take profit. Our favoured averages continue to imply further gains and while this condition exists we remain medium-term cautiously bullish.

Figure VI.4   Dax
Source: eSignal. www.esignal.com

Dax (Figure VI.4)

Today's gap opening has, thus far, seen the price action trading above the opening level and is the second gap in the medium trend since the March low. The question is whether this is a runaway gap or an exhaustion gap. If the price action can hold above the low of the price vacuum (3596) over the next few days, the probability is greatly increased that this is a runaway gap and the trend is likely to continue. However, if a gap lower, a bearish engulfing or other such reversal pattern were to occur in the next few days we would cover or partially liquidate any long positions. The price action over the next few days should help to clarify the picture but our technical bias at this time is medium-term bullish.

VII
Peter Toogood: Forsyth Reports

FORSYTH PARTNERS: EDITED MANAGERS' REPORTS

May 2000

We have been sounding out many of our trusted fund managers and strategists to reach some definitive conclusion about the future direction of markets. Unfortunately the lack of direction for markets is consistent with the lack of conviction currently being displayed by investment professionals. Many have reservations about the markets based upon strong global growth, rising inflation and arguably extended stock prices. The doomsday scenario would anticipate multiple compression (the price in the price earnings ratio contracting) and bond yields continuing to rise making equities look even more expensive.

October 2002

We must stress again that this is a critical juncture for the market. We have clearly reached the despair phase but whether we have witnessed the final capitulation is questionable. Capitulation means no fight back; however, each time that we have reached these extremely oversold positions, the market has rallied aggressively and, arguably, unconvincingly. The real capitulation is likely to be seen as investors realise that economic fundamentals are not improving and that central bankers still need to take definitive action to curtail further economic weakness in 2003. In our view, a major change of trend will be inspired by a macro-economic event or dirt cheap equity prices. We are clearly flirting with the last death throes of the bear market, but there will be many opportunities to re-enter the market in earnest once a positive trend is established.

January 2003

We are sure of two things. Firstly, given the state of confusion among commentators, we absolutely guarantee you breathtaking volatility. Secondly, the return will again be at the extreme end of estimates. The best policy for those investing on a medium-term view (3–5 years) is to acquire equities on weakness and to be alive to policy initiatives. We will do our best to recognise these changes as and when they occur and report them if they represent genuine change rather than more noise.

March 2003

We had hoped that an overwhelming response by global monetary and fiscal authorities would aid the ailing economy and offer some hope to equity investors in 2003. Instead, we have defaulted to option B, otherwise known as 'dirt cheap equity prices'. Equity valuations have been compelling since October 2002 but the catalysts are still lacking for a meaningful secular trend. At current levels, equities are deeply oversold and could well rally significantly in the next week or so. To our mind, this will be yet another rally in a bottoming phase which could take another 12 months to finally be resolved. Perversely, the great hope for equity investors remains the behaviour of the corporate bond market which has sustained its gains for the first time in this bear market for equities.

In terms of asset allocation, we have started the year trying to work with what we know and not what we hope for. Our basic allocation remains overweight in bonds and alternatives at the expense of equities. We are favourably disposed to corporate bonds and have an overweight position in high yield and lower-grade paper accordingly. The equity selections focus upon the proven stock-pickers and the portfolios are fairly fully invested. The catalysts for change may not be obvious but valuations are compelling and we must respond to this opportunity. From a technical perspective, our advisers suggest a rally into the May time-frame with a further low in July. This may well then mark the bottom for this bear market but this will only be known in hindsight. Volatility will remain extreme as we reach an emotional high for this bear market.

July 2003

So far the tone of this note would imply that we are bullish. In fact we are agnostic. The most significant event in the last 20 years occurred in a speech made by Alan Greenspan in May of this year. In this speech he turned on its head 20 years of conventional wisdom, namely that central bankers' sole mission was to fight inflation. He stated without qualification that at all costs deflation should be avoided. He even contemplated the use of unconventional means to support assets prices. Unusual yes, but unheard of, clearly not. There are many examples throughout history of bankers using monetary methods to achieve their objectives. In most cases they succeeded in debasing the underlying asset and encouraging investment in physical commodities. However, the success or otherwise of this policy initiative is irrelevant to us as investors. What we do know is two things. Firstly, that the business cycle will become more volatile as there is more interference and that the stated policy objective is inflationary. By implication, financial assets will become inherently more volatile and, if the inflation trade succeeds, increasingly vulnerable. This volatility is what ultimately attracts us to hedge investments. These are the only vehicles capable of trading on both the short and the long side and booking the profit. Trades are absolute not relative, and in a world where the cycle has never been more opaque this is a key advantage. Where mandates permit we have a full allocation to the asset class.

September 2003

The Federal Reserve is fighting an impossible cause. End-user demand will not grow at a pace needed to absorb the excess capacity from US inc. and the rest of the world. Too many goods, too few buyers. The rest of the world faces a stark choice in 2004. Stop behaving like a supplier of last resort and grow independently or face intense competition from a much weaker US dollar or, worse still, active protectionism from the US. China and Co. cannot continue to behave in a mercantilist fashion – all of the benefit none of the pain. There are some signs of hope from Japan and we assume that the recognition of the case outlined above makes Europe finally act at sometime in the next six months.

In the meantime it will be interesting spectator sport. The liquidity trade will eventually work but favours commodities and hard assets. Financial assets will struggle in this brave new world and volatility is guaranteed. We hope good stock-pickers can see us through and that hedge funds can take advantage of the volatility trade. We are investing a great deal of time and effort in both.

January 2004

Today valuations are fair, not extreme. Some year-end rotation into the laggards is inevitable but the picture for 2004 is one where, from a sector and capitalisation perspective, there are few staggering contradictions. In 2004, the big macro theme may simply fail to materialise. Yes US-led growth may disappoint and equities may be vulnerable or else growth might start to coordinate across regions in 2004 with significant implications for interest rates globally. The systematic risks to the world in 2004 remain an uncontrolled slide in the US dollar, extreme terrorist atrocities and Japan and Europe failing to shoulder the burden of growth, particularly in the second half of 2004.

VIII
David Schwartz: Dates

PROFIT ODDS FOR THE MONTH: % CHANCE OF POSITIVE MARKET

Date	January	February	March	April	May	June
1st	—	56%	44%	63%	65%	51%
2nd	68%	63%	46%	58%	61%	48%
3rd	56%	47%	53%	67%	64%	56%
4th	69%	35%	55%	68%	55%	54%
5th	58%	43%	48%	69%	43%	53%
6th	53%	40%	42%	57%	57%	78%
7th	46%	47%	43%	50%	42%	55%
8th	54%	53%	42%	43%	44%	50%
9th	53%	41%	52%	60%	47%	43%
10th	44%	53%	55%	55%	47%	40%
11th	36%	42%	38%	55%	46%	44%
12th	39%	36%	41%	44%	41%	47%
13th	55%	58%	42%	52%	51%	50%
14th	61%	42%	64%	56%	51%	45%
15th	65%	59%	50%	66%	58%	41%
16th	64%	48%	43%	59%	52%	55%
17th	53%	55%	47%	59%	40%	47%
18th	58%	52%	47%	66%	48%	52%
19th	50%	41%	61%	68%	47%	38%
20th	49%	44%	47%	58%	49%	52%
21st	51%	31%	59%	51%	43%	44%
22nd	54%	53%	43%	42%	48%	48%
23rd	36%	46%	44%	56%	43%	40%
24th	44%	49%	41%	44%	47%	45%
25th	56%	57%	48%	55%	51%	54%
26th	54%	57%	53%	59%	37%	50%
27th	47%	67%	54%	70%	42%	43%
28th	51%	64%	46%	53%	40%	58%

Date	January	February	March	April	May	June
29th	61%		57%	51%	59%	52%
30th	64%		44%	52%	37%	53%
31st	58%		60%		46%	

Date	July	August	September	October	November	December
1st	68%	61%	41%	57%	44%	54%
2nd	50%	57%	62%	59%	51%	49%
3rd	49%	67%	49%	58%	59%	46%
4th	61%	52%	58%	57%	45%	37%
5th	51%	70%	56%	54%	52%	53%
6th	61%	65%	57%	53%	54%	49%
7th	57%	69%	61%	56%	42%	44%
8th	49%	58%	47%	45%	51%	50%
9th	54%	61%	42%	33%	44%	38%
10th	58%	48%	43%	36%	67%	50%
11th	52%	55%	35%	46%	53%	59%
12th	42%	63%	42%	43%	63%	56%
13th	63%	51%	41%	51%	52%	49%
14th	49%	52%	51%	63%	58%	56%
15th	66%	50%	49%	55%	69%	61%
16th	52%	51%	35%	41%	58%	60%
17th	56%	46%	51%	49%	57%	46%
18th	43%	51%	59%	63%	53%	41%
19th	47%	42%	44%	59%	54%	51%
20th	52%	55%	52%	51%	42%	53%
21st	43%	59%	59%	58%	42%	56%
22nd	48%	47%	55%	49%	38%	72%
23rd	50%	48%	33%	48%	33%	72%
24th	49%	59%	49%	49%	50%	69%
25th	41%	56%	50%	46%	43%	—
26th	51%	48%	29%	40%	61%	—
27th	37%	40%	50%	52%	63%	77%
28th	57%	60%	50%	53%	56%	68%
29th	46%	48%	47%	48%	49%	72%
30th	51%	60%	56%	52%	47%	66%
31st	50%	54%		51%		71%

Source: Daily Stock Market Trends, David Schwartz, Burleigh Publishing 2000.

Index

Index compiled by Annette Musker